# SAGA BOY

ALSO BY ANTONIO MICHAEL DOWNING

*Molasses*

# SAGA BOY

## MY LIFE OF BLACKNESS AND BECOMING

### ANTONIO MICHAEL DOWNING

MILKWEED EDITIONS

Published 2021 by Milkweed Editions
Printed in Canada
Cover images: (boy) Anton Ivanov / Alamy Stock Photo;
(crown) ArtKio / Shutterstock
Author photo by Dave Winn Photography
21 22 23 24 25   5 4 3 2 1
*First US Edition*

Milkweed Editions, an independent nonprofit publisher, gratefully acknowledges sustaining
support from our Board of Directors; the Alan B. Slifka Foundation and its president, Riva Ariella
Ritvo-Slifka; the Amazon Literary Partnership; the Ballard Spahr Foundation; *Copper Nickel*;
the McKnight Foundation; the National Endowment for the Arts; the National Poetry Series;
the Target Foundation; and other generous contributions from foundations, corporations, and
individuals. Also, this activity is made possible by the voters of Minnesota through a Minnesota
State Arts Board Operating Support grant, thanks to a legislative appropriation from the arts and
cultural heritage fund. For a full listing of Milkweed Editions supporters, please visit milkweed.org.

Library of Congress Cataloging-in-Publication Data

Names: Downing, Antonio Michael, 1975- author.
Title: Saga boy : my life of blackness and becoming / Antonio Michael Downing.
Description: Minneapolis, MN : Milkweed Editions, 2021. | Summary: "Blending
    mythology and memory, Saga Boy follows a young Black immigrant's vibrant personal
    metamorphosis"-- Provided by publisher.
Identifiers: LCCN 2021004726 (print) | LCCN 2021004727 (ebook) | ISBN 9781571311917
    (hardback) | ISBN 9781571317643 (ebook)
Subjects: LCSH: Downing, Antonio Michael, 1975- | Authors, Trinidadian--Canada--
    Biography. | Authors, Trinidadian--21st century--Biography. | Blacks--Canada--Biography.
    | Musicians--Canada--Biography. | LCGFT: Autobiographies.
Classification: LCC PR9199.4.D696 Z46 2021  (print) | LCC PR9199.4.D696 (ebook) | DDC
    818/.603 [B]--dc23
LC record available at https://lccn.loc.gov/2021004726
LC ebook record available at https://lccn.loc.gov/2021004727

Milkweed Editions is committed to ecological stewardship. We strive to align our book production
practices with this principle, and to reduce the impact of our operations in the environment. We
are a member of the Green Press Initiative, a nonprofit coalition of publishers, manufacturers, and
authors working to protect the world's endangered forests and conserve natural resources.
*Saga Boy* was printed on acid-free 100% postconsumer-waste paper by Friesens Corporation.

*To the life, wisdom, and prayers of my grandmother,*
*Miss Excelly Theodora Downing, whose song I am still singing.*

"Give him a mask, and he will tell you the truth."

—OSCAR WILDE, *"The Critic as Artist"*

# CONTENTS

# THE QUEEN
# DESIGNED MY BRAIN

I

The Queen designed my brain.

Almost everyone I knew as a child was born at a time when Trinidad was her property. With no right to vote or make their own laws, they were all perfect British subjects in training. This meant Anglican hymns, little schoolboy uniforms, and the single greatest sanitizer of our savagery: the King James Bible.

I learned how to read by studying the King James Bible. My grandmother taught me on a veranda in the jungle when I was four. Her eyes were bad, but she still needed her salvation. She still needed her proverbs and her psalms. "The Lord is the strength of my life, of whom shall I be afraid?" I learned how to read so I could become her eyes. In this way, Her Majesty the Queen designed the framework of my very first thoughts.

As a scrawny Trini-child, I wore khaki short pants and carried a cloth satchel full of books. In my bookbag was a red *Nelson's West*

*Indian Reader*—the colonialist's handbook. Into my studies, I poured all the devotion I had for my grandmother, whose dark vibrant eyes and cunning smile were my whole universe.

I learned the Queen's lessons a little too well. And the greatest lesson was this: if you could name a thing—commonwealth, colony, savages, subjects—it could become real. "In the beginning was the Word, and the Word was with God, and the Word was God."

In 1986, I landed in Canada, a shiny-faced Black boy thrust into the tiny northwestern Ontario town of Wabigoon, near Dryden. From a jungle to a blizzard within a few head-spinning days. Wolf packs howled in the trees and black bears rummaged at the trash dump. My beloved grandma was dead, and eleven-year-old me stared, perplexed, into the wilderness. This was my first encounter with transformation: the art of letting go and becoming something new. It was an art I would become all too familiar with in the coming decades.

Throughout the years, I would give myself many names. They called me Tony in Trinidad, Michael in the gleaming boardrooms of corporate Canada, Mic Dainjah when I toured England with my rock 'n' roll heroes, Molasses when I crooned soul songs, and Mike D. when I plucked the banjo at folk festivals. Finally, I became John or J.O. or John Orpheus, my boldest, baddest self.

So this is a memoir, but a memoir of whom?

I want to tell you that it is about John Orpheus, but it's not. I want to say it's about inventing John, being John, killing John, and then watching him rise again from the ashes of the fire that destroyed all I owned. But that too would fall short.

This is a story about unbelonging, about placelessness, about leaving everything behind. This is about metamorphoses: death and rebirth. About being shattered over and over and reassembling yourself across continents and calamities. This is a story about family and forgiveness. About becoming what you always were.

Like a tree shedding its cone on the mountainside, fertilized by cold rain and deer shit, somehow growing up bold and strong, it is about creativity: that desperate act of survival. Nature's only lesson. This book is about the manure we call art and the abyss that heals us.

These are the stories that wrote me.

Oh, and it's about all that other stuff too.

## I I

There was a woman in the front they said was my mother.

She too had told me this, the few times we'd met. Her name was Gloria, and I was watching her carefully as my grandmother ascended the steps of Fifth Company Baptist Church in her casket.

Gloria was fidgeting with her handbag, in a grey dress, frowning sadness as if it were raining, but the skies were clear. The wet season in Trinidad's tropical jungle usually meant seething black clouds and rain that made the bush ripe with mango, cocoa, and pommecythere (or "pomcetay," as we called it) and that washed fat snakes into the road. But on that October day, the sun was streaming bright glory into our heavy hearts.

Among the mourners was the woman, Gloria; my older brother, Junior, who was fourteen; and my two aunties, Joan and Agnes, who had come from overseas for the funeral. Miss Excelly's death had brought us together in a way nothing could when she was alive.

Where had this mother been all this time? What had she been busy doing? Gloria said, "If I had known Mama was sick, I would've come!" She scrunched up her mouth and cheeks and half talked, half shouted to Auntie Joan: "Why nobody ever tell me nothing?"

Auntie Joan was walking just behind the pallbearers. She was a tall, erect, handsome woman who lived in Canada, a place where everyone was rich. Next to her was her sister Agnes. Agnes was as small as a bird, flimsy as a breeze, elegant orchid-pink purse to match the hat to complement the dress. She lived in America. Both sisters had faces slick with tears—raw, puffy pools of grief.

"What will become of these two boys?" asked Auntie Agnes, nodding towards my brother and me.

"Leave it to the Lord—he will provide a way," Joan answered.

Junior was walking behind us a bit, in a powder-blue suit just like mine, his brow crumpled into a knot. They used to think we were twins because we were always together, but now he was fourteen, while I was eleven. He was hanging out in Princes Town, taking maxi taxis and kissing girls. He was going places that I couldn't follow.

Junior's first memory was of Gloria leaning through our darkened door, handing a bundle of baby me to Miss Excelly, then rushing back to a waiting car and driving away.

"The young one like me better," our grandmother used to say. This wasn't fair; Junior remembered his mother. I didn't. Yet as far back as anyone could recall, I clung to Grandma's skirts always, even when she was in her sickbed, with that metallic taste of death, the smell of her chamberpot, the way her silver bracelets turned black from her clammy skin. Even then, they had to make me get out of her deathbed.

When Joan and Agnes arrived, everyone asked, "Is yuh brutha comin?" Al, their wayward younger brother—Gloria's ex-husband and my father—was a ghost, a wisp of legend that draped itself across my childhood.

Miss Excelly's tongue, stiff from stroke, almost useless, groaned into Joan's ear, "Whwwwwaaaaaaaaal." Auntie Joan leaned in to try to make out what she was saying, and her mother gripped her arm. "Whaeeeeeeal," she droned again, and wouldn't let go.

"What do mean, Mama?"

"Wheeeaarrre Al?"

And Auntie Joan was crying again. It was a question: "Where is Al?" Al was not coming, but how could she break this to his dying mother?

Back at Fifth Company Baptist Church, Excelly Theodora Downing's body lay like a monarch in her pomp. They wedding-marched her coffin through the pews and laid her down before the altar. As the mourners shuffled in, light danced off the metal rings on the pine box, the bronze wood of the organ, and the timepieces of the deacons who were watching sagely. We took our seats at the front, and the air filled with the perfume of warm bodies, starched shirts, boot polish, and lilies of the valley.

Sombrely, the reverend made his entrance. The murmuring hushed. The choir members, in their cherub robes, rose to meet him. He gestured, his arms wide as if to hold us all in one embrace, as if hugging the Holy Spirit, as if inhaling the gusts of sun pouring through the stained glass. Then, signalling to the musicians with a wink, he raised his eyes to the heavens and the choir began to sing.

Act One

# TONY

## Chapter One

# MONKEYTOWN

I

Poulourie was my everything.

Pou-lour-ree. These three delicious syllables ruled my life. I was five, and if I ever got my hands on as little as fifteen cents, I would buy poulourie, a fluffy, golden deep-fried ball of dough that was crunchy on the outside and chewy on the inside. I lived in New Grant, a village in the south of Trinidad—or "down South," as we would say. It sat between wide, muddy rivers full of crocodiles, thick tropical wilderness, and fields upon fields of sugar cane. The yellow-and-brown two-storey building where we learned was called New Grant Anglican School, and it had been established in the year 1900. To the front, there was a paved asphalt area where we played netball, rounders, and hopscotch in our neat uniforms. In the field next to that, we dashed about, made believe, and whenever possible, yelled as loudly as we could.

Next to this field was a small shop of wonders. They sold: pickled red mango, coconut sugar cakes, sticky peppery anchar, and of course, poulourie. It was pretty much neutral in taste, but it was served with spicy mango chutney or sticky sweet tamarind sauce on brown wax paper. Poulourie was my favourite thing.

One day, I had bought three or four and was fixated on inhaling them while waiting to cross the main road. I was straining not to get any chutney on my khaki uniform. Cars roared by while I stood, my mouth wet with wanting. I was captivated by the mesh pattern inside the dough balls, by the heat of the wax paper and the green mango chutney. Just as I looked up, a twenty-seat maxi taxi passenger van dashed right by my nose. My nostrils burned with diesel. A drunk on the other side of the road staggered backwards, his eyes bulging big, like guavas.

"Yuh go get kill one day!"

In Trini, an alcoholic was a "rumbo." Everybody drank rum, and I knew from the way big people talked that you never listened to a rumbo.

Still, I finished my poulourie, which was never "poulouries" even if you had several, and looked both ways before crossing to my street: Monkeytown Road, Third Branch. Which at this point was the only place in the universe I knew.

II

On a day like that, it would have been normal to hear the sound of Miss Excelly's voice drifting over the tombstones. There was a cemetery on either side of the street, and ours was the first house after the one on the left. Her voice would catch me as soon as I left the junction, drifting like a breeze.

My grandma—we called her Mama, and everyone else called her Miss Excelly—was always singing. When she woke up with the

kiskadees, when she was happy and smiling, when she was thought-
ful and laughing to herself, or when she went to bed, the bullfrogs as
her backup, she sang. Hymns, mostly. About Jesus and salvation and
redemption and power. So basically every single song in the Anglican
hymnal. "Power in the Blood," "How Great Thou Art," "Rock of Ages,"
"Abide with Me," and the draggy one that was her favourite, "Stars in
My Crown" which I didn't really understand then, except I knew it had
something to do with getting "stars in my crown . . . when at evening
the sun goeth down . . . in the mansions of rest."

What I did know was that her bright eyes and soft face got very
strange when she sang this hymn. She would smile with her whole
face but have tears in her eyes. Was it possible to be sad and happy
at once?

In those moments coming home from school, the world seemed
dim and out of focus. Everything hushed. Her voice perfumed the very
air. The tall grass across the cemetery leaned in slow motion. Beads
of sweat slid down my forehead and tickled my neck. All of creation
became her voice calling me home.


III


In those days they called me Tony, after my first name. Or often
JuniorandTony, as my older brother and I were inseparable. Junior
Aly Downing was so named because he was the first son of Alyson
Downing, our infamous father Al, about whom we knew almost nothing. We knew that he was a charmer; we knew that he dated Juanita
and that her father cursed him; we knew that he hung out with crim-
inals; we knew that he left for Canada and never came back. The rest
we had to guess from the raised eyebrows and careful whispers of people who used to know him. Some of whom watched us as if we were

baby macajuels, anacondas, who would one day grow up and try to eat them. Who would one day grow up to be Al.

At that time, Junior and I were still young enough to do everything together. He was calmer, wiser, and bigger than me, but with the same round face and cheeky smile. He did everything first and better and braver, and I adored him for it.

People couldn't tell us apart. There is a picture of my grandmother and us taken in a studio in Princes Town. She in the lacy white dress with a broad, church hat and us beaming in chalk-blue suits that were too big. To the uninitiated, we looked like twins. Yet he was three years older.

Junior knew me before I knew myself.

We would sometimes walk down Monkeytown as its asphalt crawled into the bush and go through the overgrown back trace to Hindustan, usually to get groceries for Mama. She'd send us with a list in the form of a note that I carefully unfolded and read as soon as we were out of sight:

Mista Chan,

If God willing, please give us these items on credit and I will pay you month end.

3 pounds of Ibis flour
½ pound of brown sugar
A 2 lb sack of rice

Miss Excelly Theodora Downing

In hindsight, she must have thought that sending her scrawny grandchildren to beg for credit would make it hard for the grocer to say no. Not that this mattered to us. Our faces hurt from smiling; we were getting to go on an adventure. If the trace, which was a shortcut through the tall grass, was flooded or overgrown, we took the long way. Which meant an encounter with the scariest animals in existence.

Some of the nearby houses were two levels of pretty painted concrete with verandas and were raised up on tall posts in case of flooding. Yet many were simple one- or two-room shacks held together by galvanized steel, the shiny sheet metal that in the rainy season made storms sound like a million feet trying to trample the rooftop. As we got closer to the bottom of the last hill at the very bottom of the road, Junior looked worried.

"Aight, hush yuh mouth til we pass," he said.

We started to tiptoe and whisper like thieves.

Just as we were about to breathe again, we heard the gobble gobble and our hearts sank.

"Run, Tony! Ruuuun!"

Storming out of the yard from behind a row of pomerac trees came a gang of angry turkeys. Their hard feet stabbing at the ground and closing on us fast.

"Run, boy! Stop staring and run!"

Junior was already halfway down the hill, and I turned and followed. The terrible sound of "gobble" times twenty seemed to be emerging from everywhere.

Yet by the time we hit the bottom of the hill, the turkeys did not follow. Junior and I doubled over on the hot asphalt, our chests heaving.

"Boy, dey nearly ketch yuh!" he grinned ear to ear.

"Not me! I too fast for dem."

I couldn't believe we'd survived. As we got up, Junior dusted off my clothes and finished with a playful tap to the back of my head.

"Eh!" I turned and let out a gobble and started to turkey-chase him. We climbed the rest of the way to Hindustan laughing. It had not yet dawned on us that we had to go back the same way, but this time carrying a sack of flour and some rice.

One of our best ideas didn't end well when we decided to dress up as jumbie, or monsters, and hide in the cemetery after dark to scare pass-ersby. We were having mixed results but a lot of laughs, until Olsten Hodge showed up. He was the boyfriend of Miss Monica, who lived behind us with her teenage son.

"JuniorandTony come here!" he barked, and the great mole on his left cheek seemed to grow gigantic and fierce.

Junior jumped in front of me, but Hodge gripped his bony upper arms and jerked him off the ground. I, too, screamed as he lifted me by my armpits and carried us both like wriggling fish to the whipping room.

Usually Mista Olsten liked watching us beg until our noses were snotty and our clothes hot and salty from tears of anticipation. On this day, he set to work whipping us hard. Each blow of the belt coming with a lecture.

*Smack!*

"I thought I told all yuh . . . "

*Smack!*

". . . to go to bed."

*Smack!*

"You think I have time . . . "

*Smack!*

". . . to play de ass?"

His fat round face was livid as a hurricane. The thick knotty purple welts left by his belt would last for days.

Hodge had taken on the role of disciplinarian because Al, our father, had not been seen since he left for Canada six years earlier. Our only contact with Hodge came when he beat us with whips and belts and calabash branches. Junior always seemed less scared. Sometimes, when we knew we were going to get licks, we would hide in the bush until after dark and slink back into the house long after Hodge got tired of looking for us.

Back then, in those simple days in the tropical heat, my little head had space only for Junior, for the occasional whipping, the wind groaning in the coconut trees, the preacher wailing on Sundays, the villagers gossiping in Monkeytown and Miss Excelly's haunting songs.

Yet change and great beginnings were already on their way.


IV


The bush was really a rainforest, and it spread its wings every-where. It was an ocean of thick bristling green. Bright green like a full hand of unripe bananas. Green and black like giant ripe zaboca, which Canadians call avocado. Brownish green like the zillions of grasshoppers I could see when I pressed my cheek to the hot grass. Golden green like the chest of the sik-ee-aye bird with its beady brown eyes.

Monkeytown had two seasons: dry and hot was one, rainy and hot the other. In the dry season, the sun scorched our skulls and turned the muddy riverbanks to dust. In the wet season, violent storms blew in suddenly from the sea and unloaded their fury on the world. Then just as suddenly they blew away, leaving the sun to coax us back to life with its soft fingers of light. Unlimited sunshine and rainfall meant that the trees were enormous, the insects endless, and the birds omnipresent.

By far the ugliest things in the bush were the crapauds, which is what we called the horned toads. Great fat black-brown things with rough sacks of bulging flesh everywhere. They were horrifying. Once

I avoided a part of our yard for weeks because one had crouched there to die.

Less grotesque but no less alarming were the snakes. They came in all varieties, colours, and sizes. Coral snakes glided smoothly on their red-and-black bellies whether crawling in the bush or swimming in the murky rivers. Boa constrictors grew up to thirty feet and preferred to lie in trees and fall on their prey. Some snakes you never saw, only heard of when they ate something or someone. Other snakes seemed to always be around. Everyone I knew, from grown women and men to little boys and girls, fled in terror whenever they saw one slither or crawl into the open.

My favourite place in all of this was a stand of slim tall trees with branches that embraced at the top like the arches of a cathedral. I went there to get lost in the symphony of the forest. There you heard the constant shhhhhh of the wind whipping at the leaves, the heavy music of a hundred thousand birds thriving, and the electric hum of infinite insects. It was my own secret parallel dimension. When I threw a handful of stones up into the branches, the sky would explode with colour as the giant macaws cooling off up there would erupt with noise, beating their wings of blazing red, cerulean blue, chalky yellow and silky green. Their wings painted for me a vivid picture of wonder at the murky mysteries of the jungle.

The bush was full of monsters but it was also full of miracles.

V

Miss Excelly sat on the veranda humming to herself. She was seventy-eight, and there were many days when I did not leave her side.

As I was unbuttoning my school shirt in the single-storey house, she called: "Darlin', bring de big Bible by de nightstand."

The floor was marble and cool on my feet. When I returned with the great white Bible with the golden letters, she had not moved an inch. It was a plush book that could barely fit in my hands. A picture of a blond Jesus kneeling to pray was on the cover, and the scene would move with the angle you looked at it. I loved the shiny gold leaf around the edges, the papery smell, and the texture of the words under my fingertips.

Even big people called Miss Excelly old. Her skin hung down under her neck and made rings under her darting eyes. Her mouth always seemed to be about to smile.

I pretended to open the Bible to her favourite chapter, Psalm 27, but I already knew it by heart. Instead, as I dragged my fingertips over the colour illustrations—"Moses and the Ten Commandments," "Jacob's Dream," "The Prodigal Son"—I recited the verse from memory. It began: "The Lord is my light and my salvation—whom shall I fear? The Lord is the strength of my life—of whom shall I be afraid?"

I had been doing this since I was three. She always preferred the poetic parts of the Old Testament: Psalms, Proverbs, and Song of Solomon. And when she was not looking, I read the rest too: David and his harem. Her breasts were as apricots. "My beloved is gone down into his garden, to the beds of spices, to feed in the gardens, and to gather lilies." They were love poems fashioned by ancient Jews and King James I's scholars, and I was fascinated by the sounds and kaleidoscope of meanings they unfolded.

When I finished, I put the heavy book down and wrapped myself in her skirts until the whole world smelled like mothballs. Close to her—this was the place that made the most sense. It was 1982. I was seven. And I was certain that it would always be like this.

Mama was a poor Caribbean woman, which meant she was expected to carry the weight of the sky. She regularly performed miracles, like climbing coconut trees well into her seventies. She also raised many more children than she had given birth to. In her case, six younger sisters, three of her nieces, four orphaned kids—Kenrick, Wilton (who lived with us), Jemma, and her sister, Elizabeth—and me and Junior, who were her grandchildren. Finally, the ones she actually bore: Boysie, Jestina, Agnes, Joan, and my father, Al. These were all her children that I knew of.

For her, life was a constant act of generosity and struggle.

I grew up understanding that Caribbean women were deep wells of resilience from which all around them drew water. They were spiritually tough in an almost superhuman way.

If I had slept in her bed, as I often did, I would hear her groan and roll over well before dawn, when the crapauds were still croaking, when the world was still asleep. She would lift herself up in the pitch black. Though I could never see her, I could always hear her bones resisting the call.

"Oh lawd God Jesus, have mercy on me," she announced.

Even her shadow seemed tired. Why was she getting up and taking all her warmth away from me? I squinted, confused, but not for long. She was lowering herself to her knees to pray.

Then came the soft muttering of words I couldn't make out. It began quietly enough but soon became a hymn. A song made of pledges and pleadings, sobs, sighs, and lamentations; the deluge of her misery and her fear. Every now and then, the name of one of her children cut through: "Agnes . . . Joan . . . Al." My father's name always made her cry. Soon the whole room was shaking with her voice.

Most times I would wipe my runny eyes, roll over, and go back to sleep. Today was different. I lay trembling under the sheet. Chest pounding. There was nowhere to hide from this hurricane. Soon enough, the crashing waves of her voice slowed down. She grew still. The storm passed. Then, as always, Mama rose from her knees, victorious, and got on with the day.

## VI

My room faced the cemetery, and my poor head was full of bogeymen.

I would wake up in the dead of darkness and imagine one of the awful creatures of our folktales coming for me. These stories, which I ate up greedily in the daylight, haunted me in the nighttime.

La Diablese or "LaJabless" was a devil woman who would come to parties and charm the men and leave them lost in the bush. A Douen had backwards feet and led children astray. A Papa Bois could transform into any animal and would trick hunters to their deaths. Lagahoo (or Loup-Garou) was a half-person, half-animal spirit that walked around dragging a vicious whip and chain behind it. These names, as I would later recognize, were almost exclusively French. Yet in those days they were just names to me and their strange music, which fascinated my tongue, only added to how fearsome they seemed. The scariest to me was Soucouyant. A Soucouyant was like a Trini vampire. A hag, who at night, slipped her skin and streaked across the sky as a fireball seeking innocent blood. You had to salt or burn her empty skin to stop her. The fact that I had never seen a fireball streaking across the sky did not prevent a chilly drop of sweat from sliding down my spine at the mention of that word.

This may all sound like fairy tales and superstition, but in my rural, Trini childhood, everyone, including big people, took these stories seriously. Grown people would speak in hushed tones about certain others being vampires. To me, it was just another odd part of growing up on the island that I never questioned. Perhaps it was because we lived in a tropical rainforest. There were real monsters, with real fangs, crawling around nearby, in the riverbeds, deep in the bush, waiting under rocks and on low branches and often in our very houses. So, why not in our heads too? They crowded our imaginations and gave life to our fears. A menagerie of menace that the Lord had put there to remind us that no matter how big we got, the whip hand would always be his.

And so it went. My early life was mostly an easy rhythm of reading schoolbooks and Bible books; exploring the bush; playing cricket, football, or table tennis; and hanging out with Mama and Junior. All this plus watching the blazing sun rage and the raging storms drown the earth in rain.

And also: more poulourie.

## VII

I was having the best day. I'd received a letter from Ami de Sol Downing, my dad's wife whom he'd never married. They lived in a place called Victoria in Canada, which to me was something like Sesame Street, except I assumed there were no grouches.

Everything about this letter made me giggle. The envelope had a pattern of red and blue stripes around the border. The handwriting was loopy and clear: "Mr. Antonio Michael Downing, Monkeytown, Third Branch, New Grant, Trinidad and Tobago." The stamp proclaimed, under the head of the Queen, "CANADA."

It was the first letter I had ever received. I carried it to school in my bookbag like a laurel wreath of victory. Whenever I couldn't stand it anymore, I took it out and smoothed the creases religiously, dragging my fingers over the neat little words. Little Nigel was apparently a very happy brother I now had, and baby Adrian was also doing well. The best part was the photos. There were two Polaroids: one of my dad with a Jheri curl, and one of the young family all together.

Ami was white, which to me meant she was a movie star. I had never met a white person before, and the concept was still being worked out in my mind. They seemed to exist in a world of perfection and angels and limitless exotic fruits, like apples and pears.

My dad, who I couldn't remember having seen before, also looked famous and beautiful.

Geography was my favourite subject, so I pulled out the large atlas at recess and flipped to the map of Canada, where I found Victoria Island in the Arctic. It gave me so much joy to know that my father, who before that moment was just someone my grandmother talked about, actually had a face—and a place too. Of course, he and his family lived in the city of Victoria, on Vancouver Island, and not in the Arctic, but at that time, young Tony was having the day of his life.

My best day was about to get better: it was the last day of school. My toes tingled at the thought of the hot season break which promised excursions, car rides, maybe even a trip to San Fernando, the second biggest city in the country. But that was all far off. Today I was mostly excited about getting our report cards. Mrs. Barrington, my teacher, walked through the aisles. "Now, class," she said as she handed a lime-green report book to each student, "today is the final day of your first year of primary school, and I want to congratulate you on your hard work." She stopped at my desk and tapped her nails to get my full attention. "I especially want to congratulate Mr. Downing on being first in test and excelling in reading, comprehension, and maths."

My classmates clapped politely. I smiled so hard I thought my head would burst.

Rushing out of school that day, I couldn't wait to tell Mama about finishing first in test. This was a big deal. But poulourie were a bigger deal. I waited eagerly for the Indian man behind the counter to serve them up. My mouth was already sloppy with anticipation.

As he handed them to me, the heat from the fryer and the spice of the pepper sauce filled my face. I stumbled down the stairs in a reverie, and as I got to the road, one precious poulourie rolled off the wax paper and onto the dirty ground. "Noooooo!" I yelled. I reached to grab it much too late, and then realized that I was off balance. I fell forward as I tried to right myself and maintain my grip on the other two poulourie still safe in my hand.

A car horn rang out. Tires screeched. And very quickly, my whole world faded to black.

There were no human casualties that day. No broken bones or bruising. People came running. They picked me up and scolded me, and then I continued on my way.

I survived; the poulourie didn't.

## Chapter Two

# THE DEVIL'S WOODYARD

I

"In the beginning was the Word, and the Word was with God, and the Word was God."

As soon as I heard that Bible verse, I could never forget it. It sounded like the most profound thing I had ever encountered but I had no idea why. It was also very true. The only places I could get books were in church or at school, which was an Anglican school and so also church. The Word was literally with God.

Despite all the King James we swallowed in Trinidad—or maybe because of that—it was hard to get away from the devil. He was everywhere. No place more so than during Carnival. Carnival was an annual party that lasted weeks, a cultural celebration, a kind of ecstasy in which the whole country indulged. It featured costumes, colourful and elaborate, and monstrosities marching through the streets in broad daylight. We called it "playing mas," which is from the French word "masquerade." The tradition began because the mostly French slaves could not attend their masters' masquerade balls, so they created their own. And there too, the devil reigned. Our Carnival characters included Jab Molassie, Moko Jumbie, Gentleman Devil, and Lucifer, to name a few. There were also references to Obeah, or African black magic, and the fiends from our folklore with their whips and chains and horror-show habits. It seems obvious now why they all had French names, just like the slave masters. Carnival was the slaves' reaction to the European culture they were forced to contend with. They did so by turning their torment into their entertainment. Yet the demons who amused the adults were both terrifying and alluring to my young self.

Jab Jab or Jab Molasie was my favourite character. He was a demon with blood-red horns, skin as black as midnight, and a pitchfork. We used to chant: "Yuh fraid de devil? Jab Jab! Yuh fraid him bad? Jab Jab! Well, look de devil—Jab Jab!—right in yuh yard."

These images soldered themselves to the infrastructure of my childhood imagination: God lived in heaven, but the devil was everywhere else.

It was no wonder that we were petrified of the dark. Country Caribbean dark meant blackness deep and complete. Also, it meant noise—an endless symphony of toads, crickets, night birds, and ten thousand other critters that owned the time from dusk until dawn. It didn't help that we lived next to the cemetery, and Junior and I shared the bedroom facing the graves. Sometimes if a gravedigger was drunk or lazy, he would dig a grave too shallow and it would add the rancid stink of the rotting corpse to the relentless dark.

"Yuh put de goat in de pen?" Junior asked me one night.

"That is your job." I sucked my teeth.

"Nah, boy. I put my goat in de pen. Mama say you have to put your own."

I could feel my heart start to sink. It was already eight o'clock, and the night was inky dark and full of evil.

"Yuh better get your tail outside and find dat goat."

My mouth was becoming sawdust. My heart was galloping out my shirt.

"Yuh going to get eat by a jumbie, for sure."

Hot tears were peeking over my eyelids, and my knees were trying hard not to shake.

"Noooo. Jumbie will eat de goat."

"Yuh stupid? Jumbie doh eat goat—it does eat lil boy juss like you."

Before I could break down, he hit me in my shoulder hard and started to laugh.

"Ah joking, boy—I put yuh goat in de pen too."

He cackled and hit me again.

"If yuh see yuh face right now! If yuh see!"

Tears poured down my cheeks, but I was grinning ear to ear.

"Yuh see how you wicked? Yuh see how you wicked?" was all I could say.

But all that mattered was that the devil wasn't going to get me that night.

I I

Much like Trinidad itself, Miss Excelly could surprise you with contradictions. After she had prayed her heart out until the foundations of the house shook, she wouldn't hesitate to cuss you out if you thought you could sleep in. She was an ambitious lady, so there were always things that needed doing. Although she was generous and kindhearted, she expected all of us to pull our weight.

"You two juss like yuh muddah and faddah. You think you can sleep de whole day and watch me in mih house?"

The land around the house always had some kind of small crop growing. Miss Excelly started her work inside the house, where she grew all sorts of plants: anthuriums, crotons, lilies, roses, cacti, and aloes. In the front yard, she grew mint, thyme, and fever grass. This last had a strong pungent smell and sharp leaves—she would boil it when we were sick with fever and put us under a heavy blanket to sweat it out.

At the back, we planted corn and kept a few chickens, goats, and sometimes pigs. Beside the garage, we kept yams, eddoes, dasheens, and cassavas—we called these root vegetables "provisions." Around the house, we had fruit trees: papayas, cashews, calabash gourds, and lemons on the cemetery side; pomeracs, yellow-skinned coconuts, and grapefruits towards the back. And of course, all kinds of mango trees: doudous, long mango, rose mango, and Julie mango on the cemetery side.

We had tales for every tree. Our neighbour Hodge was notorious for sending us to cut, from the thick welting calabash branches, the whips he would use to beat us. Junior once climbed the pomerac tree by the canal, only to hit a Jack Spania wasp nest. He got stung so much, he dropped ten feet to get away. Cashew fruit made your mouth cottony.

By far, my dream was always mango season. We had recipes for every form of mango. Green mango salad we called chow; it was made with bird pepper and shadow beni for spice. This just-before-ripe-mango salad we would eat at the side of some rice or provisions. The greatest thing, though, was simply waiting under the tree for a ripe Julie mango to fall, and then sucking up the golden pulp before it ran down between your fingers, sticky and perfect and delicious. You could peel the skin off and watch the yellow strands of mango cling to each strip, but I preferred mine skin and all.

You could usually find my grandma in one of the fields weeding with a hoe, cutting grass with a cutlass (which is what we called a machete), or on her hands and knees picking weeds in the dirt. The woman was dynamic. It was the 1980s. She was born in 1904. She probably had rubber boots and a hat on, and she was definitely singing a hymn:

*We are marching to Zion, beautiful, beautiful Zion.*
*We are marching upward to Zion, the beautiful City of God.*
*Let those refuse to sing, who never knew their God.*
*But children of the heav'nly King may speak their joys abroad.*

The hypnotic effect this had on everyone who stopped to listen was never lost on me. Every note poured out of her like warm honey and drifted off down the road like perfume. This was the first gift she gave me, her first lesson: she taught me how to sing. But even more important, she taught me the art of keeping an audience riveted. It was a spell. It conjured us into her sacred place and bathed us in her profound peacefulness.

This was the rhythm of the day. By afternoon, she would be sitting in the gallery sipping iced water to keep cool from the heat. When I was young, I wouldn't stray far from her side. She would watch me play, often with Junior in the yard, and call out one of her sayings: "You are very harden little boy, but remember who don't hear will feel," or "Don't put yuh hat where yuh can't reach it." Not that I always understood or behaved, but I always listened.

When she sat and recited verses of the Bible, I asked her about them and she told me. I was obsessed with the stories. The parting of the sea, why God let Job suffer, how Solomon got so wise, turning water into wine and the whole fantasy of Jesus, and most crucially, the poetry of the King James version. Every time I heard a "thou" or a "begat" or a "goeth," I felt like I was tumbling into a secret world, a puzzle that needed to be solved. The magic of the Queen's English had already hooked me deeply. This was her second gift.

I clung to her skirts as much as I could in those early years. I would hide behind her when strangers came to the yard to talk.

"Miss Excelly, you can lend me some sugar until next week, please God?"

"Of course, child. I only have a pound, but I will give you half."

"These boy, them getting big! Which one is this? Junior or Tony?"

"This is the little one, Tony."

"He acting shy, but he look like he faddah, eh? Fuss he look juss like Al."

"I feel he like me more than the big one. He doh say much, but he smart and he does listen."

On this day, Mama offered the only thing that could bring me out of my shell: an audience.

"Boy, come and tell them that ting yuh was saying the other day."

I couldn't figure out why Mama was so proud of my little speech, but I liked seeing the smile of delight on her face when I said it. I put on my explaining voice.

"Umm, well, want is when yuh feel you would really like something, like fry bake and salt fish or dhalpourie," I said slowly. "Need is when if you don't have something, you might suffer, like food or Jesus." I could feel them laughing, so I puffed out my chest even more and looked off in the distance like the pastor when he was thinking deeply. "You can want something you need and you can need something you want, but a wise man will always know the difference."

Grandma's friend shouted and hooted with delight.

"The boy talk like Solomon himself," Mama said as I slipped back behind her skirts.

Yes, one of my earliest memories of myself is a performance and a composition. In truth, many of the elements that would make up the rest of my life could be seen in that moment: clever, shy, lover of attention. The shyness, however, would come and go.

## III

My grandmother was serious about two things: God and education. Her relationship with Jesus seemed personal. He was her first lover, and they had eloped a long time ago. She was a child when he first touched her soul.

When my grandmother was thirteen, her mother died and she suddenly became the parent of six siblings. Preacher Johnny Richardson, her father, quickly found a new wife and family, and left Mama to fend for the others. They were Theresa, Olga, Gertrude, Dawnice, Sese, and little Stanley, who I saw die in our house when he was an old man.

Jesus was now the man of the house. I don't ever remember Mama pushing us to follow Christ, but education was a different thing. She pushed and pushed regularly. "A good education will carry you to the ends of this earth. Without education, you have nothing." Quoting King Solomon, she would say, "Wisdom and knowledge is better than silver and gold."

School days began early in the morning—sometimes before the sun rose. She would iron our short-sleeved cream shirts and khaki shorts until they were clean and stiff. Appearances were important. We had our workbooks and readers in our bookbags and perhaps a few pennies for poulourie, and away we went.

Once at school, we ran helter-skelter around the yard and generally made as much noise as we possibly could until a hand-rung bell began to chime for the morning assembly. We dashed to the front yard straightening our rumpled uniforms. Tucking shirt in pants or skirt and lining up breathless according to our grades, which we called standards. The two infant years were at the front followed by the first standard. The ranks rolled back, disciplined and exact and taller with each line, to standard five. I was in standard one this year.

By the third bell, you had better be quiet, neat, and attentive if you knew what was good for you. Mrs. Briggs, our principal, rose and rolled her stern eyes over us. She was the lightest-skinned lady I had ever seen. Her hair hung down in waves. Her face seemed pink. Her mouth pouted into a stuffy authority as she stared over her glasses. It was time to learn.

She enunciated in a faintly British accent: "Let us sing our national anthem." We sang the country's anthem daily. Its verses had been composed by a white Guyanese man. The anthem that predated it, which Mrs. Briggs and Mrs. Barrington had undoubtedly sung every day of their childhoods, was the British "God Save the Queen," or perhaps "God Save the King."

Tuneless but obligated, we began:

> *Forged from the love of liberty,*
> *In the fires of hope and prayer.*

The young ones shrieked with enthusiasm. The older boys muttered. The word "liberty" sounded more like "lay-bah-tee." Mrs. Briggs scowled and raised her delicate hands to vigorously conduct us. The ordeal over, we muttered through the Lord's Prayer like a horde of sleepy wasps. Ahhh-men.

Next came our morning exercise. Picture fifty children counting out as they went: "Ooone," touch toes and up. "Twooo," left side. "Treeee," right side. Our principal turned purple with rage: "It is 'th-ree,' not 'tree.' 'Three,' the number after two and before four. Not 'tree,' the thing monkeys climb! We will speak properly at New Grant E.C. School!"

We started again, making it to the end this time. A soft breeze of relief and chatter began to rise, but Mrs. Barrington, my teacher, shook the cast-iron bell and we simmered. Then a standard-four boy farted loud as a bullfrog, and the whole yard erupted in laughter. We settled down only at the thought of the sharp ridge of metal in the heavy wooden rulers they used to spank us.

School in Trinidad had one essential purpose: to civilize the savages. Here we were, rambunctious brown-skinned children descended from Yorubas and Hindus, but we didn't learn any African folktales or read the *Bhagavad Gita*; we learned of Odysseus and his voyage home to Ithaca.

The closer you could get to Europeanness—especially Englishness—the better your life would be, and the more your life would be worth. The first rule was that we couldn't speak like Trinidadians. The Creole that everyone spoke outside the schoolhouse was strictly prohibited. We were required to speak and write "properly," which meant more British. Which meant more white.

The final act of our morning ritual could be the best or the worst, depending on the day. One by one, children who had misbehaved the day before slouched towards the front to be punished. It was public humiliation. You held your hand out for the "licks"—delivered with the heavy wooden ruler with metal edging—and winced. You didn't want to look, but you didn't want to not look because you would miss the blow. If you pulled your hand away, they would flog your bum, which was always worse. This was called a "cut tail"—literally they would cut your tail. This ritual was the best when it meant watching other kids get their palms beat with rulers. It was the worst when it was your turn. I was rarely in trouble in those days. This too would pass.

New Grant E.C. School was part of the Anglican school system. Anglicanism had become the official religion of Trinidad when Queen Victoria signed the island's separation from the Diocese of Barbados in 1867. Our school was one of dozens across the country that married instruction in maths and sciences with a "proper" moral grounding. It was two floors with two rooms. Our classrooms were separated by tall blackboards on wheels. We sat with our standard for all the lessons.

Our main textbook was *Nelson's West Indian Reader*, written and printed in Cheltenham, England, and compiled by J.O. Cutteridge, an Englishman whose legacy would loom long over the history of the island. Every year we were given a new copy to learn and read from. It began with such worthy sentiments as "reading must from the beginning be accompanied by thinking." But reading and thinking soon centred on Christopher Columbus, the Queen and buccaneers like Walter Raleigh and Admiral Lord Rodney who "saved" the West Indies; it was a sanitized history of the Commonwealth. There were no mentions of slavery or kidnapping, maiming, raping, and taming of savages—just gallant white men forging new adventures with stiff upper lips and hearts full of fealty to our sovereign.

Those books were used for so long in Trinidad that my auntie Joan, at age seventy-five, could still remember this colonizer classic "The Last Buccaneer":

> Oh, England is a pleasant place for them that's rich
> and high;
> But England is a cruel place for such poor folks as I.

I remember the book well. Stories of Sir Walter Raleigh, Napoleon, and Columbus were interspersed with sections of the *Iliad* and descriptions of ancient Rome. They each had about ten full-colour pages which were always of some famous scene of English, French, or ancient Roman or Greek history, depicted by a British or Scottish painter. In *Drake Receiving the Honour of Knighthood from Queen Elizabeth,* bearded courtiers surround Gloriana Regina herself. Men in soft caps and frilly collars look on with harsh eyes as Elizabeth, with her pumpkin-coloured hair and virginal-white robes, brandishes a sword to knight Sir Francis Drake. Drake had been sacking Spanish ships in the adjacent story, called "The Buccaneer," which I read when I was six.

I consumed these tales with wide-eyed fascination. And what unfolded page after page, battle after battle, image after image, was the great river of things that explained the world. Achilles slaying Hector before the walls of Troy, Joan of Arc leading the charge against the English, cannons echoing on the high seas, raids and sackings, islands "changing hands." It all marinated my little brain like cod-fish soaking, seeping into the cracks, and floating inevitably on a strong tide back to Buckingham Palace. Back to the Crown, the curtsies, the knighthoods, the gold, the pearls, the treasure, the unstoppable velocity of destiny. And it was called "History."

All this I perceived in those pages, but if I ever tried to speak of it to anyone outside of school they would shush me. They'd say: "De boy like he books eh?" or "Clever like he faddah," or "Leave school in school arright?"

Our classroom had rows of wooden desks whose tops would open so that our books could go into their bellies. The coat of arms that looked down on us was topped with a ship's wheel and a conquistador's helmet, and it celebrated Columbus's three ships: the *Pinta*, the *Niña*, and the *Santa Maria*.

The only white face we ever saw was Jesus praying in our Bibles, yet somehow, even as a child, I understood the golden rule: there was a place called white, and it was always better.

In these subtle ways, the Queen's design was being drummed into us, even as we were trying to get the means to escape her dominion.

# IV

By the time I was five, my demeanour ranged from giggly and chatty to argumentative and stubborn, or what old folks in Trinidad called "harden" or "own-way." I liked to do my own thing—except when I was with Junior, of course.

Junior and I were always either laughing or fighting. We would fight about whose turn it was to take the enamel chamberpot, or "posy," to the toilet that morning. About who should sweep the garage with the cocoyea broom, a collection of dry sticks tied together into a hard bristle sweeper. Even though Junior was bigger, I wouldn't hesitate to swing a punch. Fear and apprehension weren't part of me back then.

Our favourite thing to do was to imitate people.

Hodge got the worst of it because we hated him the most. Back straight, belly big and fake pregnant, and a look on your face like a rotten watermelon that was about to burst. That was Hodge. Now you needed a low growly voice, like a sergeant giving orders: "JuniorandTony, I thought I tell all yuh to stop smiling!"

I was in instant stitches and rolling on the ground.

"All yuh think life is fun? FUN?!"

Not able to contain myself, I jumped in, pushing Junior aside. "Little boys should not be smiling," I mimicked. "They should be sweeping yard and studying hard."

Junior was hanging on to my neck for dear life.

"Get de belt. I will show all yuh fun. Oh shit, mih pants fall down."

By far, our best imitations were of the preachers we would see every Sunday at Hindustan Baptist Church. They were shouters who would sing songs so mournful that it was hard to figure out what they were actually saying. In the gaps, a deacon would call out the next line for those who couldn't read, and the whole congregation would sing in response. Junior and I took turns being the deacon and finally got to the climax of it all, the sermon.

The formula was simple: we started with a verse.

"In the beginning was the Word, and the Word was with God, and the Word was God."

Then we took turns yelling the nouns, as if the louder we yelled, the more we would be understood. Until finally, we were yelling the whole thing.

"THE WORD WAS GAAAAWD!"

Then the best part: you catch the power.

This might mean gibberish speaking in tongues, jumping and danc-ing on one leg, falling to the ground stiff as a corpse, or preferably, all three. "Ketching powah" was the pinnacle of the performance, and Junior and I took it so seriously that we were often covered in sweat and rolling on the grass by then.

Yet all was not always theatre and jokes. I was just like the place where I grew up: full of contradictions and prone to sudden violence.

V

When your brother offers to tell you a scary story during a blackout and there isn't any light but candles for miles, you want to say no but you can't. The blackout is cause for being terrified, but it's also like a holiday feeling. We're huddled around the candles in the living room when Junior asks, "Tony, yuh want to hear a scary story?"

"Yeah?" comes my shaky answer as a terrible noise rises from the cemetery.

He says: "Yuh know what is Lagahoo? Lapin Garou, some people does call dem. Long Boy and Pincy are hanging out one day, and Pincy say, 'Long Boy, ah so hungry. Meh belly hurting mih.' Long Boy tell him, 'Well, Pincy, ah know what to do: leh we go an hunt some wild hog.' 'Wild hog?' 'Yes, boy. Pig tail, roast pork, pig foot, and tripe. We don't have to share with nobody!' Pincy say: 'Yes, potna. Leh we go and hunt some hog.'

"So they wait until it get really dark, and then jump in the bush with the hunting gun. Pincy say, 'Boy, yuh kno where we going?' Long Boy say, 'Yes, man. Ah know where the whole pack of pig does sleep, but yuh have to be very, very quiet.'"

Junior is whispering and I am forgetting to breathe.

"So when they reach where the hog is, Long Boy give Pincy the gun and say, 'Ah going to run up de hill and chase dem down so yuh can shoot one, all right?' Pincy is nervous, and he hand was shaking on the gun barrel. 'But, Pincy, yuh have to remember one ting: don't shoot de leader of the pack. Don't shoot the wild hog in de front, yuh understand?' Pincy nod, but he fraid and all he can tink of is what if the wild hog rush him and stick him with a big dirty tusk in he backside?

"So Long Boy gone. Pincy waiting. He wait and he wait and he wait, and the bush start to get cold."

Outside, the cemetery sounds much noisier than a place full of dead bones and stones should be.

"Suddenly everything start to happen. He hear dem first, and they grunting—humpf, humpf, humpf. Then he hear the tree and branch start snapping, and they moving fast. In a rush, Pincy see the wild hog start coming down the hill. He hold up the gun, but he chest beating fast-fast-fast, and as soon as he see the first wild hog, he squeeze the triggah and—bang!—the whole pack scatter. The first wild hog drop down on the ground, squeezing out blood from he belly like a river. Pincy run up to it mouth, already dripping for de taste ah roast pork. As he run up, he hear Long Boy voice coming from the wild hog: 'Oh God, Pincy. Yuh shoot mih!'"

# VI

I cut my grandmother with a knife. Well, technically just a knife handle. It was a heavy cast-iron handle with an inch of blade left, but I threw it at her with all my strength.

It started when I walked through the kitchen and didn't say, "Good morning, Mama." Having no manners was the worst thing that could be said of a child. Before I could leave the room, I felt a hard, dull pain at the back of my head. She had hit me with a green mango. The old woman couldn't chase you, but she was deadly accurate at throwing things.

"Boy, you can't say good morning when you pass me?"

Before I knew it, I responded with my temper. I flung the handle at her.

"Why yuh hit mih?!"

The blade sliced the saggy brown skin on her arm and drew a thin line of blood.

She was shocked. I was shocked. She looked confused and furious. My ass was going to get beat. Before my crocodile tears could start, her face turned to a look she had never given me before: disappointment.

"What is wrong with you, child?"

So I ran. Out of the kitchen and into the road, my little legs seemed to be moving so fast they weren't moving at all. I ran down the road with my arms swinging and my hot tears blowing in the wind.

When I reached Miss Annette's house, I met Junior and his friend Allister preparing to leave and said, "Junior, Mama say to take me to the Devil's Woodyard."

"She say dat?" He looked at me sideways.

He and Allister were wearing rubber boots with their pant legs tucked and swinging sharp cutlasses.

"All right. Well, come then, but it's your cut tail if yuh lying."

Allister was the older brother of my best friend, Sterling. He was what we called a "red" boy. His hair had big curls, and it and his skin were slightly reddish compared to everyone else's.

"Look nah, Junior," Allister moaned, "me ain't have no time to slow down for no lil boy."

"Me eh no lil boy!"

I looked at Junior, pleading.

"Leh him come. Ah will take care of him," he said.

Then we were off. Slipping into the bush just after the bend in Monkeytown, we left the world behind.

First stop was a Julie mango tree known for having the sweetest fruit. Soon my sadness was lost in the thick, syrupy yellow-gold juice that drizzled down my arm and throat. I lost touch with everything but the sound of the wind in the trees and the sticky softness slicking down my throat. Ecstasy achieved, we continued down to the river.

The river moved slowly, and most of the logs were alligators. Crossing was straightforward only if you happened to be an alligator. We boys had to find somewhere shallow and cross fast. It was quiet tropical bush—which is to say, it was very noisy. Birds chased and harassed each other in squadrons branch to branch. Giant many-legged crawlies scuttled on the damp ground as we chopped our way through the tall grass.

At the top of a hill we came to a barbed-wire fence. Straining one by one, we held open the angry wire for each other. Then we were in a wide-open farmer's field that reeked of cow shit and had been tilled so the ground was unpassable. We walked around. This was the farthest from home I had ever walked. I was terrified and fascinated. Some farmer with his gun was out there looking for us.

The place they called the Devil's Woodyard seemed appropriate to my mood. After the long walk, I started to think about Miss Excelly and what I had done. Going to meet the devil didn't seem as bad as facing her. Some part of me was afraid, but Junior was there and he wasn't afraid.

The trees stopped. The lush green gave way to a field of cracked muddy ground. In dozens of little muddy hills, steaming liquid mud bubbled out of the earth. Is this what hell looked like? No trees. No grass. Just dry mud and bubbling hot mud. How was this possible?

I felt like I had arrived in some parallel dimension. Allister and Junior stuck sticks in the bubbling pools. Revulsion and fascination mixed my brain into a boiling stew.

"Doh be scared, Tony. Tony, yuh fraid?" they teased.

> *Yuh fraid de devil? Jab Jab!*
> *Yuh fraid him bad? Jab Jab!*
> *Well, look de devil—Jab Jab!*
> *Right in yuh yard.*

After an hour, it was time to go. The sun was falling fast and nobody wanted to be in the bush after dark. I looked back at the devil's field, but all I could think of were my grandmother's words: "What is wrong with you, child?"

The answers would be a long time coming.

Chapter Three

# WHOM SHALL I FEAR?

I

Legend has it that the island of Trinidad was "discovered" by the head colonizer himself, Christopher Columbus, in 1498. It was his third voyage across the great heaving Atlantic, and after giving shout-outs to Aragon and Castile, he swore to name the first landfall after the Trinity, or Trinidad.

Of course, like all his "discoveries," this one uncovered nothing new—there were already people living on the island. The Carib and Arawak indigenous peoples had lived there for centuries. The vegetarian Arawaks called the island Kairi, and nearby Tobago was inhabited by the warlike Caribs. Over the next two hundred years, both groups were decimated by a combination of European weapons and disease. Yet even today, a quarter of the towns in Trinidad bear indigenous names, such as Oropouche, Arouca, and Guayaguayare, where my grandfather used to work on the oil rigs. While Tobago would change hands among the French, English, and Dutch many times, Trinidad remained under Spanish control for centuries.

The first dramatic transformation of the island's population came in 1783, when the Spanish king Charles III published his Cedula de Población, or Cedula of Population. This was a scheme to settle the island with other European colonists, as long as they were from Catholic countries and paid taxes to the Spanish crown. To this point Trinidad was still mostly inhabited by indigenous tribes overseen by a small cadre of Spanish overlords. A few years later, in 1789, the French Revolution led to the mass migration of royalist French plantation owners from other Caribbean islands like Martinique and Guadeloupe and their Black Creole-speaking slaves. Overnight, Trinidad became overwhelmingly French-speaking. This is why so much of the island's vernacular is rooted in the French language. I grew up saying words like *cote ci cote la*, *la diablesse*, Jour overt (or J'ouvert), and La Romaine, but because there was no formal French taught in school, I had no idea I was speaking another language. A Rwandan DJ once shocked me by saying, "You from Trinidad? I love that place. You guys speak so much French!"

More than language, the French brought with them many of the traditions that are associated with the island to this day. The most famous, Carnival, started when plantation owners threw Marie Antoinette–style masquerades that their slaves then mimicked. That's why if you march in a band in Carnival, you say you are playing mas. Playing mas was how the slaves became free. You put on a costume—a devil, a character—so that you could reveal yourself. Lives that laboured under the burden of whips and chains were suddenly vivid and alive. This fascination with masquerade was burnt into the heart of what it means to be Trinidadian.

In 1805, Admiral Horatio Nelson beat Napoleon's navy at Trafalgar, and the Spanish and French naval powers were finished for good. The English took over Trinidad. The Queen had landed.

This was directly responsible for bringing my family to Trinidad.

In the War of 1812, or what the Americans call the "Second War of Independence," slaves from West Africa were liberated by the redcoats, who (not ones to miss a trick) then turned them into companies to fight their former slave masters. When the truce was signed in 1815, the Crown shipped the Africans to the inland wilds of Trinidad. They started so-called company villages in the most stubborn bush, where to this day there is only one real road in and out.

My family came from these companies.

We learned how to thrive in this teeming, isolated backwoods, and we gained a reputation for being resilient, spiritually devout, and a little mentally unstable.


## I I


Dragging myself home weary from school, I could hear Miss Excelly singing "Pass Me Not, O Gentle Saviour" as I hit the cemetery, which was never good. In the gallery, I watched her black-pepper plaits and her sagging jowls and her mouth hanging on to "hear my gentle cry." She looked like an old lady with no real income and three mouths to feed. And I could see that there were tears in her eyes.

"Mama, don't cry. 'The race is not to the swift, nor the battle to the strong,'" I said, quoting Ecclesiastes.

And she smiled while crying and said, "Child, you know book, but you don't know page."

I tried to wrap my arms around her as if I were holding her together from whatever big-people worries were caving in her soul.

"Darling, go and boil yuh grandma two fig before yuh go and play." By "two fig," she meant neither two nor what we Canadians call figs. She meant green bananas and not ripe bananas, cause who would boil those?

By this point, kids followed me because I was never afraid and seemed to always know what to say. For example, when the churchy people came to talk down to us and frighten us into salvation, I was the kid they never wanted to see. "But doesn't the Bible say, 'I am the way, the truth and the life: no one cometh unto the father but by me?'" I would ask. "So why do we need you?"

Annoying, right?

I headed to the kitchen intent on boiling green bananas but the sound of my friends' loud chatter and laughter soon dragged me out into the road. Soon I was jumping rope on the blazing asphalt with my bestie, Sterling, another red boy who was nothing but trouble. Sterling was the only one willing to play tricks on our older brothers, who were also best friends. The previous week, we'd found where they stashed their stolen hand of green bananas to ripen and had moved the hoard to another spot so we could have it, but also so we could watch them go mad searching for it.

Cecily was there, also jumping rope in the road. She was my girlfriend, but that only meant we talked a lot at recess. Also there was Aiesha, who was tall and dark as 90 percent chocolate, and had a Jheri curl that made her seem pretty in a grown-up way. And Natasha, who was tall and quiet but always nice. We all were around the same age and played together almost every day.

The girls were always better at jumping rope, and when Sterling got tied up, Aiesha laughed at him. He kissed his teeth hard and said, "Why yuh so Black?" Which was the worst insult.

"Yuh juss mad cause yuh can't jump rope," Aiesha said.

And I stuck up for him cause I always fought with Aiesha. "All right, Miss Pitch Oil, you stay there with yuh Black self," I said.

"I might be Black, but at least I have a muddah and a faddah. Where yours? Yuh even know who yuh faddah is?"

My face got hot. I was trying to come up with an insult, but my tongue was heavy. I was boiling over. My temper had started to throb and swell like a knock in the head when I got a thump between the shoulders. Miss Excelly was vexed.

"Boy, I thought I told you to boil two fig for me! De pot boil over and coulda bun de house down!"

My friends were rolling with laughter because I was getting bouffed up, which is what we called getting yelled at by an adult.

"Come out de road."

And she dragged me by my skinny arms as my friends fell over themselves howling with laughter.

III

My friend Sonny and I only spoke ping-pong. Sonny was a small Hindu boy from School Trace, which was the street next to my school where all the Indian folks from New Grant lived. He was like a brown doll, with a tiny round head, dark lips and eyes, and hair that swooped down from right to left. We would climb the calabash tree and sit in the sun eating mangoes. There was never much to say. He was the only person I never felt I had to prove myself to.

At our house, we had a ping-pong table in the yard. It was green with white lines around the outside, like Wimbledon, and had a bright green net. Sonny and I loved to play almost as much as we loved eating mangoes. One day we had just boiled the dented ping-pong balls back into shape and were about to start a game when Sonny asked: "Yuh want to come to *puja* for Diwali?"

"Wey is *puja*, boy?" My mouth enjoyed the strange new word.

"Dat is when we do devotions for Lakshmi. She is the prettiest goddess, and Diwali is she time."

After the British outlawed slavery in their colonies in 1833, they started bringing Hindus and Muslims from the Indian continent to Trinidad as indentured labourers. This was colonizer-speak for five years of hard labour and then a ticket home or a piece of land if you wanted to stay. Maybe it was the hundred days of cholera and ocean storms needed to get back to Calcutta, but after five years, most took the land and stayed. For this reason, a third of Trinidadians are of East Indian descent. In true Trini fashion, their traditions mixed and mingled and stitched themselves into the fabric of the country. They spoke Bhojpuri, Urdu, Gujarati, and Hindustani, and they had stories and words very different from anything I'd learned from King James.

I don't remember how Sonny and I became friends, but we liked each other a lot. He was quiet, almost mousy and introverted, and I was a notorious big mouth. We were the odd couple. "Okay, boy," I said, his invitation to *puja* intriguing me, "Ah go ask mih grandmuddah, but ah think I can come." As was usually the case back then, I was in it for the food.

Then we were playing. Caught in the dance of the bouncing ball. We spent days staring the rackets into each hit, twisting our wrists to change the spin, and pulling back dramatically for a smash. The only sounds were our grunts, the hollow bounce of the ball, and a hoarse voice calling out the score after each point. The world became this bizarre tango of limbs, and Sonny and I disappeared into it.

After forever, which was probably just a few hours, we sat in the driveway by the road, sweating and eating pomerac. The pomerac is shaped like a pear, but it's red and white and juicy when ripe. I was explaining to Sonny that I never got to eat them because there was a Jack Spania nest in the tree. (A Jack Spania is a super-aggressive wasp that breaks off a piece of its tail when it stings you. The sting makes flesh puffy and painful.)

Suddenly, the shadow of a big boy loomed over us.

"Ayye, yuh think yuh good at table tennis? Who want to play a real champion?" he bragged.

"Yuh could play?" I was skeptical.

"I is big man. I will school all yuh."

It was obvious right away that he wasn't good at all.

"One–nothing . . . two–nothing . . . three–nothing . . . " Sonny kept score.

By four–nothing, the boy was getting mad and screwing up his face. By five–one, he was cussing and slamming the racket whenever he missed shots.

"Doh slam my racket," I said quietly.

"Dis fucken ting not balanced," he said and whacked the edge on the table. I didn't like this. The Tony temper simmered.

"Just doh slam we racket."

"Eight–two . . . eight–three . . . nine–three . . . "

"Dis shitten racket eh no good! What kinda shit is this?" Whack went the racket into the side of the table.

I was over the table and in front of him so fast that I don't remember how I got there. My racket smashed into his face.

"I tell yuh not to slam my racket!"

His eyes watered and blood started to squirt out of his nose. And then he was gone, running down Monkeytown Third Branch, holding his nose and calling out about how "dat lil boy crazy."

Sonny was laughing and pointing at me. "Boy, you like Jack Spania. Yuh small, but yuh is *real* trouble."

IV

Who was the Indian boy in the bright Datsun who showed up to take Mama to the shop or the doctor in Princes Town, or dropped off money when she couldn't rub two cents together? His name was Kenrick, and that was Miss Excelly's prayer dividend. Which is like a mutual fund for faith. She prayed up a storm all day, and then helped people for no reason except that they needed it. Eventually, they paid her back.

"That is Kenrick. Ansel son," Wilton said, as if that explained every-thing.

Wilton was my adopted brother; he was much older than the rest of us and already in his man body. He ran track, and his spikes hung, temptingly, from the bedroom doorknob. But I knew that touching them would get me a stinging "tap" on the back of my head.

"Who is Ansel?"

"Ansel is an Indian girl who your grandmother used to teach to sew. She had a school and would teach many girls how to sew and knit."

"So?"

"So Kenrick was born right there in the back room. When Ansel get pregnant, she muddah put she out and Miss Excelly take she in. So Miss Excelly is like Kenrick grandmother."

"But how can she have an Indian grandchild?"

Miss Excelly had many grandchildren. Wilton, of course, was one of them, although I never knew the story of how she adopted him until many years later. After his mother was stabbed in the road and died, he was sent to live with his father. The knock-about playboy, suddenly responsible for five children, was overwhelmed and started to look for places to send them. Miss Excelly showed up bright and early one morning in her best hat.

The neighbours asked incredulously, "How are you going to take care of Wilton, old lady? You can't even take care of yourself."

She didn't budge. All she said was: "I saw this boy in a dream. God will provide. He coming with me."

And she was right. Wilton did survive to have his own kids and become the doting father he never had.

Whenever Mama got sick, Jemma and Elizabeth, two sisters she had taken in when they were young and in trouble, would come and take care of us, bringing their own children with them. Jemma was crippled from polio, people said. One of her legs was in a metal sling with leather straps. The contraption squeaked and clinked when she walked. Her skin was the colour of Carnation milk, and her eyes were coffee-bean brown.

I hated breakfast when Jemma made it. Something in me choked down the food with scorn, as if I would catch polio from eating it. Her sister, Elizabeth, or Liz, had the same colour skin but no boot-strap. I remember both being kind to us in a way our old grandmother couldn't. They would ask us questions and check our homework and not need naps in the afternoon.

Our hero was Steve. Steve was Mama's actual grandchild by her first child, Uncle Boysie. Boysie was a legend. He ran a shop in Fyzabad and would always show up with boxes of goodies: red plums, red mangoes, tamarind balls, anchar, cuchilla, and other useful stuff like flour, rice, and meat. Tall, calm, and quiet, he played mas and married a Hindu woman. Which basically meant he was going to hell, but this never seemed to bother him. Uncle Boysie had Mama's twisted sweet smile and sleepy eyes, and he loved her more than anything.

Steve was Boysie's son, but was raised in the house in Monkeytown just like we were. So Mama was both his grandmother and his mother. I'm not sure why he ended up there, but he grew up with and was five years older than my father, his uncle, Al. When I knew him, he was police. His erect stance, shiny boots, and crisp moustache made him look impossibly handsome. He lived up north in Trincity, which was close to Port of Spain and almost like another country. There were far more houses, bigger houses, packed together side by side, with cars in the driveway. Back in Monkeytown, almost no one owned a car. Going to Steve's house was like going to wonderland. On the drive north, we'd catch the sights and smells of the towns and people, the men and women selling "ripe fig," big bunches of bananas, breadfruit, fresh coconut water from coconuts chopped open right in front of you with deadly sharp cutlasses. We'd see the vendors moving slowly as king snakes, beads of perspiration bubbling on their skins, and smell the peppery scent of barrah or oysters fresh out the sea. It was a whole universe of hustle that my thirsty senses drank up lustily. Until, finally, we'd land at Steve and Vio's house and find it filled with incredible things: sodas in the fridge, candy in the pantry, two television sets—sophisticated trappings of city living that impressed and intimidated me.

We played with his only son, Mike, who we called Mauvin. Almond wars was our favourite game. We fanned out in teams among the trees of the almond grove, filled our little pockets four-deep with the hard purple-and-green fruit, and pelted one another mercilessly. The tears dried quickly, but the welts stayed for weeks.

Vio, Steve's wife, was always sharp and well dressed and professional. She had a mole on her cheek and dark, intelligent eyes. There were no women like her in Monkeytown. She didn't cuss, drink, or even yell loudly when she talked. Little did I know she too grew up right there in Monkeytown. That was how she had met Steve. But that is a story for another time.

The women on our street were legendary. Miss Annette and Miss Paula had a baby-making contest going. They were both in double digits. They were the loud, cussing, drinking women on the street, but they always seemed to keep their swarm of children fed. Miss Annette was married to a dougla—half Indian, half African—named Olwin. They would fight like cats and dogs. Physical fights with knives and broken bottles and insults that cut even worse. Miss Annette was notorious for having kids that weren't Olwin's and would tell him, "That one is not yours! Watch he face. He not yours! Look at you. You like a ram goat. Horn growing all over your head!"

"Giving horns" was an old-school expression for getting cheated on. Yet when Anselm came out looking like Mr. Placid, Olwin shut up and raised him like his own son.

Across from us and down a hill was the house belonging to Boboy and Miss Ayla. Boboy was pitch black, but short and stocky and powerful. They said that he had a gun and was "real dread," which is Trini for not to be fucked with. Of course, this didn't stop me from stoning him and cussing him one day. Wilton dragged me into the house by my neck. "Boy, yuh want to dead?" he scolded. "Yuh lucky Boboy didn't get vex."

That was my way: all chill or no chill at all.

Junior and I liked to be at Boboy's. He kept bullfinches, picoplats, and red-breasted robins in small wood-and-wire cages. The cages had chalky-white beak sharpeners and removable floors to clear away the newspapers full of shit. Boboy would whistle to the birds until they took flight in song. As a child, I'd never seen a man do something so gentle.

Boboy was enough older than us to command respect, but he never talked down to us. For Junior, this was the closest to a father he would get. All I needed was that old lady and her sayings and songs.

My father later told me that when he lived in Monkeytown in the 1970s, he had felt the same about his cousin Mikey as we had about Boboy. Mikey was older and cool and knew the streets. "My father was a mystery," Al claimed, "but Mikey taught me what was up." Long after Al had left for Canada, Mikey went mad and would wander out to the junction naked as the day he was born and eating a block of cheese. Mad Mikey, my father's role model and the person for whom I was given my middle name.

One of the few stories I'd pieced together about Al involved a razor, domestic abuse, and a prophecy. Mr. Barzy lived behind us, past Olsten Hodge and Miss Theresa, in his own patch of land. The only way to get to his land without going through the bush was along a little unpaved road we called a trace. He grew all kinds of fruits and vegetables, and was therefore always chasing thieves. Barzy had a big gun and was not afraid to use it.

The story goes that my father was dating his daughter Juanita and cut her on her hand with a razor blade to teach her not to have wandering eyes. Barzy went crazy and the police were called. Al got off scot-free, but Barzy swore: "Yuh get out of jail this time, but you will spend the rest of your life in prison!" This proved to be so accurate a prophecy that in the family, it is said that Barzy cursed Al and all his offspring that day. Maybe even went to an Obeah man to cast a spell on him.

So life was in the superstitious south of Trinidad: balanced somewhere between Grandmother's prayers and the voodoo of violent men.

## V

The first time I saw the sea, it shocked me awake in a way that has yet to sleep again. It was an enchantment. At first it poked from behind the coconut and palm trees like specks of aqua, impossibly bright. Then, piece by piece, the blue became one continuous miracle. A salty breeze hit my cheeks. Gulls called out their manoeuvres. The water glowed with life. I had heard about and seen pictures of the sea, but in person it was an overwhelming experience.

We were in the back of a maxi taxi heading north from San Fernando. I was squished into Mama's lap, straining my neck to catch more of this new vastness. She was so tired in those days. Lines splayed out of the corners of her eyes and creases of her mouth. Bright blue veins poked out like earthworms tunnelling under her skin.

"Mama!?!" I exclaimed, but she shushed me and disappeared into her thoughts.

Then, to my horror, I discovered that the field of blue moved.

It rocked and heaved and swayed and came crashing into the land. It was a massive, glistening place of possibilities that stretched on forever.

Out there somewhere was Venezuela, where I was born. Out there somewhere was England, where the Queen knighted lords in their frilly coats. Out there somewhere was Canada, where my father lived.

Specks of white sails flickered between where the blue endlessness became the sky. I squinted hard against the spraying brightness and tried to imagine my father, the handsome man in the little picture I had, but it was no good. I had no idea what he or Canada was like.

Suddenly, as if by some counter-spell, the sea vanished behind the trees and was gone.


VI


Wakes were the only chance to see rumbos in their natural habitat. They lit up the garage, pulled out the linoleum tablecloths, and set out bottles of Vat 19 and Puncheon rum. In Rome they had funeral games, but the proper Trini salute to the beloved dead was an All Fours tournament.

All Fours was a card game that only rum-drinking big people played, usually on weekends or at wakes. Men bet on it, and players performed in a trash-talking, taunting, gesticulating way that captivated me. I thought, "This is what big men did," and decided that I had to learn all its secrets.

I snuck down the back stairs and stood in the dark, peeking—wakes were not for children. So many men I had only seen stumbling home in broad daylight now sat around a table pouring sips into plastic cups. So this was what big people got up to in rum shops.

That day at the viewing, I had seen my first corpse. I knew this old lady and had played with her grandkids many times. She was lying in her best Sunday dress in a pine box with silver handles. She had been turned to stone. Her eyes were cold, and every wrinkle along her neck and jowls poked out. It didn't make sense that she was dead now. And wouldn't call out from her chair: "Little boy, tell Miss Excelly ah coming to borrow a pound a flour til Sunday, please God."

She was dead, and that meant there would be a funeral at the cemetery with slow groaning singing and big puffy hats. Mama and I would be there, and she would sing some dreadful hymn, like "Abide with me; fast falls the eventide. The darkness deepens; Lord, with me abide." By the time she was on the second stanza, there would be wailing and many cries of "Lord, have mercy," but the "mercy" would sound more like "mussy," and the ladies would smell like the mothballs they used to keep their good clothes from being eaten by insects, and the men would lower the coffin into the hole, and the preacher would preach damnation and end with "dust to dust, ashes to ashes," and the big people would go home whispering about what she'd left them. But first there had to be a wake. Bodies were boring, I decided. Rumbos were the real fun.

All Fours wasn't like our children's games, which included Go to Pack and Suck de Well—it was a big man card game. It was played in teams of two, four at a table, I had no idea what this game was all about but I needed to find out. I hid where I could studying the backs of their wrinkled hands full of cards, their alligator eyes watching each other crooked and sly, their big talk shifting with the cards played: "My jack cyah hang. I iz de hangman here," "Don't talk game. Behave yuhself."

"Yuh beggin or yuh stand up? Doh waste time, partner."

As far as I could see, the object of the game was to slap your card down as hard as you could while watching your opponent cut eye, which is to say, act as rude as possible.

"Wey yuh say? Wey yuh say?"

The game ended when one rumbo jumped up and yelled a string of nonsense that they all understood: "Dat is high-low hang jack game to gooo!" The whole place exploded in yells and laughter, and Mr. Tanal, the winner, slammed his cards extravagantly four or five more times and took the Puncheon bottle straight to his face.

Junior told me later, "Dat is how big man does operate."

I spent two weeks yelling All Fours words and practising slamming my imaginary cards down as hard as I could.

## VII

Without doubt, the house on our street that had the most impact on my life was also the one that would be the easiest to miss. It was Miss Monica's house, next to our place but set back from the road. The story goes that Mama let her build a house on her property rent-free. "Charity begins at home and ends abroad," she would often say.

Olsten Hodge, Miss Monica's man, was cruel. A sadist whose ego needed to be told he was the man of the house, even when it wasn't his house. Miss Monica's son, Dexter, was slow and epileptic. I remember watching him mouth easy words as if he didn't understand them. It was as if a child had inherited a large man's body. When Dexter had seizures, he twisted on the ground, clutching the sticks and grass, frothing at the mouth, and snapping his jaws together so that his teeth clicked loud and suddenly. Old folks called this malcadee.

Miss Monica's brother, Larry, would appear every now and then. He was clean-shaven and spoke with a soft voice in a way no man I knew did. He had big reptile eyes and an Afro shaped like a helmet. He was muscular and fit. The whispers were that he had been to jail.

One day, when the wind seemed to be everywhere, Larry offered me a pack of peanuts if I would follow him into the bush. Salted peanuts were a once-a-year treat, so I agreed. Getting a free pack of this delicacy seemed strange, but those Planter's peanuts were the most delicious so I followed him.

Then Larry got naked.

It was weird. Private parts were supposed to be private. I knew something was wrong with him, but I felt trapped.

He put a peanut on the head of his dick and asked me to eat it.

"Doh tell anybody about dis, yuh hear?" he was breathing heavy. Sweat beaded on his top lip. The world was whipping in the wind.

After I ate the peanut, he spit on his prick and sodomized me on a bed of flattened grass. The broken stalks smelled fresh and new. I felt like a ghost floating in the angry breeze. I wanted to leave so I could breathe again. When would this be over?

"Is juss a little secret game for you and me, all right?"

"All right." I could tell he was a liar.

"Yuh want more peanuts, right?" he said catching his breath.

When I left, my mind was spinning. My heart was thumping in my ears. Everywhere, the wind was howling. I ran the last ten feet from the bush. Casually at first.

Running was my favourite feeling. Wilton was a sprinter. He had special shoes with spiked soles that would hang by the bedroom door. Sterling used to run long distance. We would go out to the road to watch the runners pass. Everything seemed to speed up and disappear all at once when you ran as fast as you could.

Outside the bush, I felt my stomach begin to settle. My breath slowly stopped tripping over itself. The world slowed down, and as it did, my hardened spirit began to boil and bubble. I looked back towards the trees and laughed at Larry. I cackled my defiance.

Something inside me needed him to know that he hadn't fooled me. He hadn't even given me the whole pack of peanuts.

## Chapter Four

# THE PRODIGAL SON

I

Life returned to normal, but nothing was the same.

In Monkeytown, I had come to learn the certainty of violence if you did something wrong. Anyone in the village could spank you, and if you went home and whined about it, Miss Excelly wouldn't take your side. More likely, she would say, "Child, what did you do?" And your stinging backside would get more licks.

When I got caught sneaking cigarette butts out of the ash tray so I could pretend I was big, the ugly boy with the welt on his face slapped me so hard the whole side of my body twitched and trembled for two days. His breath stunk of blood pudding. "If ah catch yuh smokin again, I will BUSS YUH FACE!"

But even though I knew what Larry did was wrong, no one spanked him. Nothing happened. I didn't tell anyone. God did not send his avenging angel, and I had no father or mother to fight him.

Everything went back to normal, but nothing was the same.

———

The first time I sang in front of an audience was a total disaster, mostly because it never happened. I was at the Pentecostal church one Sunday after the sermon, singing "How Great Thou Art" and pretending I was in the choir, when the pastor heard and asked me to sing for the service the following week. I would finally be on the pulpit. No more pretending with Junior for the goats and chickens.

Junior said: "Tony, yuh bettah hard practice. If yuh singing off-key in church, crapaud smoke yuh pipe." He meant that if I was bad, they would all laugh at me.

I annoyed everyone by belting out the hymn all week at home, and Miss Excelly was proud, with her handsome cheeks beaming. But she cringed when I sang the second refrain of "How Great Thou Art," squeaky and bad.

"Don't hang yuh hat where yuh can't reach," she declared, telling me to sing it lower.

So I did, and it felt warm in my chest like Vicks VapoRub.

"Start quiet so yuh have room to get big in the refrain," Mama advised.

I pretended that I knew what this meant and kept basically yelling it as loud as I could.

Miss Excelly was cooking coo-coo, which is fried corn meal, and we didn't get coo-coo often, so I was waiting in the kitchen as if it would fly away if I didn't eat it immediately. Singing: "I see the stars. I hear the rolling thunder. Thy power throughout the universe displayed." My grandmother was no longer looking proud but daring me to shut up with her kind eyes that wouldn't say it cause she was still proud, and besides, she was a sucker for old Anglican hymns.

"Then sings my soul . . . "

Later, Junior and I were sweeping out the goat kennel with two cocoyea brooms. The little round black goat droppings were everywhere.

"Give dat hymn a rest, nah? God tired hear how great he is."

So I sang louder: "My saviour called to thee. HOW GREAT THOU ART!"

And he flicked me with goat dung, and I sang louder until we were sticking the nasty brooms in each other's faces. Then we were laughing, because neither of us really wanted to be covered in goat dung. "Oh, geeeeed!" we said and teased each other with the dirty brooms, and I stopped singing for a little bit.

On the morning of the service, I was in my best shirt and pants and looking ready, but inside I was in a panic. My palms were sweating. The more the deacons and the choir and the congregants arrived, the more my heart sank into my shoes.

And I chickened out. I told the pastor yes nervously when he asked if I would sing the next week instead. Mercifully, he could see in my face that next week would never come.

II

I walked through School Trace and watched the brown women in their kitchens cooking the night before Diwali. The mothers, aunties, sisters, and cousins, straight black hair pulled back, village gossiping as the pots bubbled. There were no saris or tassa drums, just a palpable excitement buzzing through the evening.

"Tell mih de story of Lakshmi again?" I asked Sonny.

The Hindu stories seemed so vast, so cosmic, when compared to Solomon and Egypt and the two loaves and five fishes. They seemed to be about the most important things.

The deities and demons had been churning the ocean of milk in the hopes of stirring up a magic nectar. Instead, out came an all-consuming poison. Which freaked everyone out. So they prayed to Lord Shiva, who promptly volunteered to drink all the poison and save them. Churn, churn, churn and out pops the most resplendent Lakshmi.

In truth, she was my first love, with her four arms holding pink flowers and sharing gold coins, sitting in a lotus flower in red silk. It was the first time I remember thinking that someone was beautiful.

The deities and demons agreed: Lakshmi was a catch. But she chose Vishnu as her husband. Vishnu had blue skin and sacred snakes on his biceps. I found all of this stunning. This wasn't the stiff upper lip and cold blue eyes of Elizabeth II. This was fire and passion and the foundation of all things personified in a goddess with eyes the colour of warm cocoa, the colour of midnight, the colour of infinite mystery. I loved it.

I missed the *puja* the next morning but came later for the dinner and the lights. (I did mention that I was in it for the food, right?) Sonny and I entered the family home, where we were each handed a fig leaf, our plate, then lavished with paratha roti, which we called "buss-up shot" because they beat it so much on the baking stone that it looked like a ripped shirt. Then roasted pumpkin, sweet rice, channa, bhaji, and callaloo, which was spinach cooked in coconut milk—all was piled on. It was a sumptuous feast of smells and sights and textures. You had to scoop up the filling with your roti while you sat on the ground. "Better belly buss than good food waste," Mama would say, so I ate every last morsel.

When we had finished, we walked out into the night, fat like pythons. The night was on fire with Mother Lakshmi's presence. On School Trace, every nook and cranny was filled with burning diya. Diya were little clay pots filled with oil and lit with a twine wick. Houses adorned their lawns and bannisters with bamboo-framed sculptures lined with diya, filling the air with the smell of burning and the flickering shapes of birds or flowers or patterns of cascading circles. The night seemed to be basking in the glow of the goddess's presence, each diya a golden blessing from her hands.

Back in Monkeytown it was not so luminous, but the big boys were bussing bamboo. The "cannons" were made of hollowed-out bamboo, four or five joints long. One end of each cannon was elevated, and the bottom end was filled with boiling kerosene. As the mouth of the cannon belched black smoke, the lower end was ignited using a flame from a Caribbean Molotov cocktail called a flambeau. Once lit, the cannon would explode with noise. It reeked of that scalding kerosene smell and roared like a raging monster. To make it boom like a cannon, someone had to put his face to a hole in the bamboo and blow hard enough to get the smoke out but not so hard that the sizzling oil would splash back on his face. This was a delicate dance that not everyone mastered.

The hills echoed with this cannon war as a dozen bamboos pelted noise into the night. Big boys patted themselves on the back and jumped and whooped when an especially loud shot went off. The loudest, fiercest bamboo cannon won.

I watched with my mind split open, mouthing the words from the cannon fight in "Benbow the Brave," a story in my school reader: "What should they know of England, who only England know?" it said, quoting Kipling. And the big boys manned the guns like those shirtless white men in Benbow's crew. In our driveway, where the ping-pong table would usually be, we stood back warily and jumped and yelled whenever our cannon fired. The most tranquil festival of peace ended with the adrenaline rush of pretend colonizer cannons.

The white stars were watching. The night creatures sang in the trees. My belly was hurting with deliciousness. Cannons or diyas? I didn't have to wonder which one Lakshmi would prefer.

III

Auntie Joan's visit from Canada was the next best thing to Christmas ham and sorrel. She was preceded by a barrel that arrived sealed with duct tape and was as wide as the door. In big letters it said: "Joan Cynthia Guevara Kenora Ontario Canada." As with every new word, I repeated "Ke-Nor-Rah," many times, tasting the delectable new syllables. But, of course, I had no idea where that was or what she was doing there. To me Aunt Joan was our hero, like Joan of Arc from Nelson's reader and Canada was Canada, the Land of Milk and Honey. A barrel from Canada was like a visit from the archangel Gabriel or a message from another galaxy. We jumped around it, waving our arms and shouting until Miss Excelly got tired of telling us to shush.

"All yuh children go kill mih," she declared and tumbled down into a chair. She needed to sit down. More and more, she would complain about "the sugar" and say her vision was blurry. I didn't know what "the sugar" was, but I knew Miss Excelly was no longer up at the crack of dawn, digging in the garden or busy about the yard. So we did what most children would do: we ran wild.

I was six and Junior was three years older than me, so he was usually gone with his friends. He was too old to be my twin now. I spent my time playing in the road, running through the bush trying to catch parakeets, and reading everything I could find.

Auntie Joan's barrel was filled not with toys but with a ton of clothes for little boys. The excitement vanishing, Mama, Junior, and I sat down to read the letter that came with it. Auntie Joan was coming to visit us. She was like a time traveller. Her letter promised that one day, if we were good boys, she would take us there too.

Auntie Joan had handsome high cheekbones and was taller than any woman I knew. "Boy, come here let me look at yuh," she said when she finally arrived. "So you are the one getting all those top marks in school?" She enunciated so clearly, with only a hint of Trini slang. A Canadian accent, I thought, smiling silly.

"Yes, Auntie Joan."

"Look at Al son. Mama, yuh don't find he favour Al? The boy is the spitting image of his father."

"Do you know where my father is, Auntie Joan? Do you see him?"

At these questions, she shifted her gaze to Mama, whose eyes were filled with tears to see her daughter.

"Child, you shouldn't worry about those things. Leave your father in God's hands. Do you say your prayers?"

"Yes, Auntie Joan."

"Where is the big one? Junior not here?"

Miss Excelly didn't know where Junior was. "He always knocking about somewhere," she said. "I feel the little one like me more."

I had heard her say this before. It was nice to beat Junior at something, but I wondered how he could not love her as much as I did.

"Just like his father," Auntie Joan said.

"Just like his grandfather," Miss Excelly agreed. Then her eyes looked through the sky and she recited Exodus: "For I, the Lord thy God, am a jealous God, visiting the iniquity of the fathers upon the children—"

And her daughter finished her sermon: "Unto the third and fourth generation of them that hate me."

They were sitting in the gallery drinking tea. I was hanging around, exhausted with excitement but determined to catch every droplet of their chat. They were saying something about "Calgary" and "Victoria" and "Al and Ami," and then realized that I was listening.

"Boy, why yuh don't go play in the yard and let big people talk?" Mama's face was sad, but her tone was stern. I was dismissed.

The legend of Al Downing—my father, her son—floated about my childhood like a ghost with no resting place. It was there in the whispers of old folks who knew him, in the handful of pictures Ami sent from Canada, and in the way that Mama always looked close to tears when she said his name.

Her youngest son, her miracle baby boy.

Miss Excelly had had many miscarriages between the births of Agnes and Joan, who came when she had given up on more children. Then, when she was forty-six years old, Al arrived. Though she already had many siblings, Auntie Joan felt responsible for my father from the very beginning—or "since Lord make morning," as Mama would say.

Good with his hands, terrible with women. Even in his early teens, Al had a reputation for being a smooth talker with a quick temper. He picked pockets; he loved to gamble. Mama lost him to the streets before he was even a man. Then he left for Canada, land of the white people, land of milk and honey, the promised land. For us poor people of the empire, such a journey was like being given a passport to paradise. It seemed as if Mama was always waiting for him to return. So was I.

At the moment, though, she was cooking a feast for her daughter's first night. She was making salt fish with onions and tomatoes, cassavas, dasheens, and eddoes—all provisions that Auntie Joan loved.

"Mama, this smells so good! Yuh don't have any avocado?"

"Gyul, what is avocado?"

"Zaboca. They does call it avocado in Canada."

I knew there would definitely be some pigtails—cured, salted pork tails. They made all kinds of scrumptious dishes, and my grandma had a weakness for them. But Joan was a Seventh-day Adventist, which meant, among other things, no pork.

"Oh, Mama, you made bake too? With coconut?"

Joan took the pan full of dough and opened the oven to discover a reeking pound of pigtails where her mother had hidden them. Miss Excelly was busted. Her eyes popped wide and her mouth turned into a guilty pout. I had never seen her face like this.

"Mama, this stuff will kill you," Auntie Joan lectured. "You can't keep eating this pork. It does cause high blood pressure—"

A huge smile was blooming somewhere behind my face. My cheeks were hot with fun. Watching the lady who always lectured me get a taste of her own medicine made me want to giggle, but I had to hold it in.

"—to hypertension, and is not good for your diabetes. The salt, the salt, the salt, Lord Jesus have mercy. Boy, why are you over there grinning like dead dog?"

The giggle roared out of my belly, and I toppled over holding my side. I must have made quite a sight because soon I noticed that they were laughing too.

Yet Auntie Joan couldn't help leaving without trotting out one of Mama's classics as a parting shot: "Who don't hear does feel."

For me, that usually meant I had a licking coming, but as I watched Mama's hands trembling for no reason, I wondered what it meant for an old lady like her.


I V


The first time I transformed into someone else, I became the Prodigal Son. It was for the school play, and being good Anglicans, the teachers had chosen a famous story from the Saviour's own lips. Jesus said (in the words of King James):

> A certain man had two sons.
> And the younger of them said to his father, "Father,
> give me the portion of goods that falleth to me."
> And he divided unto them his living.

And not many days after, the younger son gathered
all together, and took his journey into a far country,
and there wasted his substance with riotous living.

Except we were nine-year-olds speaking in Trini, so it was more like
"Faddah, Faddah, give mih my share a de money so I can go an live
mih laife."

When I got the part, I rushed home and pulled down the big white
Bible to stare at the picture of the wayward son, hands clasped in peni-
tence. This is the role I would play, but in our version, I became a Rasta
when I left, dreadlocks included, and when I returned, lo and behold:
my locks were gone. Who doesn't love children pretending to be grown?

"Oh, Lawd, is mih son. He once was dead, but now he alive; he
once was lost but now he found."

In truth, it was probably a frantic mess, but little me got a taste
of something I would later come to crave: the stage. At our first performance, I was stunned awake by the electricity of the stage. It was
powerful to feel the audience laugh at a line I said. I could feel them
respond like a wave of lights suddenly turning on.

I was always too loud and too dramatic for real life. Junior and I
rolling in the grass yelling out sermons or mocking Hodge—that just
didn't work in the big-people world. "Hush yuh mouth!" was a standard response. But on stage, there was no such thing as too loud or too
dramatic. On stage, I could be anything I wanted to be. I could mock
big people until my little heart burst.

We eventually performed the play for the Anglican archbishop of
Trinidad in a pavilion in San Fernando. I met him briefly, looking like
he was playing mas in his colourful robes.

While I was pretending to be a vagabond son wasting my substance on riotous living, Miss Excelly's actual son, Al Downing, was
in a "far country" getting wasted on substances and riotous living.

## Chapter Five

# THE GOD OF NEGRO

I

My grandfather was a saga boy.

I never met him, but his ghost stared back at me from a grainy black-and-white photograph for my whole childhood. In it, he's wearing a double-breasted suit with a soft pocket square. His fedora tilt drips with attitude. There is hardness on his brow, but his face is as smooth as his silk tie. His eyes shine like dark, hot coals. They are eyes full of chaos and charisma.

The saga-boy tradition started in the 1940s, during the Second World War. A saga boy was a West Indian playboy dandy. He needed to be luxurious for luxury's sake. If you saw him in the street, he would be wearing gold chains and rings, the flashiest Venezuelan print shirt, soft pants, new shoes. Every three days, you would catch him at his barber's, getting a "mark up."

Some saga boys played in steel pan bands at Carnival time. Some were pimps, others hustlers. Some just liked to dress up. But all were ladies' men. Granddad, people said, liked to drink and gamble, and he could handle himself in a stick fight. But by far his greatest addiction was the attention of women.

I grew up hearing stories of how tall and handsome Herbert Downing was. How he would stroll his six-four frame down the main road, singing kaiso songs with a rose in his hat. They called him Catnine because he worked in the oil fields and would climb greased poles like a cat. He was a tall, dark, and handsome man with a pocket full of money. He was full of himself. He called himself the God of Negro. Not the Prince, the Duke, or the King, but the God of Negro.

Clearly he was a humble man.

I also heard stories of how lucky my grandmother was to have such a catch marry her, especially in her condition—meaning after she'd had two children with other men.

Little Tony never understood much of this, but I would often stare at the image of Granddad in that photo, think of all the whispers I'd heard, and imagine the man. Would he have liked me? Would he have tried to beat me, like Hodge did, or would he have taught me how to crease and fold a pocket square just so?

I would steal whiffs of him in the chatter of the men drinking and playing All Fours at wakes—men he used to fight and drink and cut style with. I would hold my breath and listen as the Downings or Ayres or Richardsons invoked his name, hoping to learn something about him or about my father.

But the hardness in his face in that old photograph was what stuck out to me. It made me shudder. Herbert was not a nice man. He was a rolling stone and had many lovers besides my grandmother. From what I was told, he was always coming and going, always in between something—in between outfits, in between women, in between lives. He was also a very cruel and violent drunk, especially as a lifetime of hard living steadily clawed back his famous looks and his independence.

He was never home; the road was his home. He was always out partying, carousing, gambling, drinking, and fighting. This is the hallmark of the families left broken in the wake of slavery, like so many shattered Puncheon rum bottles a century after the party has ended.

I remember hearing a story about Miss Excelly going to his workhouse near the oil fields at Guayaguayare and finding another woman living there. Claiming her turf, my grandmother started making dinner, only to have this rival woman snatch the frying pan and toss the green bananas on the ground. The woman then began to boil water so she could be the one who made Granddad's supper, but my grandmother doused her with the pot.

Miss Excelly loved the Gospels, but she wasn't one to turn the other cheek when her man was the prize.

Mama would speak sometimes of how she cared for Herbert Downing in his final years, of how he could do nothing for himself, not even dress or use the bathroom. He would scream and swear and call down on her head every terrible curse he knew, even as she wiped and washed his backside. Time will catch a saga boy—even the God of Negro—just as sure as any other man. Yet a man so vain could not stand to live, a husk of himself, ravaged by disease and dependent on a woman.

So he vented his rage on her.

Even years after, she would grow silent and grip the arms of her bamboo rocking chair until I thought she would break it. Back and forth she would rock until the creaking echoed into the dusty corners of that house. She would rock and sing and rock and sing as if in a trance.

In years to come, her hymns would find me in my most desolate moments. They would pour out of me before I even realized what they were. I came to understand then that singing and reading were her therapy, her coping mechanism. She sang hymns and read psalms to defeat the demon she had married. When he died, dumb from stroke and crippled with arthritis, Miss Excelly could not cry.

The legacy of Herbert Downing—his wandering life, his abandonment of his children, his saga-boy style, and the songs my grandmother sang to survive him—all became silent cornerstones of my childhood. Although I never met him, I lived under his long, shallow shadow for most of my life.

This was my grandfather. This was my father. This was my inheritance. This is the model that would eventually shape my life: an endless storm of charisma married to a long trail of tears.

## II

One morning, Monkeytown awoke to the banging of hammers and the clanging of galvanize. The noise cut through my sleepy head and called me into the road like a church bell on Sunday. Big people were already there, chattering.

"Yuh see what shame he bring to she?"

Comess, we called it. Comess was like gossip rolled into a public spectacle—that could be a cussing or perhaps a cutlass would come out, but definitely a show. Like all country people, we took perverse pleasure in other people's private business spilling into the street. Comess was our entertainment.

Strange men were taking apart Mrs. Philomena's house. The hammering was the sound of them pulling out the nails and knocking out the boards that made the walls.

I heard someone in the crowd say: "Why he cyah drink rum like everybody else? Why he have to do drugs?"

Drugs? What were drugs? I didn't understand, but the men didn't stop working. Nail by nail, the shiny metal of the roof came down.

Sheet by sheet, it was loaded into the back of the truck. Board by board, the frame that held up the walls was dismantled; the men loaded that on the truck as the whole village streamed into the road to watch.

Mrs. Philomena and her daughter were nowhere to be found.

"She husband owe dem drugs-man money, so they taking the house!" Junior and I overheard. We got close enough to see the dirty overalls of the workmen, but we stayed back, wary. Perhaps if we got too close, the drugs would get us too.

People gossiped heavy under their breath. Some pretended to be very concerned, questioning the men and then running back to tell everyone what they said. People tingled with the sight of that family's shame.

I looked up at Junior. He always knew what I didn't.

"Junior, what is drugs? What happening?"

He looked at me and sucked his teeth long. A *stchuups*—a great big sucking sound that said, "Boy, don't ask me no questions."

What went wrong with Mrs. Philomena's husband? He was a regular man, not a rumbo or a bad john. He seemed quiet and normal. Yet some ominous mystery had unravelled the fabric of his life—not to mention the ceiling of his house.

I got the message that drugs and shame were close friends, and you didn't want to know either of them.

Why would anyone want so much comess?


III


Do you know how hard it is to catch a parakeet? They are fast and smart and have big, hard beaks like sharp stones. Parakeets are the same chalky bright pastel colours as parrots, but smaller. The day I caught one, I felt like a superhero.

It was the day of the stick fight, and I went up to the junction by myself. I was big enough then, seven years old, and the junction wasn't far. In the pavilion by the football field, old men, hard-faced men, young men, teenaged boys gathered while others sat beating drums to build the anticipation. Everybody gathered in a big circle. In the middle, fighting, were two men stripped down to loincloths, holding hard guava sticks and wearing white head ties. I had to weave my way to the front to see what the noise was about.

It all looked like a dance—dip and slide, swing and duck, jump in and jump back—until one of them took a stick to the forehead and came up a hot, bloody mess. It was what we would call a buss head. The man's white headcloth was now bright red, and the blood kept coming like Kool-Aid. The crowd gasped. I had never seen someone bleeding like this. It made me queasy, and I left before I could see who won.

As I walked back down the main road, I saw it hopping from branch to branch in a tree. It was rare to get close to a parakeet—much less catch one. It was a prize I couldn't resist. Step by step, I eased towards the bird, pleading: "Come nah. Jump in mih hand nah." And it flew away to another branch. "Come by we house nah? Yuh lookin hungry," I called as I soft-stepped, arm extended. Finally, it was curious enough to move close and peck at my fingernails.

Then I snatched it.

The little beast gave a couple of squawks, and then buried its beak into the flesh between my thumb and index finger. I yelled out, but I didn't let go. Pain shot through my hand, and I started to see stars. Slowly, carefully, as if I had to pee, I started walking home. But I did not let go.

Eventually, the parakeet relaxed in my hand. It sat calmly staring up at me, its beak like a grin. But it did not let go.

When I got home, no one was there. Not a soul. My excitement was over anyway; my hand was numb, and I felt like the parakeet and

I were now friends. We had survived something together. So I let him go. There was a strange feeling of accomplishment. As if I had discovered something important about myself.

Dexter, Miss Monica's son, was in the backyard. He told me that he had seen what Larry and I did, and if I didn't do it with him too, he would tell on me and that I must have liked it anyway.

He crowded into me. His eyebrows seemed thicker than most people's, and his eyes looked as if he were in a cloud. I felt certain that I had done something wrong and I didn't want anyone to know, so I went with him into the bush.

My breath was shallow and caught, and I felt trapped. So I kept still and watched him abuse me.

This happened time and time again, one or the other would take advantage of me, then life would return to normal.

Although they are fast and have beaks hard as bread knives, parakeets are not impossible to catch.

## IV

My first atrocity started as a fight with Junior. Like so many of our fights, this one began over something that neither of us could remember. Yet in the pathological mind of eight-year-old me, it made sense to try to win at any cost.

As the scrawnier brother, though, I lost badly. Junior batted me away and pinned me down like a dragonfly. Being the less stable of the two of us, I took the conflict thermo-nuclear: I poisoned his fish.

Junior's fish lived in an oil drum, which had cement poured into the bottom third to make it airtight, a Third World aquarium. The green murk bloomed with goldfish and baby koi and aggressive Japanese fighter fish. This was my target. I found a bottle with a skull-and-crossbones label—full of thick black liquid we knew simply as disinfectant—and poured it in. I'd watched this stuff kill crapauds with just a few splashes. It worked so fast you could follow their final hops and watch them keel over and croak. So I knew as certain as kobo flocked in tall trees that every single fish was doomed. Which did not make me hesitate. I was consumed with rage at being beaten. Something in me had to win, and if a barrel full of fish had to die to achieve this, oh well.

My punishment was equally devastating (in my mind, anyway): I was not allowed to go on the church excursion to San Fernando that afternoon. Miss Excelly knew precisely how to get to me. The smell of the sea, the rolling sapphire water, the palpable excitement of the trip—none of this would be mine. I wailed. I begged. I gushed up rivers of remorse, to no avail. At last I passed out, exhausted, and forgot that fish, excursions, and brothers existed.

When I woke up from crying myself into exhaustion, it was from a black-out kind of sleep. Slowly, the tragedy came back into focus. I remembered everything. Dashing headlong into the street, I saw that the maxi taxi was almost about to drive off. I ran, spindly arms swinging, for what seemed like days. When I went back to Trini in 2010, I realized that it was not that far at all, but back then I spent years running to try to catch that maxi taxi. I arrived at the junction in time to see it turning the far corner, leaving me stewing in diesel and disappointment.

Then I did what most people would consider a second act of madness: I continued to run.

"Wait for me!" I yelled. Spite and fury sent me chasing after what I could never catch. I ran and ran, and when I couldn't run anymore, I walked and kept walking. When I had passed the streets I knew, I kept walking. And when there were no houses, I still kept walking. Spite became determination then dissolved into curiosity, and I continued walking.

Dusk caught me at the edge of a sugar-cane field that did not seem to end. Trinidadian night was approaching. My legs were suddenly weary twigs. Fear of the oncoming darkness took all the fight out of me. My salty face slackened. I could see the sun boiling as it fell in the distance and the shadows started to gather. The cane was fast becoming a dark and sinister sea. What horrors were waiting on the other side? My frantic mind began to wonder.

I started to hear the voices of crapauds, water snakes, crickets, screech owls—a symphony of scary, noisy things I could not see. I was surrounded and alone, and nothing cared. It was getting harder to see, and a cold wind was coming off the fields.

I couldn't breathe. I became hysterical, standing there petrified. I wept shamelessly. My snotty face contorted in tears. The cane field began to rock and heave. Little me turned and turned and turned, looking for a way out, looking for someone—anyone—to save me. But salvation would not come. I had travelled too far. Like a douen, I had been swept so far away from home that there was no way back. My heart filled with the sheer terror of being completely alone.

"The Lord is my light and my salvation," I said. "The Lord is the strength of my life." But I wasn't thinking of Jesus—I was thinking of Grandma Excelly smiling at me. "Whom shall I fear?" My breath was convulsing in my chest. My pulse was pounding at my forehead. "Of whom shall I be afraid?"

Slowly but gradually, I started to breathe normally and calm down. Some part of me was soothed and fascinated by the emptiness before me. I felt the presence of an ancient conversation between the light and the bush. A void as big as life itself. I felt like I could hear every living thing. I felt like I was alone yet somehow connected to everything. It was like being born again. And it began with a mean-spirited, selfish act of mass murder.

I decided to blame the whole thing on Rastas. Stitched into the colonial fabric of our lives was the lie that Rastas were bad people who did bad things. Outlaws and druggies who even I recognized as great scapegoats. So I concluded that I too could blame them. My sincere apologies to Rastafari everywhere.

Soon headlights floated into view, and I waved and called and got picked up. They dropped me at a police station. Three constables in their starched shirts and government boots took turns asking probing questions. My "Rastas kidnapped me" story fell apart almost instantly. Maybe I was just too tired to sell the lie. No one believed me.

As the police Jeep bumped over potholes back to Monkeytown, I fell asleep watching the night fly by. The sound of the bush was a constant hum in the wind, and it seemed so different and strange that I had been lost out there such a short time ago. I came home to find Mama, Junior, Olsten Hodge, and Wilton waiting in the living room, burning a candle and sick with worry. They bundled me in. It was way past bedtime. I heard the constable say, "If yuh ask me, de boy just need a good cut-ass."

## Chapter Six

# SOUCOUYANT

I

Soucouyant would suck your blood. Nobody wanted a visit from one. I once saw Miss Excelly stand in a grown lady's yard and yell at her: "Yuh suck meh last night. Why yuh don't go an suck yuh muddah!?"

As a kid in a small village in the country, I didn't know whether to believe these things or not. Somebody was always whispering about creatures from fairy tales, and some people took it seriously. I overheard talk of a certain Downing family cousin named Oscar, down by the river "naked as he born" and working obeah—Trini for performing magic. People said he had a group that gathered by the river Boudicai chanting and reading a forbidden book called *The Sixth and Seventh Books of Moses*. Except in the Bible, Moses wrote only five books. Obeah was our witchcraft, and some say the few Yoruba words we knew weren't the only ancient African traditions still alive back then.

A man named Papa Neezah was a known obeah man who would make charms to curse and bless just as cruelly. If someone told you,

"Papa Neezah gimme dis," you knew it had some magic on it and you shouldn't mess with that person.

Everyone said that Baby was an Obeah woman. She lived in a small shack and never cut her grass. She was a big woman, and her skin was pitch dark. Up and down the road she would go, mumbling to herself. And if she ever mumbled at me, I would walk fast or run to get past her. People said she did obeah, but maybe she was just mentally ill and suffering. She too was a Downing, just like cousin Oscar and just like me.

While the white Jesus in Mama's Bible knelt to pray at Gethsemane, or blessed the fishes and loaves with his glowing blue eyes, or turned the water into wine with his golden locks, I was living in a very different world, where the darkness felt real and had a relentless heartbeat. No wonder Mama prayed so much.

By the time I was eight, Junior had passed the Common Entrance exam for Cowen Hamilton Secondary School. I watched with envy as he shopped for sharp new uniforms and bookbags. He was going into the world beyond our little street and two-floor school. I was jealous, but also a part of me felt like I was losing him. We'd been inseparable when we were younger, but now we rarely hung out. He would hang with bigger boys like Allister and I would kick it with Sterling and my other classmates, but more and more I spent time reading by myself.

One day, Mama was cooking pigeon peas with pigtails and rice on the stove. I was watching the peas pop in the heat and soaking up the delicious smells of the sauce as she sat nearby giving her legs a short rest.

"Boy, yuh don't have sumthing to do?" she said.

"Mama, how yuh going?"

"I here yuh know. *Cote si cote la.*" Which was based on the French expression *comme çi, comme ça* and meant "like this, like that."

"Well, Mama, yuh know, they that wait upon the Lord shall mount up with wings as eagles. They shall run and not be weary.'" I was quoting Isaiah, but really, I was quoting her.

She smiled her happy smile at the little preacher she was raising. "Lord have mercy on your humble servant," she grunted as she struggled to get out of her chair. In the end, she leaned on my shoulder and almost pulled me down to help herself get up. Her hands twitched as she stirred the peas. She seemed weary despite all the waiting on the Lord she had done.

When she noticed me watching her, she smiled and started singing: "There's a land that is fairer than day. And by faith we can see it afar."

She was wearing a cocoa-seed-brown dress with white patterns on it. The kitchen filled with salty peas and her voice. Her hair was in tiny salt-and-pepper plaits.

"In the sweet by and by," she sang, "we shall meet on that beautiful shore." And she smiled at me like a cat with a fish. "Chile, yuh grandmuddah old and will not be here always. What kind of man will you be? Remember that charity begins in the home but will carry you abroad."

My eyes rolled at the lecture. She had said these things to me a million times. It was true that she took more naps and complained about things I didn't understand, like "arthritis" and "pressure" and "sugar." But how could she not be part of my life?

Miss Excelly was Monkeytown, and Monkeytown was my entire existence.


11


By the time I turned nine, I was still an odd child.

I could tell you how long it took Odysseus to get back to Ithaca, but I couldn't make myself something to eat. I could explain why subjects should always come before predicates, but I couldn't play without trying to be the centre of attention. If you needed to know all the books of the Old Testament in chronological order, I was your guy.

Just don't tell me I got it wrong. I would argue. I would fight. I would escalate. I *had* to win.

It was generally agreed that I was a ticking bomb that could go off at any moment.

Wilton remembered a time when two men said something I didn't like. After cussing them and threatening their lives, I came back with a sharp cutlass and murder in my eyes. "Ah go kill yuh! Ah go kill all yuh!" Wilton had to drag me away before *they* killed *me*.

I was the same boy who would kiss and cling to his grandmother affectionately. I was able to switch from raging to affectionate and sweet in a breath. Sometimes instead of playing in the street with my friends, I would sit in the gallery with Mama as she sang to the road, her eyes fixed on some invisible place only she could see.

In school, I was a ringleader. Kids seemed to want to follow me. I always knew the right things to say, and I was never afraid of anyone. The power went to my head. At recess, I wanted to win every game. I would make up the rules for marbles and kick out anyone who didn't obey. My tyrant self needed all the oxygen.

Once a new kid—let's call him Richard—came to our school. He had a rich family and was very light-skinned, which always made people seem more special. His lunch boxes were shiny metal and showed Spider-Man and Superman doing heroic deeds. His sandwiches were perfectly wrapped in wax paper, and he always had five dollars to buy treats. Five dollars? That could buy . . . five times five is twenty-five, times four is a hundred, times five dollars is . . . a hundred poulourie! Who could compete with that?

The most startling things Richard had were his toys. He had G.I. Joes with moveable arms, dinosaurs that walked on their own, army men with real parachutes, and a giant water gun that lit up when you shot it. I went from stunned to boiling over with jealousy. I kept saying things like "Dat gun eh nuthin. I bet yuh he thief it." Or, "Nobody want to eat dem dutty snacks anyway." Or, "Anybody can get a Hulk lunch kit." But all my friends needed to shoot Richard's water gun, eat his red mango treats, and play with him at recess. My clout was gone.

There was a precedent for this. Every year, I had been first or second in test in my class, and the year I got third, I was livid. I told myself it didn't matter to me, but I was wrong. The worst part was the finality of it. There was nothing I could do until the next year.

Cecily—my sometimes "girlfriend"—had been the one to beat me. I never publicly acknowledged her because I was ashamed of her. She wore thick glasses and wasn't as pretty as Aiesha. I secretly liked Aiesha, but I didn't like that she needed to be the centre of attention too, so we were always fighting.

When Cecily beat me, she taunted me: "Mistah smartman, I smarter than you."

"Yuh not smarter. Yuh just get lucky."

"Ah lucky ah have a muddah and a faddah. Where is yours? Yuh little orphan."

The rage simmered. The fire turned down but never extinguished. It became something new: determination. Even if I had to wait a year, I had to win. There was a part of me that was implacable. A hardness that was harder than hard. This is what I unleashed on the new boy, Richard.

I stole all his toys. Tiptoeing up the stairs when the whole school was swarming and screaming outside at lunchtime, I went into his bookbag and took every last one of his army men with the real parachutes, and his silver cap guns too. Then I had the audacity to pull them out the next day at recess, like "Check out mih new toys."

Of course I was busted immediately and called before Mrs. Briggs, Mrs. Barrington, and a muscular male teacher who no one wanted to get spanked by. They towered over me in the principal's crowded, stuffy office. My hands were trembling.

"I don't believe this is true. Is this true?" my teacher, Mrs. Barrington, said. Her brow was thick and wrinkled.

"You are one of our most promising students." Mrs. Briggs pouted over her glasses. She had a hint of a British accent that made everything she said sound like a command. "Why would you do a thing like this? Think about your future."

I had never been this close to her. She was ghostly pale. I could see the brown powder on her cheeks and the mole under her left eye.

My pulse was racing. My stomach felt like a churning pot.

The male teacher was standing with his thick bulky arms folded. He was looking at me, unimpressed.

"Where did you get these toys, Tony? Tell us and we will let you go," he said.

"Umm . . . well, my Auntie Joan bought them for me when I went to Canada to visit."

"But I saw you this holidays, right here in Monkeytown. When did you go to Canada?"

Tears started to fall from somewhere, and my vision got blurry and wet. The jig was up. I had been thoroughly busted. I hung my head.

"Yuh didn't go to Canada, did you?" The male teacher wanted the satisfaction of my confession.

My nose got snotty and gross.

"Nooo?" I said, my voice quivering. I was sobbing.

"So tell us where you got the toys."

"Rich. Ard," I whispered. My uniform was by then a mucusy mess, my dignity shattered.

The adults' faces were fierce with disappointment. I drooped my neck down to avoid looking at them.

Lunchtime was over, and there was a burst of chattering and clattering students.

"Well, you'll have to be punished." Mrs. Briggs's face seemed to get hard as stone right before my eyes. "We must set an example about this kind of behaviour."

She went into the top drawer of her desk and took out a stiff black leather strap. At the sight of this, I lost my composure. Tears flooded from my eyes, and my teeth began to chatter.

"Nn-nn-nnoooo! Not de strap. Ah don't want it," was all I managed.

"Richard didn't want his toys to be stolen either. Hush your mouth and take your licks," the male teacher declared.

Then they pulled down my pants and spanked me ten times on the bare butt for the entire school to hear. Every lash of the strap made my backside sing with pain. I gasped and held my breath in anticipation, and then howled when the lash finally fell. In between, there was a quiet like midnight in the cemetery.

I thought everyone would be laughing at me, but when I finally left the office, there was more deafening silence. Mrs. Barrington felt sorry for her fallen star and let me go home for the rest of the afternoon.

I was made to apologize to Richard and shake his hand after giving him back all his toys. He moved away before the year ended, and my alpha status was reinstated. Tony, however, had learned an important lesson about his limitations.


III


Sterling told me so much about how he was winning at long-distance races that I convinced myself I could do it too.

The race was in a town named Mayaro. It was one of those towns I had heard about my whole life but never been to. We had to drive a long way to get there. As we ran, we passed people cheering and clapping for us along the roadside. I pumped my arms even harder when I saw their wide grins and heard them call out encouragement.

I loved to run. Feeling the world rush past my ears and the wind in my face. It felt like almost losing control. I adored the heat of the sun on my forehead and ears.

Wilton said, "Yuh running dat distance and yuh not training? Don't go out there and finish last." What does Wilton know? I thought.

A lot, as it turned out.

At first, I felt the rush of people along the streets of Mayaro and heard their clapping, then my ribs started to hurt. Jerky movements began to replace my confident stride and my breath was getting hard to pull into my lungs.

Sterling was up ahead of me. His arms were comfortably cocked under his armpits, and his steps were steady and strong. He was my source of real-life common sense. We didn't tell each other everything, but now that Junior was too old to hang with me, Sterling was the person I trusted most. Because he was one of thirteen kids, he was independent and "grown up," while I still routinely clung to my grandmother's skirts.

"Sterling! Wait for mih nah?" I called as he took the bend with no sign of slowing down. "Sterling! Wait!"

He slowed down and let me catch up. Unlike my tight black ringlets, Sterling's hair was reddish and full of large, wispy curls. They were slick against his head.

"Ah not waiting for yuh." His voice was soft and encouraging. "Yuh have to fight for yuh third place."

And just like that, he was gone. I was alone with my guts hurting and my heart kicking like racehorses. My face clenched up and my stride turned into a crippled lean. So I stopped. I gave in.

As I walked and felt defeated, I was trying to decide when I should run again. Thinking of what to tell Junior and Wilton. On the road, I passed a snake killed by a passing car. Its belly was white and its fangs still and useless. Its guts smelled ripe. I was wondering, What good are best friends if they just leave you on the road with dead snakes? It was like a puzzle. I wanted Sterling to win, but I wanted him to stay with me too.

If it were me, what would I do? What if Sterling asked me to finish seventh on a test so I could keep him company? I wouldn't do it. So I decided that I shouldn't be mad at him. The lesson I learned was that being a big boy is a place where you can't depend on anyone.

When the race van passed, it picked me up and drove me to the finish line. No more running that day.

Later, Wilton asked me, "How de race go?"

"Ah finish fourth," I lied, knowing I would not be expected to show him my medal. I just couldn't admit that he was right, and that I "got paro." I had chickened out.

He sucked his teeth and shook his head in disgust.

"You went all the way to Mayaro to finish fourth?"


IV


Even poor people have precious things. Mama had a box of silver and gold bracelets she kept hidden in a heavy box at the bottom of the wardrobe, underneath the big Bible and the pomerac wine. I didn't know why but I knew they were important.

Our family stories were like this. I knew they were valuable because of how well they were hidden. And I stitched together a tapestry out of the threads of their telling.

Junior said that Gloria, our mother, had come to the house in a car one day at sunset. She and Mama chatted by the front door, and then she passed a little bundle of baby me to my grandma, jumped back in the car, and left. He remembers distinctly that she did not hug him, or kiss him, or even call his name.

The car's engine never stopped running.

Mama liked to tell another story of once when I was two years old, Gloria came by and stayed for a few days. Mama said that Gloria held me in her arms and chewed my hot food before feeding me like a bird.

I saw her three times that I can remember, including once when I went to her father's house. He was a mountain of a man whom everyone called "Mack." In a cradle by his chair, he kept a massive bottle of Johnnie Walker and a rock-crystal decanter and glasses. Mack didn't speak. Just sipped and watched, and everyone held their breath. Later I learned that when he was drunk, he would cuss and slap whoever was near.

After Gloria dropped us off back in Monkeytown, she stood waiting by the door to leave. Junior and I hung close to her, expecting something, searching for all the answers we didn't have, all the mothering we had missed out on. "Remember," she told us, "in yuh life, yuh will have plenty peepul but only one muddah."

Junior remembered her from before he had come to Monkeytown and was really happy to see her. But I was confused: "Is she our Mama now?" But that was not to be. Once again she vanished. Life returned to its familiar rhythm.

Miss Excelly would speak of Gloria only rarely. "Dat chile come in dis house and—don't ever talk bad about yuh muddah—she would fight with Al like big man. And when she beating him and he hit she back, she bawl out: 'Excelly! Come and get yuh son. Look him dey wit he thiefing ass!' And then she break rum bottle and say she will cut he throat. 'I will make a jail fuh yuh!' Tony, don't ever talk bad about yuh muddah."

Herbert, or "Horbutt," her dead husband and my other grandfather, was another topic Miss Excelly avoided. One day, I saw her in the drawing room, oiling her Singer sewing machine. It was wooden and brass. It was scary when the needle moved up and down, so heavy and precise, the warm oil smelling so sweet. That day, she was wearing her "knockabout" wig, the one she knocked about the house in. She collapsed into her rocking chair, her voice warm music pouring into the room.

"He used to cuss, dat man, yuh grandfaddah. Horbutt would cuss mih while I was changing and washing him like a baby. He couldn't walk. Couldn't move. All he could do is drink rum and cuss. But before he dead, he repent and beg mih forgiveness, praise God. When he dead, Lord forgive mih, ah couldn't shed not one tear. Not one tear. Not one. Ah shed all de tears ah had for dat man when he was alive."

And she was in the rocking chair, rocking and rocking. And she started to sing: "Rock of ages, cleft for me. Let me hide myself in Thee. Let the water and the blood . . . "

If you had ears to hear them, there were stories hidden in the creaking of her rocking chair, stories that would never know any other language. And though I had no idea why they were significant, I hid them as carefully as Miss Excelly had hidden her silver and gold.

V

When I got home from playing down the road, the house was quiet. I came through the front gate, and the metal hinges whined as I opened it. From the front door, I could see that something was strange: there were boys in the house.

As I stood in the entrance of the living room, I looked around two of their shoulders. Junior and Allister and some of their older friends surrounded Aiesha. She was dressed in her school skirt, but one side of her shirt was untucked. She was as tall as Allister, and as I watched, their faces met at the lips, then their tongues poked through each other's cheeks.

I was confused, but they did it for a few minutes, and then Junior did the same thing with her. His hands squeezed the humps on her chest as their tongues contorted in each other's mouths.

Aiesha seemed suspended in air. So relaxed. She knew what to do. She had been initiated into something that I had never read about in any book.

Seeing her kiss my brother and his friends made me feel jealous of Junior and of Aiesha. She was my friend and he was my brother. Now they were part of something together without me. I was losing.

Allister walked out of the room and tapped me on the shoulder. He said, "Dat is how big man does deal with gyul."

## Chapter Seven

# STARS IN MY CROWN

I

The next year proved to be the maddest of Tony's young life. In June 1985, I turned ten years old.

Phones came to Monkeytown that year. We watched the telephone trucks pitching up the heavy black cables. Then one day, phones appeared. I would sit by ours, waiting for it to do something incredible. When the phones started working, we would dial each other up from across the street for fun until we made so much noise the old people banned us from touching them. "That is not a toy," they would say, but we could tell they were excited too.

One day, a crusade came to Boboy's yard. They pitched a giant tent and preached salvation while the rain pounded the world with God's fury. People went up to the altar, crying and clapping and singing, and were dunked into the pool of water at the front.

The band members stored their instruments in our front room. When I snuck in to see what they'd left, I was mesmerized. There were guitars and drums and amps and a PA. I ran my fingers along the shiny metal of the guitar strings and daydreamed about playing on stage. How did it work? How did they get the music to come out?

A few years earlier, Wilton and his friends had gone to make fun of a Pentecostal crusade just like that one and had come back baptized. He was never the same after that. Instead of hanging out with girls, he was always with his Bible and singing praise songs. But since he had grown up with Miss Excelly, that probably wasn't surprising.

Christmas season was always hot by day and cool by night. The smell of hams roasting in every house for miles around drifted over the street and perfumed the whole night.

I remember all the food that we couldn't get at any other time, like pone and sweetbread and sorrel and black cake and punch-a-crème. Mama stirred a big silver pot filled with sorrel. I would sit by the edge of the stove, watching the water dye itself bloody red from the leaves, and smell the soaking cloves, tart and warm and spicy.

Parang, parang, parang! Junior and I loved parang. This was Spanish party music we heard only at Christmastime. Our favourite instrument to pretend to play was the cuatro, which was like a four-stringed baby guitar. We also loved the maracas, which we called shak shak because that's exactly the sound they made: *shak shak*. We would jump and dance and yell Spanish words we didn't know. The bright rhythms would make us drunk and free.

The next year was my year to write the Common Entrance exam, a test that decided which secondary school you could go to. Which in turn determined what you would amount to in life. You ranked your school choices, and you got the school your marks could afford.

Junior had written the exam a few years earlier and was now in his second year at Cowen Hamilton Secondary. He got to take a maxi taxi to school. By this point, I was back to being my studious self and getting good marks. I had stopped being as social and spent most of my time alone. Mama kept reminding me to "study dem books," but I needed no encouragement.

In the run-up to the exam, Mrs. Barrington prepared us with practice tests and dire warnings about how our entire future depended on this. On the morning of the test, Miss Excelly put her hands on my temples and shook me with a prayer. Her voice rolled like thunder in the dawn. "Lord Jesus, bless this boy and his Common Entrance exam today. Yuh see his little heart, God. Yuh see dat his faddah and muddah are not here, Lord. Bless dis little boy." I felt like crying, for some reason.

The entire top floor of our school was put into service. All the dividing blackboards were gone. There were just rows upon rows of desks and bright light streaming through the windows. Our teachers stood at one end, supervised by the all-seeing eyes of Mrs. Briggs. I picked my desk and was given booklets and white answer cards with green letters: *A, B, C, D, E*. The exam had three sections: general language, mathematics, and creative writing.

"Students, you will have forty-five minutes for each section," Mrs. Briggs instructed. "Please use your time wisely. Remember to shade only one answer with your HB pencil. Any answers not properly shaded will be disqualified."

My whole body was buzzing. All around me, children who had been equally terrified by their parents had their heads down and were scratching away. I took a deep breath and let the rush of pencils and papers and sighs of relief wash over me. I liked tests. Tyrants though they were, our teachers had prepared and terrified us well.

It was mostly a multiple-choice exam. You looked up the questions in your test booklet and then shaded the answer on your answer card. We were tested on reading, comprehension, grammar, math, and sciences. The only part that wasn't multiple choice was the creative writing section. After hours of back and forth from each question to the answer card, carefully shading what I had decided was the right response, I got to write.

My story was called "Cain and Abel." Two brothers drive racecars for a living, but they never get along. They are always fighting. The day of the big race, they're in a breakneck dash to the finish line. Only one can make it through the bend. Someone has to give in, but they both grit their teeth and neither backs down. It ends in a ball of fire.

The national results for the Common Entrance exam were published in the *Guardian* newspaper. Every student in the country was ranked, with the person's name next to his score, next to his current school, next to the school he had earned the right to attend. That year I finished with one of the highest marks, and I was accepted at the best school in the country: Presentation College. This school had produced a president, a prime minister, an attorney general, and a leader of the opposition. And next to my score was the name of our little country village school: New Grant E.C. School.

Miss Excelly wept and smiled and wept and smiled for two days. "If God don't come, he does send a man!" she said, declaring it a miracle. Mrs. Briggs and Mrs. Barrington were also flushed with pride. That summer holiday, I was a celebrity.

It felt like a dream to me. I didn't really understand what secondary school was or why it was so important, but I knew that everyone said you had to go to a good one, and that my success made Mama almost explode with joy. For maybe the first time, being the centre of attention left me silent.

Little Tony had somehow, against all odds, found his way to the brightest of futures. Or so it seemed.

## II

That fall, I started school at Presentation College in the country's second-largest city, San Fernando. I had to wake up well before the dawn, put on my pressed shirt and shorts, and catch a maxi taxi. We would drive for miles—past Princes Town, where we dropped off and took on new passengers, and through the Tasker Road, where I watched the sun blaze into existence over the cane fields.

Sando was big and noisy. It had more people than I had ever seen at one time. Houses stacked up on hills. Blocks clogged with life. I was lost in the horns on High Street. There were men selling fresh fish and doubles by the road. Maxi taxi drivers were calling out, "Princes Town, two to go!" The sea air tasted salty and fresh. My head was swimming. I was a lowly form one, and that first day felt like all of creation was brand new.

I looked down at the crest on my uniform shirt pocket. It had gaudy gold lines encasing a bright navy *P* and *C*, and my black polished boots gleamed in the morning.

Up the steep hill on Carib Street, someone let me in through a heavy metal gate, and then closed it on the past I had always known.

When the list of required books and uniforms had come, Mama tried to put on a brave face. She didn't have the money, but what she did have was plenty of determination. Calls went out to Boysie and Steve asking if they could contribute anything. Then she put on her good wig and took me travelling.

In a living room sipping tea with Miss Dora, a friend of Auntie Joan's, Miss Excelly asked if she could donate to my cause. I sat up straight and performed. Just getting used to my rising-star status. Even rich people's children did not get to go to Presentation College. "Your auntie is very proud of you, little boy," said Miss Dora. "Presentation is the most prestigious school in de country. Very prestigious." Nod, smile, and beam with pride like a deacon on Sunday morning. This was my "bright child" performance.

My school shirts were so expensive and so rare that Mama couldn't get it at the local school supplies and uniforms store. "Madame, we doh carry Presentation," the clerk told her. "Nobody ever pass for dat. You will have to go to Sando and get dat."

Sure enough, when my first day arrived, I had five new shirts with the blue-and-gold pocket crests, shiny black shoes, and second-hand textbooks to devour. All I needed to do was not freak out.

There were many shocks to come at Presentation College, but the first was that it was a Catholic school. They had strange prayers and strange songs and strange rules that everyone but me seemed to know. Our principal, Brother Michael, was an ordained monk who retired years later and immediately left the church.

The school sat at the foot of San Fernando Hill, which was bordered by bush on one side and the downtown on the other. The compound had five or six two-storey buildings, each in pastel yellows and blues and greens. The buildings surrounded the football field, which sat on a plateau at the centre of the grounds.

Presentation was an all-boys school, and all my teachers were men. Our schedules were strict and precise. My classes in New Grant had all taken place in the same room, but now I had to shuffle from building to building.

Each student in form one was assigned to one of six houses. Houses competed in sports and games, and provided opportunities for older boys to mentor and monitor younger ones. The houses were named after saints, like Saint Augustine, Saint Bede, and Saint Barnabas. You would belong to the same house the entire time you were at the school.

Our classes had prefects—strong, sharp-looking older boys who were supposed to ensure that the students were learning proper values.

They were also tasked with ratting out any violators. My classmates were smart city boys, the brightest minds from the best families. They had less country in their voice than I did. They were so casual and confident that it was intimidating. I also had Chinese and Spanish classmates for the first time. In true Trini fashion, they sounded just like all the other Trinidadian kids, which at that time amazed me. What had I expected?

The absolute mad newness of everything frightened me into a corner, and it turned into a quiet, watchful first year.

That year we had a real celebrity in our class. Machel Montano was famous for a hit song, "Too Young to Soca." He was a handsome eleven-year-old boy singing that he's big enough to party, old enough to soca.

It's hard to beat kids pretending to be grown-ups. Machel had moves and style, and the country went crazy for his song.

It was a shock to realize that I was no longer special. In my little country schoolhouse, I was something, but here everyone was smart. Everyone had ambitions. Everyone was also from a world of wealth and two-car garages.

For the first time, I fell behind in my classes. Physics was especially bewildering. The teacher with the pocket protector full of pretty pens kept filling the blackboard with formulas and equations that I didn't understand. I thought, Everybody back home thinks I'm smart, but I don't really know anything. It was the first time I realized how sheltered and bizarre my upbringing in the bush had been.

It wasn't all bad, though. I discovered my true love, who went by the name of doubles. This was two soft, fluffy fried patties stuffed with curry channa and pepper sauce. Doubles came from steaming food stands by the road and were served in wax paper. You never asked for "a double"; even when you wanted just one, it was always "doubles."

More than a few times, I spent my taxi money on doubles and had to beg my fellow students for change to get home. But I had no shame. Doubles were warm, soft, and spicy, and the romance was strong. Each time I bought one, I walked away and untwisted the paper greedily. Then I blew at the heat to cool the first bite enough that it wouldn't scald the roof of my mouth. It was heaven.

I I I

Miss Excelly had a stroke a few weeks after I started at Presentation College. Some tired blood vessel that had had too much salt pork and too many trials and tribulations stopped working, and she collapsed on the living room floor.

When I got home from school, there were neighbours in our house. "Boy, yuh grandmuddah had a stroke. Where is yuh bruddah?"

I didn't know what a stroke was. They wouldn't let me see her. They were busy fussing about her bedroom and in the kitchen. Between the crush of bodies, I could see that she was lying down, but no one would tell me anything. They carried on lighting candles and sweeping the floor.

"Yuh have to go and find him. Look some money for the maxi. Go and tell yuh bruddah he need to come home."

I was in the road again with a funny tightness in my chest. What was a stroke? Why was everybody in our house? Where was Junior? School had finished a long time ago, so he wouldn't be there, but that was the only place I could think to look. Of course, I didn't find him.

"Mama, did yuh see Junior?" I asked her when I returned hours later.

She was sitting in the living room in a dress she would never have worn in the evening. It was not a knockabout dress. The room was filled with neighbours and brightly lit. She would never have turned on that many lights.

I walked right up to her. "Mama, did yuh see Junior?"

When she tried to answer me, all that came out was a grunt. I could see her tongue curled up in the corner of her mouth, useless.

"She can't talk, boy," a neighbour said. "Leave yuh grandmuddah alone."

That didn't make sense. I had spent my whole life not leaving her alone.

The right side of her face had drooped like a piece of plastic accidentally left on the stove. Her face was melting, but only on one side.

I sat on the floor next to her, leaned my face into her lap, and did what she would have done: I sang a hymn. "There's a land that is fairer than day. And by faith we shall see it afar."

My cheeks filled with the heat of her leg. I closed my eyes. It was reassuring.

"For the Father waits over the way, to prepare us a dwelling place there."

Why were all these people milling about our house like black ants? I closed my eyes and wished it was just us.

"In the sweet by and by, we shall meet on that beautiful shore."

IV

After Mama's stroke, Wilton and neighbours and friends pitched in to make sure Junior and I could still get to school with clean uniforms and passage, or taxi fare. After the second stroke, about a week later, they moved her to her sister Theresa's house in Fifth Company. Fifth Company was where she had grown up and where her father Johnny Richardson, my great-grandfather, had been the pastor at

Fifth Company Baptist Church and had preached about the Lord's grace. When his wife died suddenly, Pastor Johnny promptly remarried and abandoned his seven children. Miss Excelly was left to take care of her six siblings; now Theresa would take care of her as her face turned towards Glory. Unbeknownst to me, they were bringing her home to die.

She was in a room at the top of the stairs and could not leave the bed. She coughed and coughed and coughed into a bucket. The hacking and spitting sounded like the end of the world. Her body was disintegrating while I watched.

After she had her second stroke, I did not want to leave Mama's side, and initially, no one had the heart to make me. So I sat in the corner of her room like a haunted little boy and watched, waiting for her to wake up. Any time she tried to speak, it emerged in grunts and groans that sounded like they belonged to an animal. The effort looked exhausting.

The room smelled like sickness. Day and night, her body rebelled against life and all anyone could do was change the bucket and pray.

Uncle Boysie would often drop by, his eyes a raging shade of purple. In the week between the strokes he had driven her all over to see doctors and to get medicine, weeping the whole time. He looked ragged. Auntie Joan also arrived from Canada and sat with her, her eyes like pools of teary glass. "Mama, how yuh going, girl?" she asked. But Mama couldn't speak anymore, so Joan sang to her instead: "Will there be any stars, any stars in my crown, when at evening the sun goeth down? When I wake with the blest in the mansions of rest, will there be any stars in my crown?"

"Mama," she tried again. "It's Joan."

And suddenly Mama's tongue worked again. "Going hooome . . ." she said, but that was all she could manage.

Auntie Joan kept singing: "And I shall see Him face to face, and tell the story, saved by grace."

Suddenly, Mama grabbed her arm and said: "Whwwwwaaaaaaa aaal . . ."

Auntie Joan leaned in to try to make out what she was saying.

"Whaeeeeeeal," she said again, and wouldn't let go.

Where is Al? Al was not coming.

Not long after that day, Miss Excelly Theodora Downing died. Maybe angels were singing, maybe the pearly gates opened up in glory. But all I saw was her last gasp and her body turn stiff. She was eighty-two years old.

V

Cars lined both sides of the road as we made our way to Fifth Company Baptist Church. This happened whenever there was an event because there were no parking lots. The line started miles and miles away, so I wondered what was happening. Miss Excelly's funeral was happening, I soon realized.

It was bright midday and the sun was lashing us. I was dressed for church in a shirt and jacket and my new Presentation College dress shoes. So many people had come. I was trying to remember when I had ever seen so many people. They had come from all over Trinidad, as well as from England, America, and Canada. Why had they all come to my old grandmother's funeral? Joan said, "Child, your grandmother's kindness touched a lot of people."

So many people? Is this what happens when you spend your life giving to every stranger and taking in every orphan? Was this her prayer dividend?

Everyone at the church had all been helped by Miss Excelly in some way at some time. There were women she took in as girls and taught to sew. There were the sisters she'd raised as her children, and then their children. The entire scattered web of our family was assembled as I had never seen, before or since. Those of her sisters who were still alive were there—Great-Auntie Theresa first and foremost. All her children by blood had come, except for my father. Boysie and his wife and children from Fyzabad were there. Jestina, a short dark woman who was my aunt, had come with her two sons. Agnes came also, but too late to speak to her mother one last time. She arrived after the first stroke, and Mama could only look at her and groan. They had been apart for eighteen years.

Then all the children who were not her children: Junior, who travelled with me; Steve, looking like a tall, handsome officer of the law; Wilton, Kenrick, Jemma, and Liz, my grandmother's adopted children. There were also many people I did not know. The church was overflowing with bright broad hats, the smell of shoe polish and starched suits, wigs and handbags. The men were in black and wore white shirts and bright watches. Women cooled themselves with fans that matched their shoes. Every pew was stuffed.

A famous jazz singer, Charmaine Forde, crooned "Amazing Grace" and made every man sit up straight and the whole room gasp.

Miss Excelly lay at the front, in an open casket lined in powder blue. She rested under the lights like a saint in a pale lavender dress Aunt Agnes had intended as a reunion gift. My ears were ringing. I couldn't feel my body. It was as if I were watching from the rafters.

Then the congregation sang her favourite hymns. The singing was low and mournful, just the way old people liked it. The way Junior and I once mocked because you couldn't even make out the words. It sounded like one massive groaning voice, shaking with sadness.

*There's a land that is fairer than day,*
*and by faith we can see it afar;*
*for the Father waits over the way*

*to prepare us a dwelling place there.*
*In the sweet by and by,*
*we shall meet on that beautiful shoooore.*
*In the sweet by and byyyyyyiiiii,*
*we shall meet on that beautiful shore.*

Was she really just going to lie there while her favourite hymns rang out? Wasn't she going to get up and sing a refrain?

The preacher sermonized about death and the promised land, and about the certainty that she was resting in Glory. There was open sobbing and the big rumbling voice of the congregation sang: "Pass me not, O gentle Saviour."

Finally, they marched Miss Excelly down the aisle and into a hearse that gleamed black and silver in the sun. I don't remember the cemetery, but they told me that they buried her in the grave of her preacher father, Johnny Richardson.

"Dust to dust. Ashes to ashes."

And then she was gone.

## Chapter Eight

# THE PROMISED LAND

I

We were going to the promised land.

I was standing by the Air Canada counter in Piarco International Airport—otherwise known as "the airport" because it was the only one in Trinidad. Junior and I were flying to Canada to live with Auntie Joan, and the family had come to see us off.

I was excited to go to Canada, the land of milk and honey. We had grown up hearing about how incredible it was. We'd heard that Canadians drove cars and dressed fancy and were rich like the people on *Sesame Street*. For us, "rich" just meant there were white people everywhere.

Our cousin Judy had once come from Calgary with her two half-white sons, Andy and Roger, who spoke English so perfectly we treated them as if they were aliens. How could these creamy light-skinned boys be our family? I wanted desperately to know, but something in me understood that you didn't ask such things.

On this day, on the ground floor of the terminal building, ticket agents in their sharp suits took our bags and weighed them. But when they asked for our passports, there was a problem.

"They not going!" our mother, Gloria, declared, clutching her handbag. The handbag contained, among other things, our passports. She had asked to see them and then slipped both into her bag, declaring: "All yuh tief my husband, and now yuh trying to tief my children too? Dey not goin!"

I don't remember seeing Gloria at the funeral, but when word spread that Miss Excelly was dead, she appeared. This would normally have been a big deal to me, but now it had to play third to Mama dying and us going to Canada.

Auntie Joan had been the heart of the conspiracy. She had no claim to us legally; we were now, for all intents and purposes, orphans. Mama never formally adopted us but neither Al nor Gloria could claim to have been our parents in any real sense. Who, in fact, was our legal guardian? All the options for staying in Trinidad looked grim. No one needed an extra two mouths to feed and house and send to school. And who would pay for me to go to the expensive school I attended? Most likely, I would have had to drop out of Presentation.

Joan's plan—which she would say was the Lord's plan—happened so smoothly it seemed like destiny. According to the paperwork, our father was sponsoring us to come to Canada, but I have no idea if we were ever supposed to live with him. As far as I knew, we were going to live with Auntie Joan, our magical aunt who came from the magical country where everything was easy and we would eat exotic fruits like apples and pears all day long.

The second part of the plan involved convincing Gloria that it was in our best interest to go and get good educations and "make something of ourselves." She had agreed—kids were costly, and she already had three others to feed.

Finally, the Government of Canada, in a rare display of promptness, rushed the application on compassionate grounds, and less than sixty days after the first dirt hit Mama's casket, we were at the Air Canada desk, checking in. Or we would have been if we'd had our passports.

Gloria had changed her mind. "Dey not goin!"

She clutched her bag and put her back to the room as if she was ready to fight. Her nostrils flared. Her heavy hands looked like they could give a good cuff if they needed to. I was happy I didn't know what they felt like. I was trying to fathom how this woman could be my mother. She was a stranger. Now she was a stranger stopping me from going to Canada.

"Gloria, don't do this," said Vio, Steve's wife. "Think of the children. Think of their future. They have a chance to go to Canada." She was trying to reason with our mother. The night before, we had stayed at Steve and Vio's house in Trincity because it was close to the airport.

"Dey not goin! Miss Joan, you and dat good-for-nuthin Al make all yuh plan to tief my children from me. Yuh feel I is damn fool?" She pointed her handbag accusingly at Joan.

"Gloria, no one is trying to trick you." Auntie Joan did not look like she was up for the fight.

"Dey not goin!" Gloria declared again.

The big people were starting to back down and breathe long sighs, as if there was nothing they could do. My eyes filled up with tears. I couldn't comprehend any of it. Why would she stop us? How could she stop us?

At last, someone decided to ask us what we wanted to do. Gambling on the truth—which was that we barely knew Gloria and idolized our aunt—I went into full bawling mode and, through snotty tears, managed: "I want to go with Auntie Joooooan."

Gloria's eyes too were crying now. "All yuh always wanted to get rid of me. I was never good enough. Now yuh want to take my children just like yuh take my husband. Nobody ever care about me!"

The plane was waiting. The Air Canada attendants and everyone else in the airport were watching the drama as the jet sat fuelled and boarded and ready to go. But the two little boys had no passports.

Auntie Joan said nothing. She seemed to have hit some kind of breaking point. She moved away and whispered a prayer. If she has given up, I thought, who will fight for us to go? A dark cloud settled over me. We weren't going anywhere.

It seemed to take years, but somehow Vio convinced Gloria to give in. Our mother hugged us, crying, "All yuh boy remember yuh only have one muddah. Don't forget yuh muddah."

The attendants marked our bags with tags that said "YYZ," which was a word I had never seen before. I entered the plane so depleted that all I wanted to do was sleep. But first the seat belt, the flight attendant, the neat lines of rows of seated travellers, the speed of the runway, moving faster than I had ever moved, and the impossible liftoff right before I thought we would surely never leave the ground.

Trinidad vanished foot by foot beneath me. It was December 12, 1986. I was eleven and Junior was fourteen. We had begun a great adventure to a future with no horizons.

Or so we thought.

Act Two

# MICHAEL

Chapter Nine

# WABIGOON

I

I met my father for the first time in a dark room at the Sheraton Hotel in Toronto in December 1986. Junior and I had just arrived from Trinidad as landed immigrants, and the sun was quickly turning to dusk in the room we shared with our auntie Joan.

"Al, you looking old, boy," she said to him when he came in.

Still weighed down by sleep, I got up and turned on the light to see what this father I had looked like.

"Hello, kid," he said and patted me roughly on the head.

"Hello, Dad," I mumbled.

Auntie Joan watched us carefully as if she would cry.

He was wearing a heavy winter coat and had a thick, well groomed moustache over his lips and a Jheri curl just like Michael Jackson's. He was handsome, and the music of his voice was so Canadian. He had no Trini accent and he laughed a lot. A boyish laugh that would erupt with a breath, lighting up his face.

I stood by the window and watched the madness of snow falling outside. In Trinidad, ice began to melt the second it came out of the freezer. Here the entire world was a freezer.

My father was a sophisticated, charming Canadian. I was happy that he was my dad.

"Yuh starting to look like Herbert," his big sister teased with a smile on her face.

She was talking about my grandfather. I had never met him, so just then I didn't understand what she meant. In time, I would comprehend this more than I ever wanted to.

## II

One night I fell asleep in the tropical jungle, and a few days later, I woke up in a blizzard.

I was in a tiny place called Wabigoon, in the vast forests of Northern Ontario, Canada. It was the dead of winter. My world, which had always been set in a teeming rainforest, had become a dead emptiness buried in snow and ice.

In a way, it was just a new kind of bush. But while Trinidad was always lush and bursting with noise and fruit and vibrant colours, this new bush was as barren as the surface of the moon—a silent blanket of whiteness. Icicles hung, glistening, from eavestroughs. Snow banks were piled as high as treetops. The angry wind howled in the bluffs. I peeked out the window of our little house behind the tavern with my eyes wide and bewildered.

Nothing would ever be the same.

———

My dead grandmother haunted me.

I kept replaying the details of her death as if turning them over and over would make them less confusing. I remembered her first stroke, and the way it made the right side of her face droop like melting plastic. I recalled strangers milling about, waiting for her to either recover or pass away. At her sister Theresa's, she was in the small room upstairs with a kerosene lamp and a bed too big for the walls.

Her bracelets turned black. This happens, people said, when silver is pure and mixes with the chemicals given off by the skin of the sick. When lucid, she would try her heavy tongue at groaning out words no one could understand. When it got bad, she coughed up buckets of thick yellow phlegm and groaned in deep, booming notes of misery that struck me with dread and were still echoing in corners of my head. Her room filled with the smell of death. I clung to her skirts even still and lay down in the bed beside her until someone forced me to get up.

The grown folks looked at me, their brows knotted with pity. In their whispers I heard, "She is waiting for Joan. She is holding on until Joan comes from Canada."

I watched Mama die. Her eyes were fixed on something no one could see, and her mouth hung open as her last breath escaped. I was still clinging to her skirt.

Throughout all this, I did not cry. It did not move me emotionally—perhaps because I was paralyzed with fear, or perhaps because I didn't understand what any of it meant. I simply watched, stunned, as everything I had ever known came to an end.


Wabigoon was barely a hamlet. A handful of houses tossed across the Trans-Canada Highway like hooks in a tackle box, along with a general store, a curling rink, a tavern, a motel, and a few buildings in a field, which was the public school I attended.

How did such a singular Trinidadian lady end up in the wilderness of northwestern Ontario? Only Aunt Joan and her God truly knows. But the reason I would give was that Joan came to help the Ojibwe children. She worked for Beendigen, an Anishinabe child and family counselling agency, and Wabigoon was at the perfect distance from many of the places she would need to go: Thunder Bay, Kenora, Red Lake, Sioux Lookout, and the many tiny roadless Indigenous reserves spread out across the boreal forests.

In winter, it was a land of snowmobiles and lone foxes, of black bears pawing hills of trash at the dump, and of packs of grey wolves with glowing eyes vanishing into the forest. In summer, sport fishermen came from all over to drag forty-pound muskies, flopping, into their boats. Eighteen-wheel trucks rumbled through, carrying long brown stacks of raw timber. Lumbering motor homes rolled through as well. They moved west towards Winnipeg or east towards Thunder Bay. Snow came early in October, and in January it dipped below −20°C and stayed there until April.

The population, from what I could see, was a collection of truckers, loggers, trappers, anglers, and Ojibwe—and now the bizarre, recently arrived, Black lady had left for a few weeks and reappeared with two confused little Black boys.

Joan Cynthia Guevara loved the Lord.

She was one of the first women allowed to teach at Naparima Girls' Secondary School in San Fernando, and she could summon an intimidating headmaster's sternness at will. She was a handsome woman. At six-one, she had inherited her father's height. Her eyes were intelligent and kind, but her mouth told the whole story of her face. It smiled generously in joy. It scorned harshly in annoyance. It lectured frequently on Jesus and salvation.

"I know the devil when I see him; I used to be married to him," I once heard her say to a would-be suitor. This was the only thing I knew about her ex-husband, who was long gone before I had arrived. Auntie Joan never remarried and never spoke of him, but she also never stopped using his name.

On our first night in Wabigoon, she said: "Boys, come to the table. Let us have dinner and thank the Lord for travelling mercies."

She had taken off her wig, and her hair was short and greying and patchy. That was a bit shocking.

"Tony, you never seen your aunt's hair, boy? Don't worry, you will get used to it. Junior, sit. Let us thank the Lord for this food. Father Gaaawd, we thank you for your mercy and your providence. We thank you for bringing us safely home to Wabigoon. Father, as you said in your Word: 'Suffer the little children to come unto me.' I ask that you bless Junior and Tony tonight. By your hand, and yours alone, will they prosper in this new life you have provided for them. Send your angels to ring around them, and let the prayers of their grandmother never go unanswered. Amen."

Junior and I looked at each other blankly. Auntie Joan's lips trembled as if she would cry. Outside, the wind was raging as if the devil himself was trying to smash his way into our little house. My nose was distracted by the scent of steaming boiled lentils, fresh bake (a Trini bread), sautéed squash, and macaroni salad. It was our first supper, and the awkwardness hung thick.

Auntie Joan was a Seventh-day Adventist, which is an odd group of Protestant Christians who worship on Saturday like Jewish people do. She ate no meat, dairy, sugar, processed foods, or enriched flour. She did not drink alcohol, smoke, or swear, and she ran five to eight kilometres every second day for most of her life. From Friday sundown to Saturday sundown, we observed the Sabbath. This meant that we could not work or visit friends, and we would instead spend much of the morning reading from the Seventh-day lesson book and praying. Mama loved her Bible, but she had never forced it on us. This was new and bizarre.

We knew Joan as our auntie from Canada who would visit and bring gifts of clothes and shoes. But we had never lived with her. She had no children and was hoping her master's degree in social work and psychotherapy would help her understand how to raise us.

This turned out to not be the case.

She flew into reserves across the grand forests of Northern Ontario, trying to redress the Crown's sins against the colony's original inhabitants. It was a tough job, in hindsight. Not many single women of colour would have done it. Yet as a first view of Canada, Wabigoon taught us intimately about the hostile conditions the colonizers had inflicted on the Indigenous.

The stories my family tells of Trinidad Tony are that he was a chatty, rambunctious kid. He argued with big people, fought his older brother's friends, always finished best in class, and was not scared of much. He once rained a handful of big stones down on some older kids who had made fun of his friend Sterling. When they came after him, he rushed them with a big stick out of sheer fury.

He was also always reading and would often quote his books to outfox adults, much to everyone's amusement. In the playground, he led the games and decided who was cool enough to play. He had a place: the smart boy, the brave boy, Miss Excelly's grandson. He always knew exactly where he belonged. But in Wabigoon, none of the things that defined Tony remained. The bush, the khaki uniforms, the red reader books, Grandma's prayers—they were all gone. His compass had lost its directions.

First, they changed my name. After my quick enrolment in the small collection of rooms called Wabigoon Public School, I was dropped into grade six classes. The mousy teacher with the large boxy eyeglasses and red lips decided Michael was a more suitable name than Antonio, and suddenly, the boy named Tony was no more.

I didn't mind. Why not? If every single thing I knew about the world was irrelevant, it made sense that I would also become someone new.

At first, this new world left me shocked and quiet. There were white people everywhere. You could see through their skins! Their veins were blue and pink. Their skin changed colour in the cold and got bruised and purple like kymit fruit. It took a long time to not be frightened by their eyes, which seemed to come in all colours: green like my plastic army men, grey like stones from the sea, specks of yellow like Julie mango pulp, and most shocking of all, blue as if splinters of sky had fallen on their faces.

They were fascinated with me too. I remember being in the lunchroom when one milky pale ghost of girl touched my hair.

"Oooh, weird," she said. "Your hair is sooo weird!"

The other kids soon crowded around, trying to get a feel of my short, nappy Afro.

"Oh, man! It's like Velcro," said one. "If we put you up on the Velcro on the gym wall, will you stick to it?"

I was baffled. I liked the attention, though, so I suffered the indignity of being treated like a pet.

Trinidad Tony would not have been impressed.

Once I had relaxed a little, I became obsessed with the local accent. Falling back on the Queen's great lesson, I quickly understood that to blend in and become Canadian, which was what I wanted most, I had to master a new way of speaking. My Trini twang was a mixture of many accents, including French, Spanish, African, and English, and although I was an ace at Her Majesty's English, the avalanche of new cadences and pronunciations I encountered in Wabigoon made my breath catch with excitement.

A proper Trini hello was a sing-song "Eh, wey goin on?" That now became "Hey, guys, how's it going?" "All yuh, leh we go an play basketball" became "Do you guys wanna play basketball?" It all sounded like *Sesame Street* to me. Back in Trini, *Sesame Street* had been my top source of information on Canadians, who I assumed were the same as Americans.

In Wabigoon, I spent hours in the living room, talking to myself in "Canadian." The diction was easier than the sounds. The word "camera"—which had been "cah-mah-rah" in Trini, three low bassy syllables—was now "cam-rah." The trick was in the first *a*, which was drawn out round and full in Trini, whereas in Canadian it became a nasal, almost silent sound. I'd prance around the living room, speaking to Junior and Auntie Joan in Canadian, trying to mimic the facial expressions and repeating phrases with odd new words like "weird," "tobogganing," "buddy," "dude," and "whatever." Mimicking "Canada talk" became my hobby.

I just wanted to fit in, I think, but very soon after I arrived at school, Miss Red Lips dealt that plan a major setback. She administered my tests for reading, writing, and arithmetic and couldn't stop giggling her surprise at my test results when she met Auntie Joan. They decided to skip me two grades, and I was immediately moved to grade eight.

Socially, I was not ready for the move. The kids my age were not in my class, and the kids in my class were not my age. They were not interested in younger kids, especially mouthy immigrant kids who knew almost nothing about almost everything—which gloves to wear, how to walk on ice, which music was cool, or why corduroy pants were the nerdiest thing you could wear. I was as foolish as a newborn.

The school was laid out in an *L*: the long hall had six classrooms, the short hall had the administration offices, and our small gymnasium was attached to the elbow. Junior attended nearby Dryden High School while this became my everyday. Auntie Joan usually dressed me in preppy knitted sweaters with a button-down dress shirt underneath—church-boy chic.

One class I was never very good at was French. Although many of the words we spoke in Trini were French in origin, we never knew what they meant in the original language. The French teacher at Wabigoon Public School was a man with hair the colour of marble. He had a thick moustache but his chin was clean-shaven, and he sat at the front of the class asking questions that all seemed a great mystery to me. "*Quel temps fait-il aujourd'hui?*" he would say. My classmates would then take turns answering, "*Il fait froid*" or "*Il fait chaud*" or "*Il fait très froid.*"

Mr. Marble never spoke in English and never spoke to or tried to help me in any way. Gradually I moved to the back of the class. I wanted to be good at the strange words we said in his class, but everyone seemed to know way more than me, and I was embarrassed to admit that I had no idea what to do. For the first time, I wasn't the smart kid in school. I was the class dunce.

My winter in that odd schoolhouse was painful. As time went on, I started to have issues with bad behaviour. I would fight at the drop of a hat and yell and sulk. I wasn't special anymore—just confused and disregarded. The kids treated me like a curiosity for a few weeks, and then went back to doing whatever they had been doing before I got there.

So I lashed out.

They could change my name, but the hardened, own-way boy was still inside me. I fought a girl because she called me prissy when I said I didn't like her making fun of my accent. I remember disrupting classes by talking loudly at the back. When I graduated at the end of the year, they gave me the mock Nitroglycerin Award for being "the most trouble in the smallest space." In Trinidad, I had won awards for being smart; in Wabigoon, I won them for being a loose cannon.

Meanwhile, all that snow and ice had become monotonous. There was just so much of it. After a few weeks of making snow angels and falling every time I tried to run, my life became a struggle to stay warm. "Layers, layers, layers, boy," Auntie Joan would say. "Make sure yuh take yuh mitts and toque." I became preoccupied with avoiding that stinging numbness that everyone called frostbite. Icicles, however, never stopped being enthralling. I could stare at them forever, watching the light dancing on their glassy alien shapes.

Junior took to the new life far better than I did. He seemed to have no shortage of things to do without me. There were rumours that he had even kissed a white girl named Lisa behind the curling rink. I was jealous and felt abandoned. Like my eighth-grade classmates, Junior had no interest in hanging with an eleven-year-old.

The kid I did hang out with at school was a red-headed, grey-eyed little tough named Billy. Billy had a face built for mischief. He had chipped front teeth, ruddy freckled cheeks, and an uncombable patch of strawberry hair. He knew how to start fires and play hockey, and he would sometimes ride a snowmobile to school. I remember his earthworm-pink lips insisting that I lick the metal pole in the schoolyard in the middle of winter. "Go on, buddy. Do it. It'll be fun. You aren't gonna let everybody scare you, are ya?"

One day, Junior lost his bike. Someone had taken it, we figured, so we spent the afternoon searching for it. We were still looking by the early evening, as the three of us crossed the hill above the Wabigoon River under a gleaming full moon. Stars beamed down at us like little pricks of icy light. We took turns watching our breath emanate like smoke into the night.

Junior spotted his bike on the river just before the bridge and raced out onto the ice to get it. Billy and I watched from the bank as he made his way across the frozen river, until suddenly the ice gave way and swallowed him whole.

It was a sound like a great tree branch cracking.

"Junior!" I cried, but all that came back was the tranquil sound of the wind in the trees.

"Aw, he's gone under man," Billy said.

"Junior!" I yelled, and Billy and I began to carefully make our way towards the spot where he had been standing only a second before.

He was still there.

He had stuck his arms out in either direction, and although he was up to his chin in ice water, he was holding himself up.

"Let's get him," said Billy.

"No, don't come closer. You'll break the ice," Junior called back with only a hint of panic.

Billy and I didn't know what to do. My heart was kicking in my chest and I was certain my brother was going to die. Junior screwed up his face with effort and tilted his head back as we listened for the sound of another branch cracking.

It never came.

Guiding himself to what looked like thicker ice, Junior was able to pull himself out. He beelined for the shore. We walked him home in his wet, heavy clothes, chilled to his marrow, shivering in his skin, teeth chattering uncontrollably, goosebumps thick as the welts we got when we were whipped by calabash.

When he tells the story now, he says, "That's the moment I started to believe in God." Looking back, I realize that was the moment I started to believe in him. In those few seconds when I thought he was gone, I had learned how much I needed him. Junior was all I had left.

Billy and I eventually fell out. It was probably inevitable—he was mouthy and scrappy, and so was I.

"Do you wanna go at me, buddy?" he said to me when I wouldn't stop arguing about something.

There were other boys watching, so I wasn't going to back down. "Whatever. I'll fight you."

We were next to the tavern facing the highway, and as the other boys stood and watched, we fought. It ended with me on my back and Billy pinning me down by kneeling on my shoulders. Nothing I could do would move him. He sat comfortably on my skinny collarbone and bludgeoned me until blood leaked down my cheek. The other boys didn't stop him, and when it was done, they all walked off with Billy. I stood holding my nose, red bloody streaks covering my Kmart sweater.

In Trinidad, I had been known for having a temper. Wilton and Junior later described me back then as a hand grenade that could go off at any second. That winter, as the wind raged like demons outside, I vented all the frustrations of my bewilderment on Auntie Joan.

Junior and I were not happy children. Our trauma was that we had lost all the things that gave children their bearings: parents, language, community. For both of us, life settled into a rhythm of exploring our new world while lashing out at the loss of the old one.

One day in school, I threw a tantrum over some now-forgotten circumstance. I was dragged out of class, yelling, as one teacher pinned my arms and two others held on to my legs. All I could do was struggle and scream. The whole school went silent to hear my breakdown. Still, I fought. Some force of nature compelled me.

"I wanna go hooooooome!" I heard my ragged voice shriek through snot and tears. But as my hoarse throat and my fragile spirit gave out and no response came, I began to suspect that there was no longer any such place.

## I I I

That summer, I actually did lose Junior.

When winter seemed to have exhausted our stamina and we had resigned ourselves to eternal ice, spring mercifully came to Wabigoon. The lakes melted. Ice evaporated and ceded to us the trees and ground and back places of the woods. I graduated from Grade 8 at the little Wabigoon schoolhouse in the field. They gave all the graduates mock "awards." Mine said, "The Nitroglycerin Award for the Most Trouble in the Smallest Space." Everyone thought it was very funny and even I chuckled a bit too.

When summer arrived, we packed up Auntie Joan's Toyota Tercel, which was a shade of grey that was somehow both shiny and dull, and we drove through the relentless forests down into America, across Pennsylvania and New York State, and then through New York City to Westbury, Long Island, where Auntie Agnes lived.

New York City melted my face. So many people and sounds and traffic. I put the window down so I could get lost in the hugeness of buildings, the buzzing hum of traffic that sounded like it went on forever, and the stink of millions of people thriving. If going from the rainforest to the blizzard was shocking, that was at least trading one bush for another. This was another array of impossibilities. My head felt like it would explode. I put up the window, wrinkled my brow, and sat back, perplexed.

Auntie Agnes was nice. She was a refined woman who reminded me of Mrs. Briggs. She had straight hair, wore frilly dresses, and would enunciate her *th*s and raise her eyebrows in a way that felt more British. More Mrs. Briggs with the wood ruler.

We'd come to Westbury because Auntie Joan felt overwhelmed. Teenaged Junior was "knocking about, juss like his Fah-Ther"; I was like a pressure cooker, always ready to boil over and explode. As they had done in Trinidad after their mother's death, the Aunties were about to make momentous decisions about the future of JuniorandTony.

"Well, the elder boy must go to Pine Forge Academy." She spoke as if she were a queen or a duchess, and it was very hard to grasp that Miss Excelly had raised her. "Pine Forge is where all the smart up-and-coming Adventist children go." She beamed with pride that she would now have a "son" there too.

Off Junior went.

We drove him to that place of rolling, lush green hills where the bodies of thousands of George Washington's continental soldiers, American patriots fighting the Crown, were buried. Agnes and Joan seemed confident that they were being great parents by providing the best, and most sanctified, education to their nephew. An education they would want for their own children, if Joan had had any children and Agnes's two sons weren't sworn heathens. I am sure they prayed on it and the spirit of Jesus told them they would find the money somehow.

"What God hath joined together, let not man shall put asunder." Praise the Lord.

Junior was happy. My brother was once so close to me in size and manners that people thought we were twins. Now JuniorandTony was no more. He talked like a big boy, dressed church-pew sharp, polished his leather shoes, and tucked his dress shirt perfectly. He even had a girlfriend in Wabigoon, I had heard. A girlfriend? Someone more important than me? While I had been reading books and running alone through the bush, he had been interested in something a lot more useful: people.

He was by far the better adjusted of the two of us.

I could smell the turpentine off the shelves in his freshly painted dorm room. He could fill them with anything he wanted. How cool.

I could tell he was eager to grow up and see new things, but I was jealous and sulky. I was losing my protector, my compass, and my best friend.

"Try to behave for Auntie Joan," was all he said to me. He tapped me playfully on the back of my head and was gone. We left him in that dorm room with a roommate and a meal plan.

Ten months removed from the jungle, I returned to the wilds of northern Canada to live alone with Aunt Joan.

Chapter Ten

# THE GATEWAY
# WITH NO GATE

I

There is no arguing with a northern storm.

They are mammoth and ferocious. They dump snow, the evidence of their fury, into every corner of existence. They rage and thunder with impossible violence. They freeze and bury any hope of life.

When a nor'wester brings a blizzard, it howls at the world like a demented animal. A faceless animal the size of God. Looking in any direction will not only freeze your eyes but also replace your mind with blank, blinding snow squalls. Hanging traffic lights lean horizontal in the gale. Cars approach intersections and simply skate right through, unable to stop. Anything not battened down—your screen door, your barbecue, your sanity—is ripped into the air and doesn't stop flying until it smashes into something.

It is rude, unreasonable, and all-consuming.

Although northern storms are vast and white and I was puny and Black, we did have one thing in common: in our anger, we were both implacable.

"Michael! Have you gone mad?" Aunt Joan yelled from her hiding spot in the next room.

"I hate you! I hate this place!" I was screaming. Shredding my tonsils with rage while flinging plate after plate from the glass cabinet at the window. "You is not my grandmother!"

The good dishes smashed with awful cracking sounds and sprayed powdered china into the light.

"Child, calm down! They will call the police!" Aunt Joan peeked out from behind the doorframe in between smashings.

"You can't tell me what to do!"

It was my second winter in Canada, and we had moved north to Sioux Lookout. It was a half-Ojibwe, half-white, and all-mad frontier town. The Gateway to the North, they called it, except that there was no gate. In fact, this was where the roads and the railways ended. There was nothing farther north unless you got there in a rickety six-seater, single-engine airplane. It was literally the end of the road.

Generally speaking, I was not adjusting well.

What had kicked off this particular tantrum was that Auntie Joan had flown away to work for a few days on one of the northern reserves of the Anishinabe peoples. This wasn't unusual, but on this occasion, she had left me with a family of Jehovah Witnesses.

It was a shock.

The kids were polite, happy, and shone with the grace of God. The mother was neat and affectionate. The father was authoritative yet never raised his voice. Both parents hugged and kissed the children and prayed with them and helped with their homework. They ate dinner together at six o'clock sharp every evening. Both the table setting and the kids' manners were immaculate.

I had never seen this before. It was a family—a normal family—and surprisingly, the parents were kind to me and treated me as if I were one of their kids. I gleefully did my dishes and chores. I said goodnight to the mother with a loving smile. I was on my best behaviour with the children. For the first time, I tasted the quiet reassurance of having parents who were present and engaged.

The brief brush with a caring family was enthralling, as if I had been dying of thirst and someone gave me a taste of water.

So when Auntie Joan came to pick me up, tired and worn from helping the broken families of the Crown's Canadian victims, I did not want to go with her. Why did I have to lose my new family? Why did I have to go home to this lonely woman and her empty house? But my new family was watching, so I somehow managed not to cause a scene. I wouldn't dare let them down.

In the car, I bawled. I cried until the words became a stream of snotty groans. The whole river of brokenness that had been my life that year poured out of me. Auntie Joan wept too. She didn't know what to do. It must have just dawned on her that she had inherited a mess and brought it with her to the ends of the earth.

"Child, come inside and eat some food, nah? Yuh grandmother would want you to eat. I know it hurts, but come inside please," she pleaded.

When we got inside, the geyser exploded. I stomped and fumed like a mad bull. "This isn't fair!" I hollered. "Why are you doing this to me?"

I started throwing chairs and plates and pots—anything I could get my hands on. Dishes shattered, bookshelves toppled, and pots went clang-a-lang clanging down the stairs.

"I don't want to be here! You're not my grandmother. I hate this place. I hate you!"

Finally, Auntie Joan ended the tantrum in an unexpected and highly effective way: she sat on me.

"Lehmegoooooooooo!" I yelled when I realized that my spindly little arms were pinned and no amount of bucking would work. "Get off of meeeee!"

"I will NOT get up until you calm down," she said, and that was that.

My face drained. My breath levelled out. My limbs lost their adrenalin charge, and the tear streaks dried in salty tracks down my cheeks. Physics had defeated me. She sat on my crazy until it faded.

If only we could have sat on winter and made it go away.


I I


Auntie Joan's singing voice arrived with the morning: "What a friend we have in Jesus. All our sins and griefs to bear." It drifted up the stairs to my room, and I floated downstairs towards it and crumpled into the couch.

"What a privilege to carry everything to God in prayer." She was humming the hymn's refrain as she put on her boots to go outside to shovel the driveway, and she smiled at me both sweetly and sadly, as if I had not tried to smash her living room to bits the night before. "Don't feel bad, child," she said encouragingly. "Your auntie loves you."

My limbs felt exhausted, and lying on my side, I squinted against the dazzling spray of daylight and listened to the *chunk-chunk-chunk-scrrraaaape* as she chipped away the night's maelstrom.

Sioux Lookout was an endless blanket of trees broken up by massive rocks and vast glistening lakes as pretty as they were ubiquitous. The town sat on a lake and a tree-covered hill, which is where the local Ojibwe would "look out" for invading Sioux warriors. It was a railway town and a frontier town, a place where in winter kids drove to school on snowmobiles and in summer Americans came to hunt and fish. On summer nights, the streetlights glowed purple for the

Blueberry Festival and many signs about town were in the stick-and-block lettering of the Ojibwe alphabet. Indigenous people were roughly half the population.

I was initiated into a world of gun racks, fishing tackle, loons cooing at sunset, maimed and dying stags on the highway, sweat lodges, pow-wows, ugly long-mouthed fish called muskie, and Canadian rumbos fighting in the street like broken stick figures dangling from strings.

There was a tense coexistence between the white and Indigenous populations. I couldn't understand why this was Ojibwe land, but the white people ran everything. The Ojibwe were an enigma, their long bodies, flat faces, raven hair, and dark eyes remained a puzzle to me. A language I couldn't speak; a mystery I couldn't penetrate. The Ojibwe were in my school but never in my classes. They did not mingle with the white people or with me. White people treated them with a cool contempt, but every now and then, the hatred would spill over. Once I saw a pickup truck chase a group of Indigenous kids down a side street. "Boguuuun!" the truck's occupants yelled, taunting. Which was like "nigger," I thought—I couldn't understand why a person would say it to someone else. Why do they get treated like this? I wondered. Why did white men find it so funny when the Ojibwe cowered so? And hid their eyes in fear?

I would stare at the letters on the Ojibwe signs for hours. The S that leaned to the right. The B lying on its belly. The teepee triangle. They were on stop signs, street names, and park placards. The pictures were animals in motion—a goose with a circle in its abdomen, a moose with a speaking man in its guts, birds with the outlines of fish in their outstretched wings, a man flexing before a flaming sun. What did these perplexing letters mean? In school, our teachers taught us that French was Canada's second language, but in the Sioux, this was not the case.

Aunt Joan lived between the Ojibwe world and the world of the whites. She had her white church, her white hymns, and her white

Bible, but her job was to help an Anishinabe child and family agency save a generation of children from the hopelessness of the reserves. I didn't understand what these places were, but I could tell by the stories she told that it was not always nice to live there.

One day, she announced that two girls would be living with us.

"But why do they have to live with us?" I asked her.

"Boy, these Ojibwe children have no high school on their reserve." She sounded like Miss Excelly often had when explaining to me that some new stranger would be staying with us. "They have to fly hundreds of miles from up north, and they need a place to stay."

I was having trouble understanding. "Why don't they have any schools, though?"

"Child, no more questions," she chided. "This is all part of God's plan, okay?"

The two girls stayed in our basement for a few months, but they never spoke to me. They were shy and scared and probably missed their grandmothers too. I didn't understand them, but for the first time I thought I knew how they felt. Like I had been given a window into the mystery.

This was my introduction to northern Canadian towns: places split between the colonizers and the people they colonized—who, contrary to the cowboy movies I'd seen in the Caribbean, were still very much alive.

III

I was perhaps the weirdest child at Queen Elizabeth District High School that year.

I was an immigrant boy who had no idea of anything: what certain words meant, what gummy bears tasted like, what to do if you saw a bear. I was a newbie, a freshie. I had no clue, and every time I opened my mouth, we all knew it.

I was also the only Black child. I got so sick of kids touching my Afro that I started playing with their hair whenever they did.

"What's wrong with you?" they would ask.

"Well, you touched my hair. Do you like it when I do it to you?"

"But . . . well, your hair doesn't get messed up like mine. Look at it!"

Sigh. White people, I was learning, were used to taking what they wanted.

Having skipped ahead two grades, I was also one of the smallest kids in high school. They took a scrawny seventh-grader and made him a hundred-pound ninth-grader. It was very hard to be taken seriously by either boys or girls. But possibly the worst cause of my otherness were the terrible church-boy outfits Auntie Joan dressed me in. I was a bizarre mini immigrant boy wrapped in ugly dad sweaters.

I gravitated to the long-haired white boys who wore leather and long earrings and listened to loud music. "Dude," they would ask, "what are the chicks like in Jamaica?" Their hair was so soft and flowy when brushed, just like the hair of the people on *Sesame Street*. Except with headbanging, beer crushing, and Guns N' Fucking Roses. They still made fun of me, but they tolerated me because I was a little crazy, which was something they could relate to. I started listening to hair metal bands. Megadeth, Iron Maiden, and Slayer became my passion.

This, of course, horrified Auntie Joan. As far as she knew, metal was the devil's music, filled with backwards Satanic messages that would corrupt and destroy my young mind. "Child, heavy metal is for devil worshippers and fornicators."

What was a "fornicator"? I wondered.

I liked these bands because their response to the world was "Fuck you." Little Tony understood defiance. I mean, I already had an affinity for jumping around, yelling profanities, and breaking shit. Hail, Satan.

I put all my academic powers to work on learning how to be a rock 'n' roll badass, kind of. I never swore or got wasted on vodka, yet I would headbang my nappy Afro and knew the lyrics to every song. But like every teenager, I first needed to look the part. This meant a leather or denim jacket with some wicked band's patch sewn onto the back of it. I wanted to wear my allegiance.

When I finally got my hands on a backpatch, it was the sunglasses-wearing skull of Megadeth's mascot. I stitched it to the back of my blue church-boy jacket and hardly ever took it off. I was so proud that I didn't even care the jacket wasn't denim. I was the preppiest metalhead ever.

My aunt was sure I was possessed by the devil.

My schoolmates were dumbstruck that I didn't listen to rap music and talk slick ghetto jive like the Black people on TV.

In the eyes of whites, I was failing miserably as a Black person.

## I V

That winter I got two new brothers.

Well, they weren't exactly new—Nigel was nine and Adrian, or Adge, was six—but in one evening, they went from names in letters I'd read in Trinidad to warm bodies hugging me like their long-lost big brother. It was as if the cold had conjured them out of a storybook.

My stepmother, Ami, would not stop talking in her soft, polite white-lady voice. "I have always raised the boys to be respectful, and they are so well behaved that I have never—I would never—lay my hands on them." She was judging Auntie Joan for sitting on me, a tale Auntie Agnes had told her. Little did she know, she would witness the wrath of Tony at first hand in years to come.

My brothers were tiny, bright-faced little sprites. Adge was chatty and outgoing. Nigel said nothing. He spoke so rarely that it was a shock when he opened his mouth, but his smiles were so cheerful and heartfelt that I instantly adored him. Both had round faces, big curly hair, soft brown skin, and chipmunk cheeks, but Adge's were puffier.

"It so good to meet you, big brother!" he said and buried his chin in my stomach with a hug that squeezed its way into my heart.

I was a big brother? I had little brothers? Two perfect, Canadian-talking little brothers? Who clung to me, watched my every move, and listened to my every word as if they actually looked up to me? I was bowled over.

"The boy look juss like Horbutt!" Auntie Joan exclaimed, staring at Adrian. She meant Herbert. Her father. My grandfather. And her face lit up with joy as if she were six years old and her tall, handsome dad had just returned to Monkeytown from a fortnight at the Guayaguayare oil fields. It was as if she were seeing an apparition. "Juss like Horbutt!" she couldn't stop whispering.

"So how is Agnes?" Ami asked, and they soon got lost in big-people talk. I led the charge to put together the Tyco racing tracks so Nigel and Adrian and I could zoom my tiny electric cars around it. Little Adrian detonated into laughter when his car rounded the bend and crashed, flipping into the carpet. His face squeezed up with so much joy that his eyes became slits. Nigel watched carefully and occasionally mumbled something and smiled to himself.

We spent the next afternoon sliding down an icy hill in our snow-suits. We all had the soft, padded onesie kinds that zipped up in the front and then buckled with little black clips. Adrian's had a hood so big his grinning head was completely swallowed into it. The sun was glittering off the slick, frozen whiteness of which the world was made. How odd it seemed that sunshine, which in Trinidad I had always associated with sweltering heat, was now accompanied by flesh-numbing cold.

Nige tumbled down the precipice, sliding left, then right as he gathered velocity. I held Adge to my chest as I gathered a head of steam, and then dived feet first to send us both howling down the hill. The day echoed with our gleeful cries.

Brothers? Brothers! As Aunt Agnes would say in her colonial duchess accent: "What a thing."

Early the next day, they piled into their car. Ami, her eyes brimming with tears, her soft, friendly voice cracking, declared that I would have to come visit the boys in their new home once they got settled in Ontario.

I didn't know at the time that their exodus from Victoria on the Pacific Ocean was part of Ami's mad quest to bring Adrian and Nigel closer to my wayward father. Al had ditched them on the West Coast and pimped his way east with his main prostitute and soon-to-be wife, who was also Ami's former friend. In time, I would learn the sordid tale of her desperate, repeated uprooting of their lives in a mission to get closer to Al. But on that day, as the nor'wester poured its frigid wrath into the morning, I just sighed and squeezed my strange little siblings until I felt I might break them.

As they drove off, my aunt was still shaking her head in disbelief. "But the boy face juss like Horbutt."


V


"How you doin kid?" I was still getting used to my father's voice crackling on the other end of the phone line. It was 1988, a year of many firsts.

"Ummm . . . good." My chest would not let me breathe. I was talking to my father. The excitement and nervousness made me stutter.

"How is everything up there?"

"Ummm . . . cold."

"We have a nice place down here in Toronto. You wanna come live with me when the snow melts, right?"

My world lit up. Living with my father seemed like a mad dream that I shouldn't hope for. "Ummm . . . yeaaah."

Auntie Joan was watching me with her serious face. Which is usually what she did right before she mumbled something strange to herself, like "attention-seeking behaviour" or "obsessive–compulsive" or "grieving his grandmother." Except that she wasn't mumbling to herself because I often overheard. These were her work words. What was she saying about me? What did they mean? And she watched and thought and mumbled.

That day, she took the phone from me, and I eavesdropped.

"Al, a child is not a pet. Do you have the resources—the financial and emotional resources—to take care of him?"

She was using her schoolmaster voice. It was hard and preachy like Mrs. Barrington's used to be.

"I know that he is your son, but the child is fragile and explosive. Is Hailey ready to deal with that?"

"Fragile," "explosive"—I turned the odd words over my tongue. I wanted to be offended, but I didn't know what she meant. Then she noticed me listening and shut the door to the dining room. Her voice softened to a whisper, but I could tell she was still lecturing him.

I couldn't have known it then, but brother and sister were having the same conversation they always had. The one they had been having since they were kids. Joan had been big sistering and cleaning up after Al since he was born.


VI


That year I got on stage for my first rock 'n' roll show—kind of—I was dragged up by an Alice Cooper impersonator holding a massive boa constrictor.

The Trini fear of snakes made Alice Cooper the scariest of all shock rock stars. He painted snake lines around his eyes and snake fangs below his lips, and he wore a massive snake as a necklace during his shows. Terrifying. Yet when I heard that Just Alice—a real-life rock band with leather and amplifiers and a light show—would be at our school, I couldn't resist.

There I was, crushed up against the front of the gymnasium stage. The metal around the colourful drums glistened, the amps were alien consoles floating atop stacks of speakers, and the guitars sat like wands waiting to be waved.

When it all began, I was awestruck. It was all decibels, distortion, hairspray, devil horns, and white-boy posturing. My eyes ate it up greedily. I was finally in the middle of the madness called rock 'n' roll. It was going so well until "Alice" brought out the snake.

The crowd gasped and then screamed in approval. I was horrified. Alice strutted about, parading the beast, which curled around him like a feather boa made of death. Petrified but unable to look away, I simply froze. I don't know if it was because of this or because I was the only Black boy in the front row, but Alice lunged forward, reached down, and pulled me up unto the stage.

Big mistake for Alice, for me, and for his long scaly friend.

I kicked. I screamed. I cried bloody murder for what I assumed was my certain death. My chest was thumping with panic and adrenaline. Alice fought it. He was determined to add a small Trini boy to his circus of oddities. But little Tony knew how to kick and scream.

Alice soon clued in that he had chosen the wrong kid, and that this wasn't going to be fun. He set me back down, and in a rush of hyperventilating panic, I pushed my way to the back of the crowd and dashed out of the gym. I ran out into the night with the cold stars marking my way. I didn't stop running until I was clear of the infernal hell my school had become.

Almost as soon as I had regained some form of dignity, I burst out laughing, as if I had just fought off a bear, or as a mountain climber would at the summit of Everest. I rolled with demented glee. I had survived! Alice with his sour leather smell and his terrible pet boa wouldn't get me. Yet when this ecstasy receded, something unusual remained. Something in me had been activated. The lights, the spectacle, the way the crowd went mad for it, it all came back to me. Dashing home, my imagination ran wild. What if that was me? Then everyone would love me too, wouldn't they? I wouldn't be weird. It wouldn't matter if I couldn't pronounce words right. It wouldn't matter if I was small. It wouldn't matter that I lived with my aunt, who sang embarrassing hymns and dressed me like a dweeb. I would be one of them. Better than one of them—I would be special.

For the rest of my life, this desire to be transformed by the stage would prove difficult to resist.


# VII

The day before Auntie Joan put me on a train to Toronto to live with my father, we went to a powwow. I was so transfixed by the spectacle that I almost didn't notice how she watched me with her sweet, sad look the whole time.

Under the monumentally tall trees, in a clearing by a lake, we were called in by the sound of the drums echoing up through the branches and towards the heavens. Then came the voices soaring above the thumping rhythm, sharp and bright, in a kind of high-pitched chanting cry that pierced me.

I ran around the edges of the crowd, trying to get a glimpse of what was happening inside. I pushed between two men to see the drummers' mallets making the skins of the drums blurry with vibration.

The singers' mouths were open and their jaws were wide and working, as if they were trying to swallow something invisible. Behind them sat the mothers, aunties, daughters, and grandmas, singing the higher notes above the men. Their eyes were fixed on something vast and unknowable.

I saw the colours of the costumes—the blindingly bright reds, yellows, and blues. I saw the circles spinning from head to toe, the feathers, the headdresses, the braids on young girls chatting excitedly. The announcer called the dances in a booming voice. The lines of the women's shawls spread out like the wings of the Canada geese I had seen in Indigenous drawings. The men bounced proudly, throwing their heads back to the beat, sudden and fierce, while their bodies leaned and their feet trotted in a slow-motion run. I saw the hawk and the beaver and the muskie, and I felt as if I had peeked behind a curtain, as if some unseen barrier had fallen away and I was face to face with a terrific mystery.

These people—whom I had seen turning their eyes down and away from the whites, trying to make themselves small and unnoticeable, shying away from my hellos, stumbling drunk from the tavern to fight and yell in the dirty alleys of the town—these same people were now bold and upright and proud. I felt the casual normality of the people watching spill into the surrealness of the performers being watched, and back again. Being surrounded by drums, songs, and costumes had transformed them somehow. How powerful and free they all seemed. Was this a mirage?

My body said that this wasn't an illusion. This was the answer to an enigma. They were the land, the lake, the animals, the sky, the winter. This was all part of them before the Crown had come for it. "Savages," "colonies," "subjects"—the British had done to them what they had done to us. But they were still here. They were still part of the land,

and they belonged with the land the way the moose and the muskie belonged.

The powwow was a Crown-free space. It breathed life. It celebrated what things were before and what they would be for eternity.

And as I turned to face my uncertain future, my mind rang like ten thousand bells with the power of it all.

I too wanted to become something exalted and new.

## Chapter Eleven

# SAGA BOY

I

In 1988, Junior and twelve-year-old me moved in with Hailey, the former call girl, and Al, her former pimp now husband. I left Auntie Joan and the endless forests and lakes of Northern Ontario to live in the Greater Toronto Area, Canada's largest metropolis. Junior returned from his failed adventure at the Adventist boarding school in Valley Forge, Pennsylvania. He had become a silent and distant boy who I felt I hardly knew.

Auntie Agnes had sent Junior to their fancy Adventist school but either wouldn't or couldn't pay the tuition bill for his second term. Junior was no longer permitted to go to class but still lived, for the time being, at the boarding school. He was there, but he couldn't go to class. This meant that everyone knew that his family couldn't afford the fees. He never speaks of that year but I knew the judgmental cruelty of church "sisters" and "brothers." I understood that in a place like that, being too poor came with a heavy dose of shame.

This is where I first began to be skeptical of my Aunties' plans. It taught me that prayer and good wishes didn't always work out. God, apparently, did not always provide.

It seemed to me that once Aunt Agnes had gotten her use of him, Junior had been discarded like a candy bar wrapper or an empty milk carton.

Later I learned that my father, too, had once been discarded by Agnes.

Al was Miss Excelly's "surprise" baby; he came when she was in her late forties. "Send the boy to live with me," Aunt Agnes, his older sister, had said. "At least he will have his nephews to play with." Yet when he arrived, Agnes treated Al like a second-class citizen. Auntie Joan remembered seeing a photo of their family with little Al standing on the outskirts with a crumpled look on his face. An outcast.

When Agnes and her family left to live in New York City, they abandoned Al completely. He was sent back to Monkeytown to fend for himself. From then on, he began to "run in the streets." "I gotta take care of myself," he'd decided, and the allure of street life, easy money, rampant women, and fast cars never lost its power.

His talent for heartbreak was born from his own broken heart.

But I knew nothing of this when Al, Hailey, Junior, and I settled into that two-bedroom duplex in suburban Aurora. Little Tony started the experiment boiling over with excitement. A new city! A new school! A father! I finally had a real family, and things were going to be perfect.

But this was not to be.


Alyson Fitzherbert Downing was what he called a "player," not a "pimp." As he explained it, a pimp sends the girls out to work, while a player gets customers and brings them to the girls. Having been shattered himself, he had an instinctive nose for brokenness in others and took full advantage.

He'd rocked three-piece suits and butterfly collars in the 1970s as he pimped, pushed, and pistol-whipped his way to over a dozen felony convictions. Yet by the time the forgotten sons his mother had raised for him arrived on his doorstep, he was only a recreational crook. He and Hailey had nine-to-five jobs and were living the "square" life.

I was ecstatic to have a dad.

Waking up in the dim morning, I would force my sleepy limbs upstairs as Al and Hailey were leaving for work and pass out on a corner of their waterbed. Its gentle waves would rock me back to sleep. As Al stroked my head, he'd say, "Good morning, kid." He was dressed for his job at a garage and smelled of Old Spice aftershave. Specks of silver salted his black moustache.

"Morning," I would mumble, trying to motivate my eyes to stay open so I could see his face. I wanted to inhale all the father I could get.

His Jheri curl dripped. A pack of green-and-white Export "A" cigarettes peeked out of his work shirt. His eyes were dark, and you could always sense a hidden smile in them. They seemed to hide a joke and offered the promise of letting you in on it. Eyes full of charm and chaos.

Hailey was a harpy. A petite, curvy dirty blonde from a small town in Southern Ontario, she was permanently manicured and had blazing blue eyes that could shoot daggers. Her small mouth hid little coffee-stained teeth, through which she would chain-smoke menthol cigarettes. Her voice went from luxurious and seductive when relaxed to shrill and biting when pissed off. She was often pissed off. My cousin Ray, who stayed with us for a time, dubbed her Hailey the Hellcat.

At first, Hailey seemed to enjoy the idea of having kids. She showed affection in ways I was not used to, giving me hugs and kisses and looking at me approvingly when I was well dressed for school. She made exotic foods like pancakes with real maple syrup and piles of chewy, salty bacon. Pork and meat and sugar? Auntie Joan would have sent us straight to hell.

It felt nice to have something like a mother. But these happy moments were soon few and far between.

The truth was that Al and Hailey were more interested in the cheques they could get from the government for having us than they were interested in having us. She tried, in her way, to show me some motherly affection, but she knew only one way to love males.

One day she called me into the kitchen, where she had been sipping wine and smoking. She approached me, her mouth twisted into a smile, her breath perfumed with tar from the menthols. Her hand brushed my nipples through my thin shirt. Her eyes flickered over me and her smile twisted the corners of her mouth until her face was a mischievous mask. Her pointy nails described excruciatingly delicious circles around my nipples until they felt sharp and erect. I had never been touched like this. My breath stopped. Electricity leapt from her fingertips down my spine. The sensation paralyzed me. Her face hovered inches from mine, but I kept looking down and trying to breathe. I could smell her breath, heavy and close. Suddenly she seemed to get bored and moved away.


My favourite times were rolling in Dad's Cadillac DeVille sedan. It was forest green and the seats were cushion soft and smelled like new pillows, warm and fresh. I loved the way he leaned as he drove, scanning the street from behind his ashy cigarette. That casual grip of the dart, the soft pull of his lips, and the crackle as the flame glowed and released its smoke. His eyes narrowing here, his lips grinning there.

He seemed as cautious as a predator. Like a shark cruising a dark and turbulent sea.

"You know Marvin, kid? No? You gotta know Marvin Gaye! *Here, My Dear*? What about Bobby Womack? *The Poet*? No? No Stevie Wonder either, huh? What kinda music they teaching you at that school? All that Bach and Beethoven shit? All right, listen to this. You're a music dude. I want to hear what you think of this. This is Isaac Hayes's *Hot Buttered Soul*."

And he would listen to what I had to say. He cared about what I thought. My father—the man I knew only from photos and tales—cared what I thought. I eased back in the seat and tried to lean like he did, sneaking peeks to make sure I got it right. I studied the hair on his face where he had shaved that morning, the brown tinted sunglasses that obscured his eyes but not his vision, and the confidence, as if nothing as square as worry had ever touched him. The way laughter would jerk and explode out of him in a spasm, as if he were four years old and hitting a bike rim with a stick as he dashed down Monkeytown Third Branch. It was the first time I had felt that close to him.

It was also one of the last.

Back at the house, I was mostly neglected. I slept in a room with nothing but white walls and a mattress on the floor, my tiny black bass guitar, an amp, and stacks of books. Somewhere between hungry and a belly full of frustration.

One day I squeaked through clarinet practice one too many times, and Hailey waved an annoyed fingernail at me: "Shut. The. Fuck. Up." She hissed at me as vicious as a viper, but defiant to the last, I kept on squeaking my way through the music.

Junior started coming home very late. Hailey would scream at him for waking her up in the middle of the night, so he just stopped coming home at all. He would leave for days at a time without telling anyone where he was going or getting in trouble. Some part of me knew this was wrong. No rules, no punishments, no meals together—this was not the way it was supposed to be.

After a while, it felt as though he had vanished and no one had gone to look for him. I didn't understand why, but I knew that whatever had happened at Pine Forge Academy had changed him for good. There was no point in waiting up to listen for the metal of the storm door clanging in the dead of night.

Our cousin Ray was now living in Aurora too. He was Steve's brother and Boysie's son and had come up from Trinidad. We lived together for a time with Al and Hailey.

Ray had the same large, droopy eyes as his father and a thick Trini accent that made me look down on him. I had been on stage with a fake Alice Cooper, so I felt like an expert on the white world. Besides, Canada was mine and I didn't have to share it. I was here first.

Not long into his stay, he branded her Hailey the Hellcat. "Toe-nee," he would say, grinning and still calling me by my Trini name, "dat woman will kill a man one day." And he would cackle, a south Trini cackle that sounded like the call of some giant bird, except this bird loved his rum and would cook until the stink of salt cod sat like a cloud on everything. "Yuh bettah hope yuh is not dat man!" He kept cackling.

Hailey hated all of us dearly.

When I loudly complained that her birthday present of a stamp collection was "stupid," she went full-on street corner, spitting curses at me. "You better learn to be grateful, you little fucking prick!" I was certain that she loathed me.

Finally, she urged my dad to discipline me. Yelling, he charged through the basement door and started bashing me with the bass guitar he'd bought me. It was a small-scale Atak "Artist," and all I could play then was U2's "With or Without You" and some blues songs. He screamed in rage and I screamed in fear: "No, Dad! No. Stop." By the time he was done, the bass was in splinters and my foot, which I had used to block his blows, was bloody.    ·

It was not a whipping—I'd had plenty of those in Trinidad—it was an attack. A revelation of the frustrated, vengeful thing that lived inside him.

I didn't understand what it was, but something inside me never trusted him again.

11

"THE NIGGER KEEPS GOING OFFSIDE!"

The first time someone was blatantly racist to me, I was thrilled. I was playing football at my new high school in Aurora. It was gym class and I was sprinting my little self up and down the field while the smell of the wet grass filled my face. I thought it was going splendidly, but I was also confused.

I didn't understand why playing "football" in Canada involved strange names like "quarterback," "tight end," and "guard." In Trinidad, football was, of course, soccer—a very different game. After my third time crossing the line of scrimmage too soon and going offside—a concept no one had explained to me—an Italian kid with a frizzy mullet pointed over at me and yelled: "THE NIGGER KEEPS GOING OFFSIDE!"

My inside voice said, "I think I've just been racisted. Yes!" Overjoyed to finally have an experience to go with the word "racism," I burst out laughing.

Dr. G.W. Williams Secondary School was the third high school I'd been to. I showed up for grade ten as a scrappy, mouthy thirteen-year-old. My head was still half in Monkeytown. I was still mispronouncing words regularly. Like I had to try really hard to say "thief" and not "tief." Or when I said "Sarah," it came out as "Sai-ir-ah."

Too small for high school, I made up for it by talking loudly, lying outrageously, and posturing as a wanna-be metalhead with all the wrong clothes. Basically, I'd do anything for attention.

I was still getting on Hailey's last nerve with my squeaky clarinet. The instrument, black wood and sparkling silver keys, seemed like a magic wand to me. If I could touch the reed the right way with my tongue, finger the stops and keys just so, and blow at the proper angle, I could unlock a clear, pure note. It was a burst of extraordinary light that soothed and puffed up my chest with pride.

But it was Junior who showed me how truly seductive music could be.

"Put this on," he said and threw me a pair of blue jeans with a little dude in Rasta colours stitched into the leg. "We going to a party tonight."

My face lit up. "A party? For real?"

He watched me as if to say, "Don't make me regret this." But what he actually said was, "Be ready for six."

The house was like any other suburban house on the icy street. Winter had drowned the world in white powder, and a crisp, nasty bite came with each breath of air. Everything seemed normal except for this vague throbbing pulsing from the house like the heartbeat of a giant. Sketches of people's shadows peeked out from behind the snowbanks, puffing smoke or pressing up against each other, sucking at faces in the dark corners of the cold.

The closer I got to the pulsing throb, the more it peeled my head open. At the top of the stairs, the heat and smell of perspiration and music lifted out of the basement. Down the stairs, it was like we had crossed through a portal to a parallel galaxy. Darkness and bass filled the room like a womb. Everywhere people danced. Some backed up against the walls—men with beers dangling from loose swinging arms, their other hands gripping the hip bones of wide-waisted girls who were tilted over, faces focused, grinding their asses into the men. Gold-link chains, bright gold smiles, fades and flat-top hair, Clarks and Timberlands on feet, girls in mesh and underwear, flesh searing into my brain, making my body hot and rigid, yelling out when the big sound start, yelling out together, then back to grinding and expressing their own selves.

The sounds coming from the stacks of black speaker cabinets in one corner were rearranging my atoms. Every thud exploded into my chest and seemed to disintegrate and reassemble me from the inside. In the centre of the room, a rich cocktail of colognes and perfumes clashed as the grinding came with lifting, hot stepping in dark shades, front foot, back foot, left foot cock-up; knees open and close slowly, that's a buttahfly; hands stabbing in circles is "bogel"; the silver furnace, exposed and too close to our heads; the DJ talking over the song right when it got good, cutting the beat out so everyone could sing the lyrics to the big "choon," which is what you called a song.

When a song everyone loved came on, they all went mad at once. Yelling, bawling out, gunshot salute, and then reaching up and banging on the furnace pipes again and again. Bang bang bang bang bang. "Wheeeeeeeeeel selektaaaaaah!!" Which meant, "Start it again so we can lose our minds all over."

When the banging got out of control, the owner stopped the music and got on the mic: "All massive in general nah badah bang pon de furnace scene? Wintertime cold. Don't bang pon de furnace." Then back to the choon. But when another hit came on: "Wheeeeeeeel selectah!" Bang bang bang bang bang.

The sight that stole me away from everything was Junior leaning, half hidden by weed smoke, hands gesturing gunshots at the roof as he and King Man performed their songs. Seeing him there made me feel like I could be there too. I could be a king in this magic dimension without stepmothers, without classmates calling me "nigger," and without squeaky clarinets. Maybe that's how everyone there felt—like they were somewhere they could be free.

It felt like a puzzle I had to solve. It had everything I had a taste for: attention, words, and music. But I was a tourist, a stranger in this world. I was dorky and bookish, and I listened to loud white-boy music.

King Man asked my brother: "What wrong wit de yout, Junyah? De boy possess?"

"Leave him alone. He yung still." Junior would look at me, frowning, a little embarrassed, a little concerned. But he wouldn't let anyone make fun of me.

Things changed when they realized I could write songs.

One day, I showed up to their band practice with two marked-up pages of lyrics.

King Man sucked his two gold teeth absentmindedly as he read them. He had flat-top hair with little shapes chopped into it. "Dis choon artical," he said, which meant it was good. Then, reading some more, his eyes got wide. "Yow! De lickle yout is a dan! Risspec." Which meant he liked it. And he looked at me again as if seeing me for the first time.

Junior just nodded as if he wasn't surprised.

They ran through the song a capella. It was the first time I'd ever heard someone rap one of my songs. It was something about having power—"jah gimme power." Except it was "powah" and terrible, but it was mine.

I felt sky-high watching them nod and sway as they spit the words, posturing and shaking, then giving each other a "bounce," closed fists touching to salute how cool the choon was. When they finished, King Man yelled, "Wheeeeeeeeeeel selectah!" And they pointed their gun fingers at the sky. Bang bang bang bang bang. And they started into it again.

These big kids—who knew things I didn't know about girls' bodies, underground parties, knife fights, and being a man—were repeating the words I had thought of and written down. Miraculously, somehow, I knew something they didn't.

In the beginning was the Word, and the Word was God.

Life for me that year was like this: perched precariously between the wrath of Hailey the Hellcat, a father I loved but could not trust, and a lost brother I recognized less and less every day. But from then on, whenever I could, I escaped into words and songs.

It never occurred to me that these were the two things Miss Excelly had taught me—how to read and how to sing. These were her gifts.

The things she, too, had needed to survive.

## Chapter Twelve

# THE QUICK
# AND THE DEAD

I

Living with addicts is like living with zombies: you never know whether they'll eat you or ignore you.

By the time we had moved to Scarborough, closer to downtown Toronto, the wheels of our calamitous little family had come off. Al was managing another muffler shop franchise, while Hailey was the sly chain-smoking secretary at a real estate office. Junior faded in and out like a distant radio station. He came home every now and then for a night or two, but mostly he was a ship with no shore.

His home was the night.

My room was my sanctuary, and that day, I was in it yelling my face off to Public Enemy. "Too Black, too strong," Chuck D was calling out from my cheap red boom box with the broken rewind button. I was listening to Chuck and Flava Flav and hopping from one foot to the next, pretending I had a huge clock hanging from my neck like Flav.

Fun is made of moments like these when you're a nerdy loner kid.

The room was a mess of books, tapes, and musical equipment: a Yamaha RX21 drum machine, a Tascam four-track recorder, microphones on makeshift stands or duct-taped to boxes. Cords and power adaptors ran from the closet to the recording machine beside my bed, which flashed pale green, yellow, and red when the signal was hot. Guitar magazines were piled high in one corner, and thumb-tacked to the wall was a schedule: "Monday—sight reading, Tuesday—scales, Wednesday—ear training . . . "

It was the laboratory of a mad scientist.

Beside the bed, displayed like a staff of power, was the white bass Al had bought me out of guilt to replace the one he destroyed. In the closet, though I took it out only occasionally, was my grandma's white Bible with the gold letters with which I had learned to read.

Cars were slushing by on Warden Avenue, and my little window let in the haunting glow of the streetlights and let out the noise of my thrashing about. Chuck D was rapping about getting a draft letter from the government.

He didn't give a damn.

All the equipment I had was stolen, I presumed. Junior and his hoodlum homies would slink by and drop off some new piece of gear every once in a while. He stashed the stuff in our basement at first, and with a suck-teeth stchuups, he'd say, "Don't touch this stuff, scene?" Which meant, "Do you understand?"

He always talked Jamaican now.

When I could persuade him to hang, he loved to watch Clint Eastwood movies like *The Good, the Bad and the Ugly*. They were filled with hard men who didn't laugh or play. Tough-talking, whisky-guzzling shooters who kicked up dust across hellish deserts and shot people just for fun.

You were either quick with your hands or dead.

That day, when I was tired of listening to Public Enemy, I passed out on my single bed and listened to my stomach groan itself into knots. There was nothing to eat again. Cupboards, it seemed, didn't produce food on their own, no matter how many times you checked them.

I eventually heard the key in the front door, and my breath tightened until my chest hurt. Al and Hailey were home. I listened, ear to the dusty grey carpet, nose sniffing at the crack under the door. I heard them trudge in, heard the closet door slide and clang into the stop, then slide back closed, and then I heard the folding kitchen door slide open, then the clang and clink of pots on the stove.

They were cooking something, and I twisted my neck into a pretzel trying to catch a whiff of what it might be. Kraft Mac & Cheese? Fried chicken, maybe? Hailey had sometimes cooked spaghetti and meatballs in Aurora, but in Scarborough, everything had changed. I sniffed and listened and tried not to breathe, until finally I heard them retire to the master bedroom.

Then I descended on tiptoes to scavenge for food.

I slowly pushed back the sliding door to the kitchen. The place smelt like burning. Beside the stove was a Pyrex pot of boiled water, but there was no sign of food in it—just hot water with a blackened spoon on the counter beside it. This happened a lot lately, and I had no idea what it meant. Why would you boil water with no food? Then Al and Hailey would disappear for days after.

I didn't know anything about crack or cocaine or freebasing, but I did understand hunger. I never spoke to Al and Hailey anymore. I never even wanted to be seen by them. I lived in constant fear of their vacant stares, their fatigue, and their complete loss of interest in me.

It was as if they were dead.

So I built my own world and filled it with music, books, and basketball.

Now fourteen, I was in grade eleven at L'Amoreaux Collegiate Institute, my fourth high school. L'Am was in the centre of the Canadian immigrant mash-up and had students from seventy different nationalities. But even there, I was an odd boy. I was a shy, bookish kid who listened to heavy metal. What Black guy did that?

Having not been Black enough for the whites, I was now failing at being Black enough for the Blacks.

So I read. C.S. Lewis's Chronicles of Narnia, Conan the Barbarian, fantasy novels with titles like *The Black Cauldron*. The books I read the most were the Dragonlance novels, with twin brothers Caramon, the brawny warrior, and Raistlin, the sickly smarty-pants wizard. The novels were about weird lands shaken by medieval battles and cataclysms, dragons, and powerful sorcerers in towers.

I wanted to be a mage. Someone with secret words of power. Someone fierce and terrible who wouldn't have to cower upstairs until his parents got high and left him some scraps to eat.

When I wasn't in my room or at school, I was playing basketball.

I found purpose in the hollow ringing sound of leather on asphalt. I'd heave jump shots until the sweat left trails of dry salt down my cheeks. I'd flick my wrist quickly to get the shot off, and then chase the rebound all day. I'd play so long in the hot sun that dehydration would make my eyes throb. If anyone ever wanted a game or needed an extra man for their team, I would stay. If I could, I would never go home.

Home was a mess.

My favourite person at school that year was a slightly autistic savant named Matthew. He was gangly, scruffy, had unruly acne, and spoke with a vaguely British accent. He could play classical piano flawlessly and loved to explain to me why each section was "quite good."

One day, he stunned me in the music room by playing Beethoven's *Moonlight Sonata*. The bass notes punched me in my chest, while the haunting melody unfolded slowly, like a rose opening to meet the sun. His hands danced over the keys in a hypnotizing pirouette. His head dangled and swayed. He hunched over and struck the keys in a way that seemed both delicate and forceful, both violent and completely in control. His body jerked back from the drama of the notes as if they were playing him. My eyes dimmed with tears.

I was crying. I didn't know why. I thought I was too old to cry.

And for a tiny slice of eternity, I forgot who I was.


## I I


Heavy metal may not be the devil's music, but one day it brought out the devil in my father and an entire station full of cops.

I was sitting in the foyer of Midas Muffler, the garage where my dad was assistant manager. I was bored and smelled like floor cleaner from my part-time job across the street. Al was under a car with a tool that grumbled and whirred loudly.

I said, "Dad, can I go to the mall?"

"Sure, kid." He didn't look up.

I had said the mall, but I knew exactly where I was headed: the big store with the flourescent lights and rows and rows of everything from broomsticks to underwear to TVs to tapes.

A quick look and scoop, and I had two tapes under my sweater: Ozzy Osborne's live double album with Randy Rhoads, and Metallica's *Garage Days Re-Revisited* EP. In those days, stores put tapes in long, hard plastic cases, and I felt them digging into my ribs and my hip bone and down into my underwear.

My heart started kicking up a storm. I'd gotten away with it before, but these anxious moments between stealing something and getting away with it always made me panic.

The man coming towards me was looking right at me. I looked down to make sure the plastic cases weren't sticking out and giving me away. Stay cool. That's how you do it. Breathe. You're just a kid browsing. When I looked back, the man was still looking at me. He's just browsing too. He is browsing. I am browsing. My hands started to sweat and shake. I put my head down and he passed me by. Phew. When I looked up, another man turned the corner and said, "Come with me, son," and I felt the hands of the first man on my shoulders. Busted.

From the back of the cop car, I saw my dad's forest-green Cadillac driving ahead. A moment of indecision gripped me, but I quickly decided that I was more scared of jail than I was of how pissed he would be.

"That's my dad," I yelled. "That's my dad's Cadillac."

The cop pulled him over, but my dad said, "Well, you have to process him, right? I'll be back to grab him after I go home."

"What?!" I said, "You're leaving me?" And I watched with desperation from the back of the cop cruiser as Al's Cadillac rolled off. He was trying to teach me a lesson.

I waited so long in the room that I'd napped on the white table and woke up groggy. I was too sleepy and terrified to cry. I mumbled and shook. I was a pitiful thing.

When my dad finally arrived, about a year later, he was pissed. He looked at me with thunder and disappointment on his face. He was tired. He also hated cops. The cop was tired. It was two hours past the end of his shift, and he hated crooked little sons and their crook fathers who kept him waiting as if he didn't have a life to live. This was a recipe for calamity.

It didn't take long for my dad to mouth off to the cop at the desk, and then reach over and flick the brim of his hat. That drove the cop wild. Soon, police were diving over the counter and wrestling my dad to the ground. There was a lot of "Fuck you, pig" and "Grab his legs" and batons swinging and kicks getting in.

Whatever chance I'd had of talking or crying my way out of this evaporated. I watched the cops beat my dad bloody and then charge him with assaulting an officer.

Yes, my father caught three charges and a beat-down so I could listen to Ozzy Osbourne shredding.

Perhaps I, too, was a bit hooked.


## III

That Christmas, Hailey and Al decided to do it big.

They bought a Christmas tree, decorated it, and steadily began to stack presents under it. Junior and I had grown into complete skeptics, but the little boys in us couldn't help but be thrilled. We had never had a Christmas tree before. There were no pine trees in Trinidad, and Auntie Joan believed that Christmas was idolatry. Here at last was a proper tree with pine needles, ornaments, and a beaming little angel on top and piles of presents in shiny green, red, and silver wrapping underneath.

Surely we were going to get tons of amazing toys and gadgets, right? I even dared to sneak downstairs and peek at the boxes and shake them to try to guess which were mine. As the holidays approached, I watched the pile grow, salivating at the possibilities. This was going to be the best Christmas ever, we thought.

We were very much deceived.

That Christmas morning, present by present, the truth was revealed to us like a yuletide fog lifting: none of the colourful boxes were for us. Hailey and Al exchanged presents and kisses in between sips of Riesling. They stopped only briefly to give us each a lamp and a blanket. They were only interested in each other.

We were deflated.

Soon after that, Junior, still just seventeen, stopped coming home completely. I stood in the hallway, watching him move his clothes and comic books out in boxes. I didn't know him anymore, but I still felt sad. He was all I had left of my childhood, of Trinidad, of that time when things were as simple as my grandmother's lap and five-cent poulourie.

"You guys are forcing me to choose between you and my wife," Al complained.

"Well, I guess you made your choice, then." Junior was dark and angry in his silent way that felt like the whole sky was full of boiling clouds and thunder.

Before he left, Al stopped him at the door and reached into his box to take back the lamp and blanket.

"She say you can't take these," he said, and sheepishly slipped back into the house.

I watched alone in the dark hall as my brother drove away.

He, too, was now officially running the streets.


IV


Soon after Junior left, Hailey and Al lost the house in Scarborough and we all had to move out. No one explained anything to me. They just packed me into that same forest-green Cadillac DeVille and dropped me off at my brother's basement apartment.

"We have to take a trip," Al said, as if that explained why he was sending me away. A trip to where? I thought, but the words died on my tongue. "You gotta go live with your brother, kid." He shrugged. He was wearing his tight work pants, but his face had not been shaved for weeks.

None of my books, guitars, amps, mics, magazines, posters, or tapes came with me. All the things that gave me security were gone. I was tossed, barely clothed, into the rough Scarborough wilderness to fend for myself.

Despite the horror of living with them, I was terrified by the thought of facing the world without the safety of my room to hide in. I had not realized how much I hid behind my ability to create music in my sanctuary beyond the reach of my parents' chaos.

"Just for a little while, kid," my father said. Then he and Hailey, who was wearing a big-collared striped shirt with the chest buttons undone, rolled off slowly into the watery sun.

It would be five years before I saw Al again. Hailey disappeared from my life forever.

Chapter Thirteen

# NEW TESTAMENT
# LOBOTOMY

I

Things did not go well at Junior's.

His apartment had no furniture or food or curtains but was filled with stolen things. One bedroom had piles of speakers, turntables, and amplifiers stacked up in a wall. Then one night, the other bedroom was suddenly filled with suede and leather jackets. The treated hides reeked and I could see the store tags peeking out of the plastic. These items had not been purchased.

Junior and his homies ran a scam called a swarm. Ten of them would rush into a store and grab two or three jackets each. The sheer speed and numbers would overwhelm the staff before they could call security.

"Yow, take a jacket from the pile nah. We moving them soon," Junior said without looking at me.

I couldn't believe my luck. Even in his tough-boy phase he was still, in his own way, looking out for me. I chose a hickory-brown suede coat. It was so stiff that my fingers had to work hard to button it up the first time. My slight shoulders swam in it like I was wearing a blanket. It was the nicest thing I'd ever owned.

The place was soon raided by the police. I watched, horrified, as an officer put Junior in a headlock. "Stop resisting! Stop resisting!" the cop said while he wrestled my brother into a painful-looking hold, his limbs chicken-winged, his face growing purple. Junior never stopped resisting.

He did, however, continue to grow cold and distant, a stranger who was busy doing things I never knew of and probably would never understand. *Stchuuuuups*. He kissed his teeth when I asked him if he wanted to play cards. "I'm not about dem lil boy flexes again," he said, sounding more and more Jamaican every day. His expression grew hard. He never spoke of Trinidad or Mama.

My brother was a space I no longer recognized.

## I I

"Child, I didn't bring you all de way to Canada so you can grow up in a jail," said Auntie Joan.

She used her stern headmaster's voice when I called to tell her about the basement, the contraband, and the police raids. She immediately sent me a train ticket. In a heartbeat, I found myself back in the bitter freezing north, living with my aunt again.

Instead of dodging addicts and police raids, I had to dodge Joan's pop-up prayer meetings.

"Father Gaaawd," she droned in her dramatic "word of prayer" voice, "we want to thank you for delivering your child Michael out of the lion's den. We thank you that you are a God that hears and answers prayer. For you said in your word, 'Whatsoever ye shall ask in prayer, believing, ye shall receive.' So we want to lift this boy up in a very special way. Deliver him from evil. Ring your angels around him. Let him be as the tree planted by the rivers of life, that will bring forth fruit in his season. Amen."

"Amen," I said with a great exhale of air.

She was living in Thunder Bay now, in a ground-level two-bedroom apartment with a sturdy kitchen table and her bookshelf full of Jung, Freud, Adler, and the blue Adventist Sabbath school books with the artfully cheerful white families on the cover. These books contained the lessons we had to read every Sabbath, when, from sundown Friday to sundown Saturday, we cut ourselves off from the world, sang hymns, ate lentils, and meditated on the Lord. Yikes.

Thunder Bay was tucked away in the western corner of Lake Superior, and with more than a hundred thousand residents, it was the second biggest city in Northern Ontario. "The Largest Grain Port in the World," read the sign leading into town, because apparently all the grain from the Great Plains ended up there on one of those never-ending trains that took fifteen minutes to pass.

Those fifteen minutes felt like fifteen years when they were spent sitting in Auntie Joan's Toyota Tercel, listening to Evie sing "In the Garden" for the thirty-seventh time that week. On the cover of her cassettes, the startlingly blonde Swedish woman was always in soft light and smiling. "I come to the garden alone while the dew is still on the roses," she sang. "And the voice I hear, falling on my ear, the Son of God discloses."

It was embarrassing the way Auntie Joan sang along as if it were the greatest thing ever. It was not.

"And He walks with me, and He talks with me, and He tells me I am His own."

It was so corny, but like her mother, the woman loved her hymns.

"Child, why you screwing up your face at your auntie's music? Don't you know Jesus walks with you too?"

I turned up my headphones on my yolk-coloured Walkman so I could hear Dave Mustaine, Megadeth's lead singer, snarl the lyrics to "Devil's Island," and she turned up Evie's *God Anthems*. Yes, God and Satan had a Battle of the Bands right there under the clackety-clack of Saskatchewan grain leaving to feed the world.

Auntie Joan cracked a smile as she sang. Her Afro wig framed her beaming eyes, and she punched me playfully and smiled until her handsome cheekbones shone, then punched me harder and smiled more until I cracked an annoyed smile back. I was back among the snowmobiles, the Canada geese, the black bears, the ugly muskies, the Ojibwe, and my God-mad aunt.

She and Jesus were the only parents I had left.


That year, I attended my fifth high school—Westgate Collegiate and Vocational Institute. The boys liked to drink beer and "get shit-faced." The girls came around expecting a Black guy, but got me, a geeky metalhead in all-new church-boy sweaters. I quickly disappointed the white kids who wanted a breakdancing, shit-talking rapper boy.

In the music room, where light sprayed from high windows and music stands littered the floor, I fell in love. I started playing the string bass, the elephant of the orchestra, in the school concert band. It seduced me fully with the weight and coolness of the honey-glazed wood, the horsehair bow bouncing on the strings, the resin dust suspended in air, and the deep booming sound that trembled in my spine, rumbled in my chest, and enveloped me like a womb.

I lost myself in music, a habit that would stand the test of time.

One fateful day, Mr. Yaciuk, our Polish music teacher, asked me dismissively: "How good at basketball are you anyways?" He asked this while meticulously draping his suit jacket over the back of his chair. Then he looked me squarely in the face and said: "From what I hear from your coach, you are a much better string bass player."

I had just made basketball team for the first time. I was ecstatic, but it's true that I wasn't very good. I knew I would likely never play a game all year. I didn't care, though. I was on the team. I had a shiny new uniform, and I was finally a real baller.

"I have spoken to him," Mr. Yaciuk said, "and you are off the team." He turned back to his papers as if he had just flicked the page on some sheet music.

My face tightened and flushed. I sprinted to the gym, confirmed this news with the coach, and then sprinted back to the music room. Mr. Yaciuk hadn't even lifted his head.

"I quit!" I declared, stomping away. I never went back.


One morning soon after that episode, I couldn't get out of bed.

The terrible northwestern winter wind howled in the snowbanks. It moaned and whistled right through me. Auntie Joan called, then begged, then threatened, then prayed, then simply gave up and went to work. The next day was the same, and the next and the next. I spent weeks dragging myself through our small apartment, falling into sluggish sleeps on the coarse, scratchy couch.

My heart was broken and I didn't know why.

More to the point, the brokenness that lived inside me had been exposed. After bouncing from Trinidad to Wabigoon, to Sioux Lookout, to Aurora, to Scarborough, to Thunder Bay in five years, I had lost any sense of my specialness to the vast, black heaving sea of chaos that seemed to follow me everywhere.

I dreamt of Monkeytown, of the light fading over fields, of an old lady serenading the tombstones, of mad feral things chasing me through tall grass. My wings wouldn't fly, my guns wouldn't shoot, and my legs wouldn't run fast enough as Jumbie chased me through the bush.

Every morning, my aunt got ready for work and looked with concern at me still bundled on the couch, but then she'd just shake her head sorrowfully. She had run out of things to say. The depression lasted weeks. Finally, I got up one morning, showered, and sheepishly asked, "Tanty Joan, can you drop me to school?" ("Tanty" was what I called her when I was sucking up.)

"Thank you, Jesus!" was all she said, and just like that, I was back from the dead.

But there was no going back to either music or basketball.

With no extracurricular activities to fill my time, I started hanging with the boys who drank beers and smoked weed all weekend. At one of their parties, I threw a boulder that smashed a front window. Everyone else was throwing pebbles, but Little Tony needed to escalate. I was charged with a misdemeanor and had to go to court.

Auntie Joan refused to help me. "Excelly rolling in she grave," she said. "This is what she spend she last days to raise you for you to become? This is the law. I cannot help you. You will learn your lesson yourself. You ever hear she say, 'Who don't hear does feel'? Well, you didn't listen to me, and now you have to feel."

True to her word, I went to court alone. Running late, I begged a ride on the back of a speed bike because it was the only way I'd get to the courthouse on time. The engine was grumbling and whining when the biker revved, and we flew through the morning across town, hurtling into my precarious future.

I finished the year as a young offender.

## III

That summer, Aunt Joan sent me to live with Aunt Agnes. The idea was to keep me "out of the devil's reach." And once I got there, possibly because I felt guilty for causing so much trouble, or perhaps just because I was bored, I got baptized. Despite having no desire to be lobotomized by the New Testament, I decided that if I made my aunts happy, perhaps I would become one of the good Adventist kids—the ones they always praised. After all, my aunts just wanted the best for me, right?

"Do you accept Jesus Christ as your personal Lord and Saviour?" the pastor asked, big and clear. Westbury Seventh-day Adventist Church was arrayed with flowers and bright dresses and the light of the Lord. The deacons had erected a container filled with water for the Baptism. There we stood, in God's swimming pool, its bluish water sparkling in the holy brightness, at the centre of the wide altar, before the congregation and under His watchful eyes. There were six souls to be saved that day, and mine was one of them. I was bewildered by the spectacle but determined to play the role of the good Christian boy my Aunties wanted me to be.

Aunties Joan and Agnes sat in the front pew, full of sighs and stray tears. My anointment made them feel they were finishing their mother's work. They were proud that after all the "devil music" he had listened to, their promising nephew, who passed for Presentation College and could quote chapter and verse of both testaments, was giving himself to Christ. Praise the Lord.

The deacons' robes looked light and pretty, and the choir was singing "Amazing Grace" because I had said it was my favourite hymn. I'd said that because Charmaine Forde, who was famous, sang it at Miss Excelly's funeral, and somehow I felt this was really all about her.

"Boy, Mama would be so proud of you," Aunt Agnes cooed as she obsessively smoothed my tie. "All her prayers are being answered today." She was almost ready to weep. She pressed her present—a pocket-sized King James Bible and a matching hymnal with "Michael A. Downing" embossed in gold on the covers— into my hand. The leather felt both soft and rough when I ran my fingers along it. The Bible smelt like new pages. It reeked of the Holy Ghost.

"Do you accept Jesus Christ as your personal Lord and Saviour?" The pastor was in his full regalia. The organ was soaring. The whole firmament rang out with one voice: "Ahh-eye ooonce was looost, but nooow I'm found . . . " His soaking robes were floating on the waist-high water, and I could smell the chlorine, which I assumed had been blessed and was now holy.

"Was bliiiind, but noooow I seeee."

"I do," I replied, and he dunked me backwards and my eyes filled with chlorine and grace and the congregation moaned "Amen."

"Hallelujah, another soul finds its way back home."

Aunties Agnes and Joan were smiling and weeping. It was the summer of 1992. I was seventeen and finally saved.


IV


Now that I had achieved salvation, I assumed that my life would simply glow with the Lord's blessings.

I was wrong.

I settled into a room in a house on Rockland Street that Aunt Agnes and Neville owned. It was a spacious house with a corner yard, many floors and rooms, a den at the back, and a yard full of flowers fenced in with decency. Neville's face was hard as nails and his voice barked like a drill sergeant's.

"Children are to be seen and not heard," he shouted when I commented on something he was watching on TV. Then he snapped to Auntie Agnes, his voice rough as boulders, "Dat boy has no respect."

Agnes lived like a woman brought up in the time of the Queen. She was tiny, almost to the point of frailty. She had bags under her eyes—permanently, it seemed. She dressed like Queen Elizabeth, in colourful silks with sharp handbag-and-shoes combinations, a large array of pearl necklaces, and of course, hats. She had an attic full of hats in hat boxes. Meshy ones, broad-brimmed ones, flower-decorated ones, teal, purple, peach, mango—and all reeking of the mothballs she sprinkled liberally to protect them. She recited verses in an accent that was somewhere between the Hamptons and the House of Windsor. "What a thing," she would say, emphasizing *th*.

Yet Aunt Agnes's greatest extravagance was other people's children. My sweet but vain auntie had a habit of taking in strays, just like her mother, but then leaving them stranded, unlike her mother. She did it with her grandchildren, she did it with her great-grandchildren, she did it with Junior, she did it with Al. Auntie Joan would say, about that picture of their family with a miserable little Al on the outskirts, "The boy looked like a lost puppy."

Every Sabbath we spent at Westbury Seventh-day Adventist Church. Black people dressed to the nines and loving the Lord. I had grown up believing that generosity and kindness were the most Christian things, but here it was all about what you were wearing and how important you were. To me, the congregants were all hypocrites, the kind of people Christ would have kicked out of the temple.

I soon attached myself to brothers Everton and Chris Hudson. They were funny, well dressed, and from a family the aunties approved of. We spent the summer playing basketball relentlessly. If we had played as well as we talked shit, we would've been legends. As it was, we bombed around Westbury talking shit well, playing ball badly, and laughing our heads off.

Soon, I started sleeping over at the Hudson boys' home. Their mom, Joyce, was kind and welcoming. She said my name with an easy Atlanta drawl—"My-kiil"—that immediately made me like her. "My-kiil, boy, you can sing with us today in church, but them squeaky notes got to go, darling." Singing together at church was how the Hudsons showed off the family, and as an honorary member, I too was expected to hit those notes.

I felt like I had in Sioux Lookout when I stayed with the Jehovah Witnesses—a normal kid, part of a normal family.

Joyce had wanted to adopt me, Auntie Joan told me years later. But her husband vetoed the idea. One day, she told me: "Why don't you go spend some time back at your aunt's place?" It stung. I had felt as if I were one of them, but I wasn't. I was just a castaway.

I went back, sullen and dejected, a lost puppy.


Where was I supposed to go now? What would I do? I wondered. The aunties were wondering this also, and had cooked up an answer: Cambridge, Ontario, home of my stepmother Ami and my brothers Adrian and Nigel.

It was August 1992, and once again I was being sent away to live somewhere else. This time, Auntie Joan was not coming with me. At Grand Central Station as we waited for my train, she seemed to know something I hadn't yet grasped—our time together was over. She was always bad at goodbyes.

"Did you pack your Bible and your hymnal, child?"

"Yes, Auntie Joan."

"Don't be eating any of that pork. None of that bacon, ribs, or ham-burgah either, you hear me?"

"Yes, Auntie Joan."

Her eyes creased with big teardrops that somehow refused to fall, and her lecture voice grew weak and flimsy.

"You know that red meat is a source of high blood pressure and stroke." She hugged and squeezed me as she had never done. "Ring your angels around him, Lord," I heard her whisper. "Let me look at you. Be nice to your brothers and Ami, okay?"

"Yes, Auntie Joan."

It was hard to process what was happening. Once again I was being sent to a new parent, a new start, in a new place. A dance that had become sad but familiar.

I wouldn't see Auntie Joan again for almost ten years. And the next time I saw Auntie Agnes, it was in Trinidad, almost twenty years later. By then, she was crippled from a stroke, unable to walk or cut style in one of her Queen Elizabeth hats.

The wheel of time was turning.

I was being sent back to Canada.

Chapter Fourteen

# GLENVIEW PARK

I

All I wanted was a home. For the ground to stop shifting beneath my feet. For something, anything, to stay the same long enough for me to feel rooted.

By the time I'd landed at the train station in Hamilton, I was seventeen. Since my grandmother's funeral six years earlier, the parade of new towns, new schools, new guardians entering and leaving my life had not stopped. The old lady's death had cut my anchor and set me adrift.

"You are my son, and I treat all my sons equally," Ami said. "You will be no different." She was a short, ghostly pale white woman with thick glasses and a heavy foot on the gas. We were driving to Cambridge, my new home. "I have only two simple rules for you, the same as I tell the boys: let me know where you are, and let me know when you'll be back." She was talking so fast I couldn't keep up.

Her "other" sons, my brothers Adrian and Nigel, sat in the back, pretending not to listen. They had greeted me at the station with so many hugs it felt as if they had been waiting their entire lives for me to come home. Adge was all charming chipmunk cheeks, and Nige was stoic but cheerful. These, I would come to learn, were their default settings.

"Aunt Agnes said the train would take twelve hours, and I told her she should have packed you some meals. Did you even eat? Oh, you must be famished. You must be exhausted."

She spoke as if she had always known me—which in a way, she had. I wondered: Who was this woman, really? And why did she claim me so strongly?

We settled into a crammed townhouse in a subdivision for destitute single moms and their screaming children. Few fathers visited. It took forever to fall asleep that night; my mind was numb. Once again, a new place, a new room, a new family.

As I floated off to sleep, I could hear Ami quietly weeping tears of joy.


## II


The ballad of Al and Ami was as colourful as it was sad.

Ami had met Al in 1975. It was a wet Calgary day when she, just seventeen, was approached by the fiery-eyed boy with the strange accent. Her heart skipped, but with fear, not adoration.

"Do you want to go for a drink?" he asked.

"No, thank you," she said.

Ami was a practical girl, new to the big city from a prairie farm. No scoundrel was going to take advantage of her. But the boy was persistent and kept talking and smiling that breezy smile, the impish smile of a child. Eventually she said yes to a coffee.

And that was that. Her life had collided with the intoxicating mystery of Monkeytown's bush. As she would tell their sons all their lives, Ami was a swan. Once she had selected a mate, it was for life.

Al, on the other hand, was a player. Fresh to the land of milk and honey, he'd completed his criminal apprenticeship as a Caribbean pickpocket, card shark, and knife fighter, and by 1980, he had graduated into a full-fledged hustler. He dealt in women. In a city awash with oil-boom money, he weaponized his charm and turned abandonment and vulnerability, two things he knew well, into cold, hard cash. I pictured him cutting through the flat landscape in some purring vintage machine, head blazing with cocaine and possibilities, pistol in the glovebox, money on his mind.

Ami knew all about it. "He never lied to me," she told me. "Whatever terrible things he did, he always told me the truth."

When I had first met them in Sioux Lookout, Ami and the boys were moving across the country, following Al. This was their pattern: Al went to jail, she moved the kids to follow him, he left to go hustle somewhere else, she moved the kids to go after him.

In 1981, Al went to jail for attempted manslaughter. According to newspaper reports at the time, he'd stabbed his "girlfriend" and her mother many times when the girlfriend had refused to "work" that day. Baby Nigel was two years old. My brother Adrian was conceived on a conjugal visit in 1983.

After Al helped instigate a small riot at Matsqui Penitentiary in Abbotsford, he was transferred to Williams Head Penitentiary just outside Victoria, British Columbia. Ami, as she would do several times, picked up the family and followed him there. "I had to keep everyone together," she told me once.

In 1985, just as I was studying for my Common Entrance exam, Ami signed papers and vouched for my father's parole. Yet Al was also in touch with Hailey, my future stepmom. On the streets, they called her Dani and he was Kim Brown. With her help, Al started hustling again.

"I don't know where he is," was all Ami could say when his parole officer called. Then, in Al's words, Ami "got aggressive." "She came down to the stroll introducing herself as my wife and blew my shit right oughta the water," he said. This was a hustling no-no. You weren't allowed to live the street life and also have a straight life. Al had to choose: the family or the streets, his children or the high life, Ami or Hailey. There was never any choice.

Al left.

And yet, a few years later, Ami was trying to "keep the family together" again by following Al across the country, from British Columbia all the way east to Southern Ontario. That was how I met Adrian and Nigel for the first time on that icy, bright winter day in Sioux Lookout in 1988. Ami eventually settled herself and the boys in Cambridge, near the larger city of Kitchener. Even though Al was living with Hailey by this time, he would secretly visit Ami and their sons on occasion, and once he took Junior and me to see them. The only picture of us together features me in a shiny teal jacket, hands in pockets and facing sideways, Junior hugging Nigel, Adrian grinning so hard his cheeks looked like they would pop, and Al crouched in the shadows between us, eyes full of chaos.

He kept up that double life for years. It was classic Al—balancing the two women meant never having to be fully vulnerable to either of them. The two were bound to him forever, or so he thought. He was wrong about Hailey, but when it came to Ami, he would never be more right about anything. With one brief exception, she never dated anyone else.

Ami was a swan. Al was a player.

III

Hungry.

My time at Glenview Park Secondary School, my sixth and final high school, could be summed up in a word: hungry. I was hungry to prove that I belonged, hungry to feel like I fit in, hungry to make everyone believe I was a tough New York kid who took no shit. But mostly, I was hungry for something our house never had much of: food.

"I'm from New York, man. We all about dat hustle," I lied to anyone I met, emulating the boys I had seen at the ball courts in Westbury.

The driving force of my existence was basketball, which I called the Game. And there, too, I played like I was famished. That is to say, as if my life depended on it. It's not that I believed I was going to the NBA, but I also didn't believe that I *wasn't* going to the NBA.

To me, basketball was the only thing I could rely on. The court was always flat. The ball was always round. The rim was always ten feet tall. For someone who couldn't even control where he lived, this was a precious thing. But it was also a place to express my rage, to fling my body at my problems in a way no one could criticize. And finally, because I had no instruments to play, it was my only outlet to prove that I was good enough.

I sized up bodies for their speed, height, and jumping ability. Grandmothers, bus drivers, fifth-graders, guidance counsellors— everyone. I measured all humanity by whether I could back them down, fight them for a rebound, or cross them over and score. I had no idea when I might see you on the court, but I was gonna be ready.

Over the course of my two and a half years at Glenview, I would go from being two grades ahead to being the same age as my classmates. My struggles with being consistent were quickly overwhelming what used to be the easy part of my life: doing well in school. So I dropped classes, stretched out my senior electives and, because I was still young enough to do so, I came back the next year.

In my first year on the basketball team, I met my best friend Dave Beneteau—I called him Benfoot because all my friends needed a dance-hall name. He had a baby face and a sweet jump shot, and most importantly, he had my back. We dribbled one ratty leather basketball through an entire summer, no-look passing it back and forth as we talked shit or sang Disney songs on our way to play. We were relentless: jump shot, spin the ball, hook shot, square up, pump fake, foul line, 45, corner three, crossover, jump stop, finger roll, behind-the-back dribble, eyes forward. "All summer. All summer. All summer . . . " I said to Dave while crossing left-right, right-left behind my back. He was losing it, laughing.

One year, I shocked him by singing and dancing in the school play. He shook his head in confusion. "You're the toughest guy I know, not afraid of nobody, but you're in the school play, guy? Tony?!" Benfoot was the only person who called me by my Trini name. "Dawg, it's like I know you, but I don't know you." The artsy theatre kid and the tough New York street baller were warring in his thoughts. Then he looked at me sideways, grinning: "How many Tonys you have in there?"

Our coaches, Lillie and Wyman, felt to me like good coach, bad coach. Lillie believed: "It's our job to prepare these kids for life." Wyman's philosophy was: "We need only good kids in our program to help us win."

"It's Coke in a can, Pepsi in a bottle, Michael," white-haired Barry Lillie would say with a wink, wink, nod, nod that made you feel he was on your side. "Get it right or you'll never get to play ball here," he'd chuckle.

Mr. Wyman didn't trust me. He thought I was a time bomb waiting to explode. And he was right.

During a home game in my second year, I came off the court furious after a horrible shift. Two girls started giggling in the stands behind me. My temper was buzzing in my ears, and I picked up a long bench and threw it at them. Everyone in the bleachers screamed and scrambled for cover.

I was suspended for three days.

In the privacy of the empty change rooms, Coach Lillie said to me, "You need to take these three days and think about what you're doing here." He was gentle and stern all at once. "You're very close to not being able to play anymore, all right?"

"All right. Thanks, Coach," I mumbled.

He acted as if somehow he had let me down, as if he could see some part of me that no one else, including me, could see. I wasn't a bad kid; I was hurting. The kid who threw benches at people needed to hear this.

"But I tell ya, if benches were three-pointers, you'd be an all-star," he wink, winked, nod, nodded me.

This would not be his last fight to keep me on the team.


IV


Ami was a machine.

Every weekday, rain or shine, sick or well, she left for work in the morning before dawn and came home after a full work day and a two-hour rush-hour drive back. She was an entry level secretary for the federal government. "Imports and Meat Products, Doctor Yo's office," she would say in her office voice whenever I called.

From the beginning I understood that supporting all of us on her salary would be a stretch. She drove a modest grey Chevrolet, shopped at thrift shops for the boys' clothes, and what few treats she could afford—a trip to Arby's, a tub of Rocky Road ice cream, the occasional holiday turkey—were treasured and fastidiously shared. No one took any more than his share. Yet, despite all of this, she was willing to make the sacrifice for the sake of adding me to family.

Nigel and Adrian loved having a big brother, and I adored them. There was a beaming, sweet quality to the light their eyes held for me. It was total, unquestioning love and I had never been offered such a gift. Nigel was so good at math and so stealthy in his movements that we called him SuperNige for the way he made difficult things look easy. Adrian, who we called "Adge," was all baby cheeks and charisma.

We would spend hours in the basement watching gangster movies like *Carlito's Way*, *The Godfather*, and *Goodfellas*. Then we'd entertain each other inventing games like "Godfather Death Trivia"—"Why did Michael kill his brother Fredo?" "Who said, 'Luca Brasi sleeps with the fishes'?"

When we watched *Scarface* for the first time, Adge lost his mind over Tony Montana. He spoke with a coked-up Cuban gangsta accent for a year. For Halloween, he dressed in a cheap three-piece suit and would slay us with lines like "Say ello to my lil fren," and "Say gudnite to da bad guy." It would have been annoying if he wasn't so hilariously good at it. "Adrian, could you pass the sugar?" "Fuck da fuckin' Diaz brothers. I bury those cockahroaches!"

"That's not the way I raise my sons to behave," Ami said to me from behind her glasses, and I felt ashamed. I had stolen a muffin from a neighbour's countertop. "Is that what your grandmother would want?" she continued.

Ami was a single mother with three boys, eleven, fourteen, and seventeen, whom she fed on a small salary. She grocery-shopped once a month, and everything was rationed down to the spoonful. There was rarely extra money, extra food, or extra anything.

But my body, constantly pushed to its limits on the ball court, needed calories. Soon I started breaking the locks on the freezer. I would devour chicken fingers, chicken nuggets, frozen pizzas all by myself. It was selfish and I knew it, but hunger was a beast that respected no morals.

"Yeah, okay," I said, but what my chilly tone really communicated was: "What the fuck am I supposed to do?"

Ami shook her head at the disrespect. This is not how I raised my boys, I could see her thinking.

There was a silent battle between us. She insisted that I call her Mom and introduced me as her son, which struck me as strange. Maybe I had Gloria's brash voice in my head: "Yuh will only have one muddah." I didn't understand it then, but I see now that clinging to the fact that she wasn't my mother allowed me not to care. After feeling discarded so many times, I needed not to care. Brick by spiteful brick, I was building a place where no one could reach me.

Music was our maddest bond as brothers. In the basement, there was a collection of tapes of groups from the 1970s and early 1980s that Ami and Al used to jam to. It was old-people music, but for Nigel, Adrian, and me, it was an education in funk and groove and everything Black and soulful. Al Green's breezy falsetto, Barry White's deep baritone, Bobby Womack's gut-wrenching inner-city blues, Curtis Mayfield wah guitar on *Super Fly*, Rick James's badass sassiness, and on and on.

We would listen to Al and Ami's classics and sing along as if our lives depended on it. The fact that they were mostly cocaine-fuelled sex anthems didn't faze us. There was Nigel crooning "It's my duty to spank that booty" like Marvin Gaye, or Adge dancing crook-legged, shaking his head to "Me and Mrs. Jooooones," or all three of us jumping and screaming "Ra, Ra, Rasputeeen, Russia's greatest love machine."

The old music was ecstasy and made us forget our hungry bellies. Although no one said it or thought it, it connected us to our missing father. It was the music he had played as a suave street dude back in the day.

He was what connected us, what made us one, and this was the closest thing we had to being with him.

## Chapter Fifteen

# FIRST IN TEST

I

The summer of 1994, age nineteen, I left the townhouse and moved into my friend Benfoot's basement.

"Why don't you get a factory job or something? Start making some money?" Ami suggested this because my marks weren't good enough for any of my university choices. At this point I was eighteen years old and ready to leave high school.

"A factory?" Is that the best she thought I could do? "No, I'm gonna go back to school and get better marks."

"Another year in school?" she said, in a skeptical tone.

What my face said was: "You're not my real mother. You don't know me." But what my mouth said was: "Yeah, another school year." And my defiance swelled up inside me. There was an ultimatum in her words. She was fed up. Fed up with the tantrums, the stolen food, the boiling anger that often could not be contained. Little Tony was just not like Nigel and Adrian.

She had done her best.

Even though I had made the choice to leave, in my head it was her fault. I have no idea why I was so mad at Ami, but there was some painful thread connecting my departure with Agnes and Joan's surrender of me, with Miss Excelly's death, with Al and Hailey's disappearance.

Deep within me, something terrible was stirring.

I I

I had always understood the pecking order of our basketball team. Certain boys were always given the benefit of the doubt. There was a place called "white," and it could get away with murder.

On the bus ride back from a basketball game we were supposed to win but didn't, I was silent and fuming. How could we win the league if we lost easy games? It was early winter and the sun had fallen on the frosty horizon as we made our way down Highway 401. Myers and Stewie started flicking people's ears to see who they could piss off. When they got to me, I wasn't having it.

Flick. Chuckle, chuckle. I sucked my teeth. Flick. Ha ha. Chuckle. "Stop." Flick. Hee hee. "Leave me the fuck alone, you assholes." Flick. The more I tried to hold it in, the more they came for me. Flick. And I detonated.

"You fucking dickheads! You think you can fuck with me?"

They tried to laugh it off, but my switch had been flipped. I went nuclear. I lunged at them, full of rage.

"Fuck you, Stewie. Fuck you, Myers. Who do you think you are?!"

I was yelling, screaming, lunging, and swinging. For twenty minutes, the whole rest of the ride, I knew no chill.

"I'm going to fucking kill you. You hear me? I know where you live. Just watch!" The savage creature at the heart of me had crossed over some invisible line. There was no going back.

When the bus pulled up at the school, everyone was as quiet as a church mouse, but I continued wailing at the night. Spewing all my hurt and spite out into the universe. The coaches hustled the team off the bus, but I waited outside the gym door, still screaming: "I am going to kill your mom. Kill your dad. Kill your goldfish. Kill your dog. You think this is over? It's not fucking over!"

Coach Lillie sent Benfoot over to talk me down. But I was too full to listen—too full of towering hatred for them, for life, for porridge for supper, for shitty parents, for every awful thing I'd ever felt. Ami told me years later that the police had spoken to her but decided not to press charges. No one ever questioned the boys who'd bullied me. No one ever asked why I was so mad.

"Child, what is wrong with you?" I could hear my grandmother asking.

### I I I

Barry Lillie didn't run away. The day he heard that Benfoot's mom had kicked me out of her basement, he offered me a ride.

"Will you go back to your stepmom's?"

We were sitting in his car, parked sideways in the parking lot, listening to the autumn wind whipping the rusty yellow leaves about. His shirt sleeve, as always, was stained with ketchup from his lunch.

"I don't think so. I don't really feel comfortable there anymore."

His eyes watched me as if they were measuring me, inch by inch.

"Elaine and I had a talk, and we think you should come and stay with us."

My shock leaked into the silence.

"We can only do this for a little while—until you get on your feet, all right?"

I sat dumbfounded while he looked out the window deep in thought.

"Now, don't feel any pressure. But if you think you're up for it, we'd love to have you, okay?"

Live with a teacher? Why would anyone offer me this? I was overwhelmed. All I could manage was: "Sure, Coach."

I moved in with them. It was only for a few months, but the lesson would last a lifetime: Barry Lillie didn't run away. Someone believed I was worth something. And that small kernel of faith might have been just enough to save me from myself.

Elaine, Coach Lillie's wife, was as tiny as a doll, with a wit as sharp as a laser beam. She was kind, but she didn't suffer fools. Yet for some reason, our awkward first chat got me talking about my grandmother. "She was always singing, always giving away her last meal to strangers," I told Elaine.

"That sounds just like my dad," she declared, taking a sudden sad breath. Her eyes grew glassy with tears. Her dad was terminally ill. "I wish you could've met him before the Alzheimer's, Mike. He was a darling of a man."

We hugged. She felt small and brittle in my arms, but the greatness of her spirit reached across the space between us. And we were one in our grief.

Coach and Elaine stocked me up with Eggo waffles and chicken fingers, which I gobbled down even when burnt or half frozen. I'd eat whole boxes of waffles drowning in maple syrup. I was fragile and teetering and dangling at the edge of something dire.

Years later Coach would say: "I could feel something dangerous was building inside you."

That spring, their faith and my defiance got a win: I was accepted to all the universities I'd applied to.

Since arriving in the blizzard of Wabigoon eight years earlier, I had attended six high schools in six different cities and had had six different guardians. Yet by some combination of mad-Tony grit, Eggo waffles, and Miss Excelly's prayer dividend, I was on my way to the University of Waterloo.

Somewhere in the grey morning, Auntie Joan was saying, "Praise the Lord."

## Chapter Sixteen

# THICKER THAN WATER

I

My father was like a Canadian winter—just when you forgot how bad he was, he showed up again.

"Nah, not my dad," I said when Benfoot told me some kid he knew had met Al at Milton penitentiary. The tension in my voice surprised me.

He said, "Dawg, do you even know where your dad is? How do you know it's not him?"

"It's not fuckin' him, okay?" And I hung up and called Ami.

Ami knew better. In her mind, Al and prison went together like coffee and cream. She took the news seriously and called the jail. Sure enough, Al was just twelve minutes down the highway from us.

He was a tightness in my face, a knot under my ribs, a ball of fury I had bundled up and tucked away where no one could ever find it. Yet somehow it had found me. I didn't want to go, but I wanted to see him more than anything.

Ami, Nigel, Adrian, and I waited in a fluorescent visiting room, bright enough to scorch every secret into the open. In the car, no one had spoken except for Ami—that's what she did when she was nervous. We signed in, the dull grey doors clicking with finality, and moved past a room with thick double glass, hard-eyed guards, and cameras creeping in the corners. Jail. The system's trash heap. The monster at the heart of my fear of police.

I had never seen my father locked up.

I hadn't seen him for nearly six years.

He walked in wearing his jail shirt, rough bags under his eyes, speckles of grey on his chin, and his nerves on his sleeve. Deep lines had dug themselves along the sides of his mouth. His Jheri curl, which I'd adored when Ami sent a picture to me in Trinidad, was a mess: dried out at the roots and tangled at the edges.

"How you doing, kid?" His eyes twinkled with a smile. They were boiling dark brown, just like mine. When he laughed, it was my own laugh in my own voice that burst out of him.

Ami conducted the visit. She seemed quietly gleeful. This was the only time she could ever nail Al to one place. She was already planning to be his surety for parole, already resurrecting her sunken vision of a perfect family. Just as she had done in Victoria almost a decade earlier, she was already daring to dream.

Adge looked up at Al longingly. For most of his life, his dad had been a myth. Now he was starstruck. He was about the same age I had been when I first met Al in that downtown Toronto hotel room. Adge's love was clear, unclouded by painful memories.

SuperNige said nothing but saw everything.

I looked down at my feet, looked back at Al's face, looked up at the clock, looked into the corner, looked back at his face. The world was blinding and surreal. I felt like I was suffocating. I couldn't reconcile the image of my dad, who I'd always thought of as strong and free, locked in a tiny cell, unable to move or run or go for a walk without permission. Just thinking about it made me claustrophobic.

How did he end up in this place?

As we drove back to Cambridge, my mood plummeted. I felt dark, invisible fingers fumbling at my composure. They pulled on angry threads that stitched up wounds I wanted to stay closed. This visit had ripped them wide open again.

What had put him in there? Did he fight someone? Lose his temper, like I sometimes did? What else did we have in common? Was I just a convict waiting to happen?

Under all these thoughts was the terror that whatever had put him there would put me there one day too. I can never end up like him, I thought to myself. I can never be an animal in a cage.

Milton penitentiary burned this into my brain: whatever my father was, I had to become something else.

## I I

"Who is dat white lady to you? Ami?"

By 1995, I had not heard my mother's voice in almost ten years. So when Aunt Agnes offered to give me her number, I was filled with trepidation. But I took it and called anyway.

When Gloria's voice came crackling out of the phone, she offered her classic line, which was both a reminder and a warning: "Boy, I is yuh muddah. No matter what yuh do, ah will always be yuh muddah."

I had no idea who she was. I knew her name. I knew her face. But I didn't know her. The only of her family members I knew were her brother, who rocked LL Cool J Kangols and went to jail for murder, and her dad, Mack, the mountain of rage and Johnnie Walker whisky. My only clear memory of her was of that day at Piarco Airport in Trinidad, when she'd tried to steal Canada, the promised land, from me.

Now she asked me, "Who is dat white lady to you? Ami?" She was trying to convince me that Ami was not my real family. "Blud is thicker dan watah. Yuh understand? Blud is thicker dan watah."

By this time, Gloria was living in Brooklyn. She was a clever, gritty lady. She owned a garage on Fulton Street, though she had no papers and was in America illegally. Yet she was a boss. She kept the books and hired and fired, while her boyfriend managed the mechanics work. She was a bold, loud woman. Almost everything she said—whether in joy, sadness, or anger—was shouted, but her laughter was infectious. Good or bad, she could fill a room with contagious energy.

"Yuh want to talk to yuh brothas? Cardo, Ronald, look! Yuh big brutha in Canada on de phone." More brothers. These brothers sounded just as old as Adrian and Nigel and just as happy to have me as a big brother. How many secret siblings did I have? It occurred to me that I knew almost nothing about Gloria's life.

My mother had me, but I never had her. I wasn't mad at her; I just didn't think about her. All I had were questions: Why did she abandon us? Why did she leave us with Miss Excelly? Where had she been all this time? All the mothers I had come to know would never have left their kids. Not for a day, much less for twenty years.

"Boy, yuh coming Brooklyn for de Christmas?" she asked me.

"I don't know."

"Yuh should come. All these years I didn't see yuh. Come for de Christmas."

She sent me the money and I booked the ticket. At the age of twenty, I was going to spend my first Christmas with my mother.


It was mostly my fault that Al and Gloria got back together that year.

Al got out of jail with a head full of dreadlocks and quickly found the dirty underbelly of Cambridge. He went by the street name Dread, a generic Caribbean term for a Rasta.

It hadn't taken long for him to wear out his welcome at Ami's. One day, he borrowed her car and never came back. It was the car the family depended on—the one that got her to and from work every day. After three days of not hearing from him, she had to report it stolen. When the police found it, a week later, it was in scraps: windows broken, seats peeled off, smelling like an alleyway.

"Dread" and I would talk every now and then. He was always positive, except when he spoke of Calgary or Trinidad. "Boy, I wish I had finished my degree. I had two years left. Two years. That seemed like too damn long. Now look—it's more than fifteen years later. Get your degree. Stay in school."

"What was it like with you and mom in Trinidad?" I asked.

"Your mother was my wife. I loved she. But when I come to Calgary, I just forget all about her. That was my biggest mistake."

I was sitting in my room in the Waterloo co-op residences, talking to him on the phone and wondering if I should tell him about her. "Do you ever wish you could talk to her?"

"I wish, but she don't wanna talk to me," he sighed heavily.

I dropped the bomb. "She does ask me about you."

"How? When? You does talk to her? She does ask for *me*?"

Al and Gloria, childhood sweethearts, first-time lovers, could never resist asking about each other. As kids, they fought like cats and dogs in Miss Excelly's house. Cuss and break bottles and threaten. But twenty years later, they were still asking about each other. I connected them, and soon they were talking regularly. Before long, Al was also coming to Brooklyn for Christmas.

I left Al at my student apartment. He needed a place to stay until his flight to New York, and my roommates were all gone for the holidays. He was trying desperately to get his wife back, to patch things up with Gloria, and Gloria had banned him from staying with Ami. He was back to where he always seemed to find himself: between the wrath of two women who loved him.

Coach and Elaine weren't happy that I would miss Christmas with them, but they didn't try to stop me. They were worried about me meeting Gloria. They didn't say it but they were wondering the same things I was: What kind of mother leaves her child to grow up without her? Where has she been all this time?

## III

"This boy! This boy!" Gloria cuffed me playfully until her bracelets jangled and the flesh under her arm shook. She hugged me and then stepped back, looking: "Lemme watch yuh, nah? Lemme see dis boy!" She was so happy that she was chuckling, and we laughed as the car sloshed across the Brooklyn Bridge.

My mom had a tough face when she wanted to. Small black eyes, big jowls, a flat bell-pepper nose, and a poutish mouth. She laughed when she saw me, and her whole face widened and shook.

My brothers Kurt, Cardo, and Ronald were there too. Kurt was affectionate and chatty and wild and looked just like Mom. Ronald was long and lean and had a warm but quiet baritone voice. Everyone was jumping with excitement.

In the land of abandonment, there are no half-brothers. So many of us were raised by grandmothers, aunties, older sisters, stepmothers, or distant cousins that the Caribbean family was often a hodgepodge, a pelau, a mix of odds and ends. You found your family where you could. And if you had the same mother, you were brothers, that was that.

"Look, Kevin," she said, indicating the driver, and sucked her teeth. Kevin, a middle-aged Trini man with a greying moustache, was her boyfriend. He put on his best grin, but his eyes looked splotchy, a dead giveaway for a rumbo.

"Eh!" she shouted at him. "Don't watch me so! Yuh good-for-nuthin wretch!"

"Woman, leave me alone, eh?" And the whole car got silent.

Once we got home, we ate roti and doubles and poulourie. Real poulourie, which I hadn't had since I left Trinidad. When she and Kevin went to the garage, the boys and I played and laughed. I was good at entertaining my new brothers, I thought.

When I asked about Mom's boyfriend, Ronald got dark and fierce: "I doh like how he does deal with Mum," he said, though he didn't elaborate.

Soon, I knew exactly what he meant: Kevin was abusive. That very night, a messy fight happened. "I finish with he," Gloria declared. "He feel he can hit people? I will do for him!" Their tension exploded into a drunken fight. Ronald wanted to stab Kevin. Kevin got kicked out into the cold, and I never saw him again.

Our happy Christmas went on without missing a beat. One night we were sitting in a roti shop eating aloo pie and drinking punch-a-crème. The streets of New York were crammed with shoppers and carollers and bright Christmas lights. I was so drunk with happiness that I kept singing and singing. Gloria could belt them out too. She knew every parang and could sing them in perfect Spanish. We sang all the "long time" choons we used to sing at Christmas. "Drink a rum and a punch-a-crèmah, drink a rum! It's Christmas mawnin!" Every song I sang made me feel more and more Trini. More Trini than I had felt since Gloria took away our passports at the airport.


A few days later, Al arrived.

He gave me $112 but wouldn't tell me why. "Merry Christmas," he mumbled when I pressed him. I was so happy to be under the same roof as Al and Gloria that I didn't care. It was a miracle.

I watched the two of them in the kitchen—him trying to sweet-talk her, her pushing away his hand and scowling at him, and then him trying again and her again pushing him away, but this time without the scowl. It was a mating dance. They had been apart twenty years, but their childhood love still smouldered like coals from yesterday's fire. They moved around the kitchen blowing on those embers, and from a distance, I watched the unusual sight of my parents courting.

Seeing them separately would have been weird, together even weirder, but together and happy was a fantasy. I think it was then that the dream of having a "real" family—*my* real family—was kindled in me.

"Look, Mykaal," she said and handed me a pair of shiny gold rings. Al was standing next to her, grinning sheepishly. These were their wedding bands, from the first time they got married. Somehow, improbably, they had both hung on to them.

"Boy, you get us back together. So these are yours now."

"Mine?" I said in disbelief.

I looked at them, then looked back at the rings in my hand to make sure they hadn't disappeared, and then looked back up at them again. I put on the rings carefully, as if they were precious relics of power from one of my wizard books. They were more than rings; they were a connection to a past I had lost, and a promise of a future that had returned. A physical sign that all of this was not just a pipe dream.

They glowed like a talisman.

We had a fun Christmas, full of Trini food and laughter and goofiness, and I left soon after for Canada. Al was staying on.

When I arrived home, I found that my new stereo, our DVD player, my roommate's Sega Genesis console, and all his games had disappeared.

Al had pawned it all for drugs.

## Chapter Seventeen

# THE GRASS CROWN

I

"Dude, I need to fucking paint you," the guy with the baby face declared.

If God don't come, he does send a man. In the fall of 1997, Chachi was that man. That year, after two years on the University of Waterloo Warriors basketball team, I was cut. My great romance with the Game was over. I felt like basketball had fathered me. I had soaked up second-hand daddying from my teammates. Between the sweaty practices, the nail-biting games, and the breathless sprints, I had absorbed the lessons their fathers had taught them. My father would never see me play. The Game was my church, my ambition, and my ego trip. What could fill such a void?

Chachi had the answer. Its name was art.

By this point, English literature was my major. The Queen's English was now officially my area of expertise. My days were filled with reading the canon, the centuries of sacred history of England's books. A lot of dead white men. It was as if I were back in the Anglican schoolhouse in Monkeytown. And as I read these classics, it seemed natural to me to try my hand at making my own versions of them. I littered my notebooks with bad renderings of Spenser, Donne, and Oscar Wilde. Words, as always, cast an enduring spell over my imagination.

It was this instinct to express myself that Chachi would latch on to and nourish into a mad passion. Cristian Snyder—Chachi—had a German baby face and permanent black bags under his eyes, and he lived in overalls splotched with acrylic paint.

He came up to me at a party where he was showing his paintings and I was reading some poems, and insisted, "I need to fucking paint you." And that was that. We became inseparable.

Chachi could balance a coffee, smoke a dart, shift gears on his Volkswagen, and not drop a breath of conversation. He had survived cancer, been a human shield in Nicaragua, worked as a commodities manager, and danced in booty shorts at Renaissance, Waterloo's queer club. He was an existentialist anti-hero, and if his life had been a show on cable, I would've never changed the channel.

I wrote, he painted. Day and night for an entire summer, that was all we did. We would drift by his parents' house on Pandora Street to scrounge for food and then pass out, depleted from days and nights of working, talking, smoking, and dreaming our biggest dreams.

Our first show together was called *Children on Cato's Mountain*. It was a reference to Dante's Purgatory, the mountain where sinners were sent to suffer their way into Paradise. The idea of suffering your way to the land of milk and honey resonated with me.

The story I wrote for the show read like a Latin soap opera: A dying man blows into a bar with lightning and thunder storming at his back. He mistakes the bartender, Natalia, for his lost love, and to ease his suffering, she pretends to be the woman who haunts him, his muse. As Beatrice was to Dante. Chach painted five scenes from the three-chapter narrative poem, and he unveiled them at a coffee shop in downtown Kitchener as I read, accompanied by a Spanish guitar.

The real Natalia, a long bombshell of a bartender, was Chachi's muse. He made her the subject of his most ambitious work, an enormous linen-and-acrylic portrait. In it, she had her hands clasped firmly but casually, and the green of her sweater was like fields of rolling grass. Her oval eyes beamed back as ethereal as those of a Greek goddess.

This painting was the final reveal when I read the line "My God, why have you forsaken me?" and I could feel the audience gasp and exhale, but I kept my head down, reading.

The drama of the moment made my head swim.

Unbeknownst to me, something had subtly nudged itself into place at the back of my brain: from then on, music and art be the new Game.

## I I

"Mike, I know it's not your birthday yet, but I want you to have this." My brother Nigel's present for me was sitting on the fireplace with a note that ended: "Don't fret. I got it on sale. SuperNige." Nigel was now taking chemical physics at the University of Waterloo and he and I, with the help of Coach and Elaine, had rented a townhouse close to the university.

On the cover of the book, called *Caesar*, Gaius Julius Caesar sat on top of a horse, surrounded by painted enemies. He pointed his sword towards the sky. His face was grimacing with determination. "Danger knows full well that Caesar is more dangerous than he," he'd bragged like a battle rapper in Shakespeare's play *Julius Caesar*.

The real Caesar, I learned, was good at everything. The real Caesar was Rome's greatest general. He never lost a battle, never lost a war. No matter the odds or the terrain, Caesar always won. And the thing he loved winning most was the grass crown.

The grass crown was Rome's greatest honour, the rarest of the many crowns Romans bestowed on their military leaders. This was the only one awarded to a general by his soldiers, and it was given only to a general who had saved his troops from certain death. And I wept when Caesar won it. Oh Death, where is thy sting?

As was the custom, his soldiers fashioned him a crown of leaves and flowers from the bloody battlefield and placed it on his head. Then he was given a triumph, which was a victory parade through the streets of Rome, and the entire city partied for days in his honour. It was such an ego boost that they hired someone to sit in the chariot behind a *triumvere* and whisper: "You're still just a man. You're still just a man." Caesar won the grass crown so often that when he died, the Romans made him a god. They deified him so that his spirit could protect Rome forever. Oh grave, where is thy victory?

From the day Nige gave me this book, I too worshipped Caesar. This great white Übermensch with the cold omnipotent eyes stared right into me and said: "Win and everyone will love you." "Win and you'll never walk alone." "Win and you will always have a place to belong." In the chaotic currents I called my life, Caesar was the raft onto which I piled my hopes. My secret, sacred colonizer hero.

Was this a bizarre hero for a young Black kid? Not to me. European history was the only history I knew. Sir Francis Drake, Admiral Nelson, and a host of English buccaneers had been part of my little red book of colonial education. Where else could I look for my heroes?

Claiming the white conqueror's mythology felt as if I was accessing the Crown's clandestine coding, the language of violence that had been imprinted onto my neurons. In fact, it was the software, and my Black-boy body—thick lips and booty, muscular lithe shoulders—was the hardware. It fused itself to my core. This was who I was, a creature of the Commonwealth, neither Black nor white but a mutant who had forgotten his ancestors. I was the realization of the Queen's great dream: the civilized savage. Amen.

So what if I would never have white man privileges? Caesar wouldn't have let that stop him, so why should I?

## Chapter Eighteen

# GLORIA

I

I loved Brooklyn. I loved it because of the people hawking bootleg movies on Fulton Street. I loved it for the ball courts that were never empty. I loved it for the shit-talkers, the corner store professors, the malt liquor freestylers, the roti and curry goat takeout. I loved it because it was so Black. As far as the eye could see, there were Black people.

Black people in Brooklyn weren't scared of anything.

In 1999, I went to Brooklyn to live under the same roof as my mother and father for the first time in my life. I was twenty-four. They had rented a three-storey house between Marcy Avenue and Tompkins. This wasn't the slick *Wall Street* banker New York or the *Sex in the City* brownstone New York or the Upper West Side *Seinfeld* Jewish New York. This was do-or-die Brooklyn, the home of Biggie and Chris Rock and Jay-Z, and nicknamed Brooknam because it seemed as dangerous as Vietnam. Every lil homie had three things: a hustle, a jump shot, and some rap verse he could spit. The cops always patrolled, and the backstreet boys were not a boy band but the kids in the back street juggling rocks—or selling crack. The block was always hot.

My mother would sit by the back window of the kitchen in her nurse's uniform, smoking a cigarette at the end of a gruelling workday which included rush-hour commutes back and forth to Manhattan. Gloria seemed indestructible to me. She had no papers and no legal status, yet somehow she owned businesses, maintained bank accounts, and was paying taxes. A tough, resilient woman.

"Boy, come here. Don't feel yuh too big for me to beat yuh!" She was laughing, but when she was tired, her whole face would say it and her eyes would close to dark slits.

I sat down at the table to keep her company. Pooch, our red-nosed pit bull–rottweiler sniffed at us and then barked at the fading light of day.

I liked these quiet times with just my mother and me.

"Out of all my children, you and me supposed to have a bond because you was de one that I had de most trouble wit." Gloria pulled on her cigarette, and it glowed orange in the dusk and made that burning crackling sound.

What trouble? I wondered.

"Al left me in Venezuela to go to Canada, with you newborn. Then he stop sending money, and dis Spanish couple want to take yuh from me. So I leave. Not a cent to my name, couldn't talk a word of Spanish, but I didn't want nobody taking my child."

Her face screwed up against the pain of remembering. "It hurt me, hurt me bad. To even think about it." Except her Trini accent said, "It hut mih, hut mih bad . . . " Her voice grew low and trembled. "Ah sit on a park bench with you for days. De man by the bakery let me sleep in the back but tell me ah have to leave before sunrise. And was only cause God who send two children to save we. They used to play with yuh. Then when they see ah didn't have no place, they come back with they parents and beg dem to take me in. And dat is how we survive. Ah was like a dog protecting a puppy."

A dog protecting a puppy. I had never heard this story.

Outside, Pooch let out a barrage of barks at something we couldn't see.

"So when Miss Excelly write me to bring yuh to Monkeytown, I went and I drop yuh there." This solved the mystery of Junior's first memory of Gloria handing me to Mama and hopping back in a car. This is how I came to be raised by Miss Excelly.

I leaned back, thunderstruck. My tongue was dry in my mouth. Out the back door, the sound of Brooklyn traffic scrambled into the evening. Pooch had gone silent. My mother shut her eyes as if to ward off the curse of evil memories.


My dad skulked about as Gloria told these tales. He had the sense to make himself scarce. He was the one who had left her, over two decades ago. Now, in that house in Brooklyn, Al and Gloria lived with my brothers from different fathers, Ronald, Cardo, and Kurt, and my sister, Shanice, who was the oldest after Junior and me.

While Gloria was away at work, Al bombed around the back streets on a BMX bike like a scheming ten-year-old. He had a grin on his face as if the sun would never stop shining. He was selling crack in the alleys and knew every lowlife for ten blocks around. How could he be so happy?

Gloria, meanwhile, would go to work on 14th Street in Manhattan as a home care nurse, and inevitably would return cussing at what went on while she was gone.

"Ronald, yuh tink yuh is Al Capone!" she'd yell. "Stop running around with dem gyang boys. Dey done nearly kill yuh already!"

Ronald showed me the scars where he'd been stabbed three times with an ice pick. "Yeah, boy, de nearly kill me." His voice was casual, but his eyes kept checking to see my reaction. "Dem Crips corner mih and dey stick mih three times." It seemed surreal, but those angry scars right under the homemade tattoos of guns and crosses spoke of real danger.

We all adored Shanice. She was cheerful, beautiful, and the only one who could talk sense to our mother. She was the Gloria whisperer. Whenever you had something difficult to talk to Mom about—something she might blow up over or cuss you out about—you talked to Shanice first.

Most days, my siblings and I kicked it on the stoop in the yard and watched the drama on the block. The sun rose high and sprinkled light and heat between the thick leaves of the Norway maples. Chirping blackbirds mingled with hazy traffic sounds in the distance as we lazed and laughed and teased our days away under the awning. In the park two streets over, the main activities were drug sales and basketball.

At first, I was mesmerized and intimidated by the basketball rhythms at the park: the Black bodies colliding, stocky boys backing you down in the post, lanky boys dunking and smacking the metal backboards. Dribbling was called handles. Everyone needed handles. "You can't hold me, kid. You can't hold me. You too soft." The Game was just as much psychological as physical. Even the worst players talked trash, and you got no props if you scored off the backboard and didn't call "Bank." All the cunning, drama, and struggle of hood politics played out in a furious dance where the only rule was never to lose. Hail, Caesar.

I loved the speed of life in Brooklyn, and how being Black was no big deal because everyone was. I was just a person. Which, as simple as it sounds, was crucial information for me. Since leaving Trinidad, I had never lived anywhere I wasn't a visible minority. In Brooklyn, my Blackness hung lightly on my shoulders.

By day, we saw fist fights, a few stabbings, and some crackheads running up and down the block. At night, it wasn't unusual to hear the hard pops of weapons or the sirens blaring. We hid behind a heavy black iron gate that locked from the inside. One night, I woke up in the suffocating heat with my shirt sticky on my skin. The digital clock read 3:32. I had to get out. I had to breathe. When I opened the gate, I thought I was dreaming an action film. Both sidewalks were covered in men in black Kevlar vests, shotguns out, moving down the block, completely silent. It was a raid, and only the SWAT van in the street told me that these men were the police. I was frozen, welded to the spot, my breath caught in my throat, and all I could do was watch them pass.

A few weeks earlier, my parents' wedding rings had disappeared. I was distraught. I had grown used to their weight on my fingers. How could I have been so stupid to take them off? Hysterical, I raced from floor to floor of the cramped house, trying to remember where I last saw them. My mother watched me with pity.

"Boy, stop look for dem rings. Yuh faddah pawn dem," she said.

What? He pawned them?

"Sorry, kid," was all Al could say. "It's just for a few days. I know where they are."

They were only rings, right? I sighed. Nothing could ruin this magical summer. Yet a residue of sadness remained. Those rings were a symbol, a talisman, physical evidence that things had changed, and I was the one who'd made them change.

I never saw my parents' wedding rings again.

## 11

"I'm going to make Mom an offer she can't refuse." Junior twisted his mouth into a sideways grin.

"You mean like the Godfather?" I asked.

"Nah, I'm going to ask she to move to Canada and manage the barbershop."

"What did you call it again?"

"Nubian Headz. With a z." His eyes twinkled a satisfied smile at his own cleverness. Subverting the Queen's English is the slyest form of resistance. We both took pleasure in this.

"Is that a good idea?" I asked, brows up.

We were in a suburban townhouse when he told me. Even though he had made his money hustling, he had set up a legitimate barbershop. I never asked him about his criminal enterprises but I had heard enough to know that I probably didn't want to ask. And I recognized in his refusal to ever tell me much a familiar pattern: my big brother was still trying to protect me.

"I hope so," he answered, his doubts printed on his face. Alone was something we knew how to do, but having a family? Here?

His white girlfriend was at the kitchen counter, doing her nails and watching me "cut eye," which is to say with disapproval. She had dirty blonde hair and hoopy earrings, and she talked Jamaican patois even though she was born in the suburbs of Toronto. She curled up her mouth at my off-brand sneakers. Junior had found his own Hailey even as he was becoming his own kind of Al.

The barbershop he owned, Nubian Headz, had the bright, antiseptic feel of all barbershops, the black spinning chairs and the jars filled with green cleaner fluid and scissors. You could get your fade or your weave or get your hair relaxed while the latest dancehall banged out and sly barbers sucked their teeth. They never seemed to pay attention but somehow always lined your cut up perfectly. I was impressed. And now he was proposing handing the shop's care over to our mother as a carrot to bring the family together.

"You think she will say yes?" I asked.

"It looking positive." Junior was sounding more Trini these days, which usually meant he was taking care of himself. We didn't see each other much because I was living "all the way out there" in Kitchener, but I could feel the optimism he gave off.

The germ of something had infected us.

Gloria and Al, our mother and father—who we grew up knowing as legends and phantoms and tales as thin as smoke—could be living together and close by.

What could possibly go wrong?


### I I I


Gloria accepted Junior's offer.

In late 1999, the family moved to Canada, to a town north of Toronto called Newmarket and a modest three-bedroom house Junior had arranged. This would be home to Al, Gloria, and my brothers Ronald, Kurt, and Cardo, while Shanice and her young family stayed behind in Brooklyn. The deal was that Mom would run Nubian Headz, freeing Junior to do other things.

Yet as I was quickly learning with my newly present parents, there were always other angles to consider. In this case, it was about something every immigrant valued: citizenship in the land of milk and honey.

In America, my mother and brothers had no status; in Canada, Al's citizenship could be the key to getting citizenship for everyone. Plus, Al was still a bit of a loose cannon, according to Gloria. "Yuh faddah runnin' in de street like a lil boy with he old ass," she told me. Gloria wanted something valuable she could keep if he decided to bolt.

A shrewd move, as it turned out.

That December, I told Elaine and Coach that I wouldn't be at the traditional Lillie Christmas brunch that year. "Okay, well, you know we're all gonna miss you," Coach said. Then he added, "Be careful." He wanted to support my decision to have Christmas with Gloria and Al, but he feared my disappointment.

"My-kaal, come an sing some parang, boy." Gloria was singing in her sweet shouting voice. We were all belting songs out loud and drinking punch-a-crème and White Oak rum.

We were all Christmasing in Newmarket, sitting at the table in the bright kitchen of the house Junior had rented for my parents. My mother was bursting with gladness at the sight, which lit the entire room up.

Gloria said: "You eh know no Spanish? Ent you is supposed to be a Venezuelan?"

"Brother, what did you bring me?" This was Kurt's standard greeting, but this time he wrapped me in a tight hug, his big eyes shining, his big teeth spread in a wide grin.

Ronald was tall and long with a deep, resonant voice that stayed tender even when he was angry. He never said much, but his gear was always on point. Cardo was also quiet, but he had our mother's hustle and would quietly absorb everything. The vibes were up and full of jokes.

Junior played Father Christmas and made sure that everyone got presents. Jovial Junior was the best—he play-acted, did Italian gangster impressions, and even broke out some Trini jumbie stories. The last time I'd heard him talk of LaJabless and Soucouyant, a night like this would have seemed like a fairy tale.

I gave my mom the portrait Chachi had painted of me because I thought it was the most precious thing I owned.

Dad hovered cheerfully. Everyone called him Dad now and loved him, especially Kurt. Kurt was fully attached.

"Dad, you want to play chess?" I said teasingly.

"With you? I remember teaching you how to play when you were twelve or thirteen, and then you started beating me. You too good for me!"

"You haven't played me since."

We were laughing the same laugh.

I stared at him intently, trying to take a mental snapshot of him so happy.

His face was starting to crease around his mouth and he was going grey at the temples. Still, a restless energy crackled in him, in the way his fingers would not rest, in the mischief behind his eyes that always seemed to be threatening to take over.

But I had a family. I had a home.


IV


After twenty-five years apart, my entire lifetime, Al and Gloria got remarried that spring. Because the bride and groom didn't have a lot of friends in the area, the wedding reception, at a hall off a country sideroad, was filled with many friends of Junior's. I dashed across the floor to hug Gloria when she arrived. My excitement bubbled over and I didn't care who saw. This woman had begged strangers for food to feed baby me in Caracas. Who was this person? A stranger, my mother, I didn't care which. I was ecstatic.

Yet even her re-nuptials couldn't stop her cussing about something: "Sha-Neece, why yo don't wipe dat ugly look from yuh face? Dis is supposed to be a celebray-tion." My sister, Shanice, gorgeous in her gown, her skin deepest brown, her eyes pretty and sparkling, had on her most sour face. She had not been chosen to be the maid of honour.

"I is she only girl-child," she pouted. "I suppose to be maid of honour." The maid of honour was some random friend of Ronald's my mother wanted to curry favour with. I agreed with Shanice, but I wasn't about to provoke one of my mother's legendary cussing-outs.

Gloria and I took a dance at the wedding, and she twirled and bounced like a pro as soft beads of sweat pooled on her forehead. I had never danced with her before, and the whole wedding was watching. I tried to imagine her as a young lady, twirling and striving and struggling her way through Caracas, San Fernando, Brooklyn, and maybe many other cities she might tell me of one day. Gloria was always her own woman.

My parents were married again. A glimmer of hope had blossomed into a new beginning. We had passed another milestone towards recreating a real family. It was not perfect but it was real, and it was here to stay.

Or so I allowed myself to believe.

V

The deal with Nubian Headz fell apart almost as quickly as it had come together. The problem was gambling. Every chance they got, Al and Gloria would take the money from the shop and make their way to the gleaming slot machines of Casino Rama, Woodbine Racetrack, or Casino Niagara. It didn't take long for them to gamble away the payroll, leaving Junior stressed and scrambling for money. I could see the worry digging into his face. "They gambling their lives away," he told me over the phone.

Gloria complained to me on my next visit. "Dis damn boy bring me from quite New York to dis cold, shitten country," she moaned. "I shoulda never come here. What if something happen to him? What if police lock him up? What will become of me? Talk to yuh bruddah, yuh know? Talk to him!"

Mom was pressuring Junior to put the barbershop in her name and was trying to enlist me in her cause. If Gloria didn't take your money, she would send a man.

"Stay out of it," Junior warned when I casually brought it up. "You don't know what's really goin on here." His mood was ominous and brooding. As if the hustler in him was fighting with the loving son he was trying to be.

At some point, my brother Adrian, Ami's son, became Al and Gloria's casino chauffeur. He had been making weekly trips to visit his suddenly available father. He had a sleek red coupe with a bag of five-cent candy in the door and soft R & B crooning on the stereo. Day or night, he would be at their beck and call. Adrian even became friends with Gloria, his mother's sworn enemy in the competition for Al. Gloria quickly realized that Adge's trusting nature would give her more than I ever would. She lavished him with praise and he lapped it up. "You're my favourite son," she said, buttering him up. When I heard this, I laughed, imagining Ami saying Gloria's favourite line to Adrian: "Boy, I am yuh muddah. Yuh only have one muddah."

The situation was surreal. Adrian told me, "I feel like I have a dad again." Hearing this made me scared for him, but he needed to learn his own Al-and-Gloria lessons. That winter, he did. Al had put his arms around Adge and told him, "Son, I know things haven't been great, but I am working on something, and if it works, everything will be all right." Adge had had only wisps of a father, so even this drugged-up, hustling, pipe-dream-peddling version was like rain in his desert. He wanted to bask in all the father he could get.

His loss of faith was gradual, but it was sealed one night when Gloria called.

"You have to come and get yuh faddah!" She was demanding that Adge drive from Cambridge to the Newmarket police precinct, where Al was in handcuffs. Apparently, he had set up a bank account and then tried to pass a couple of fake $10,000 cheques. The bank alerted the police, and when Al showed up to collect the cash, the law was waiting.

"Why would he still be doing stupid things like that?" Adrian wondered out loud.

Al and Gloria fought like cats and dogs that night. Screaming, accusing, bringing up long-past beefs while Adrian sat despondent, listening to Trini cuss words fly and cupboards bang. His heart sunk lower than it had ever been. He told me later: "I felt like a means to an end. Like he just used me. Like my own father scammed me."

Adge slammed the door on his way out and never came back.

V I

The Newmarket experiment ended in catastrophe. As Miss Excelly would say, "Some things, if you don't laugh, you will cry."

Nubian Headz closed permanently. Employees weren't getting paid, the rent was past due, and Junior could no longer make up the difference. For him, this was a daunting loss. That barbershop was the sum total of everything he'd risked his life to build.

For Gloria, there was suddenly no way to make money and no way to feed Kurt, Cardo, and Ronald, who were all teenagers but weren't going to school. Unfazed, Gloria took advantage of my father's androgynous name. She took his social insurance card and, posing as Alyson Downing, began working as a nurse at an in-patient care clinic.

She always knew how to survive.

Meanwhile, Al started getting high in crack houses. He had avoided jail since the 1990s, but that was before he became a slave to the pipe. His life was soon ruled by the white smoke from the glass tubes. No one knew what hell he had tumbled into, but the streets, which he had always chosen first, had consumed him body and soul.

"My-kaal, if yuh see yuh faddah, yuh would nevah believe it's him. Like a skeleton in a bag-a-skin. Fo' shame. Fo' shame!" Gloria was lamenting his loss and building up to borrow money from me.

"I can help you, Mom, but I really need it back by the end of month."

"No problem," she said.

She never paid me back. I kept calling, but there was no answer. I stopped caring about the money, but I kept calling until finally the number changed. I just wanted to see them for Christmas and sing parang in the kitchen, hear Junior talk about Lagahoo dragging his chains and Soucouyant flying balls of fire, see Al happy and glowing every time we called him Dad, hear Gloria's shouting voice shaking with laughter. But when I showed up at the house, they had moved. No one had bothered to tell me.

I blew around Newmarket that week before Christmas like a plastic trash bag, failing to find them and watching the festive lights of everyone else's joy.

It takes a special kind of scandal to disturb a crack house. Yet by all accounts, the climax of this saga was a rare kind of comess.

Al crept in like a cat burglar while Gloria was sleeping, her bones weary from her long shifts at the clinic. When the sound of a starting car woke her, she dashed out into the yard, nightgown and all, and stood between Al and the road.

"Eh! Where yuh think yuh going? Yuh good-for-nuthin' wretch! Yuh have no shame?"

Al revved the engine and tried to drive around her. "Get out of my way, woman!" he declared, as hardened and own-way as Tony.

What happened next is hotly disputed. Al says: "She jump in front of the car like a mad woman!" Gloria says: "Al run mih over to get to de crack house!" What they agree on is that Al left Gloria wailing on the ground.

Junior was a volcano when he found out. "Where him? Where he gone?"

The advantage of father and son doing illegal things in the same small pond was that it was never hard to find each other.

Junior kicked in the door and lunged for him, wrapping his hard hands around Al's neck. "You think you can kill my muddah? You is not my faddah. I will fuckin kill you!"

Al strained a gasp. "Who the fuck you think you is, boy?"

Crack pipes splintered, hot rocks and glass sprayed everywhere, crackheads dashed for the floor to save themselves and their precious poison. Father and son wrestled like Jacob and the angel, like some primordial war that had been going on between fathers and sons since time began.

It takes a special kind of scandal to shake up a crack house.


VII


My entire family was deported the following year.

When Citizenship and Immigration somehow found out that Gloria had been working illegally, the jig was up. The whole clan was arrested, children and all, and marched onto a 737 bound for Piarco Airport, Trinidad.

Soon after they had arrived in the country, Ronald, who was barely nineteen at the time, had married a young Jamaican girl named Olivia.

Strangely, the wedding ceremony was in a makeshift church in a mall. The minister recited her own ghastly poems and said none of the obvious things you expect to hear at a wedding. There was no "Dearly beloved, we are gathered here today . . . " or "Does anyone object . . . " or "I now pronounce you . . . " Gloria had to call out in her shouting voice, "You may kiss the bride!" They kissed, we clapped, and everyone was relieved.

Olivia got pregnant three times in less than three years and ended up having three boys. Then Ronald was gone. Cardo, then twenty, left a young baby with a Filipina girl who was even younger than him. The fathers gone, the women remained to fend for themselves and the babies. The cycle was repeating: the abandoned kids were abandoning their kids.

Al, a Canadian citizen, didn't have to go back to Trini, but he decided to stick with the family, I imagine after significant cussing from Gloria. Or maybe he just needed a break from the streets. Whatever the case, my fragile, fractured, dysfunctional family boarded a plane and flew off forever. If truth were told, I had already lost them—I had no idea where they lived, much less how to reach them—but now they were really gone.

After the initial shock passed through me, I was ashamed to admit it but I felt relieved. It was easier to have them gone. Al and Gloria were a vortex that would eventually suck me in and pull me under.

Junior said a similar thing. "Man, ah sorry to say this, but ah happy that they gone. Ah couldn't take it anymore."

Alone was something we both knew how to do.

Act Three

# MIC
# DAINJAH

## Chapter Nineteen

# BERLIN BOOT CAMP

I

Tony loved to run. Arms swinging, the world rushing by in brushes of light, sweat stinging his eyes.

I am running with my friend Sterling in Trinidad, chasing him, but his strides are too fast. I am running after the maxi taxi after I killed my brother's fish. I am running towards the shoreline when Junior disappeared under the frozen lake. I am running down a loose ball on the basketball court, desperate and insane. I am running from side to side of the stage, a blues shouter in a punk rock band. I am running away from seventeen memories of seventeen girlfriends, a track meet of the heart. I am running, business-dude fresh, to catch my plane in Terminal 1.

I am racing through my options fast.

If I wore a suit and caught flights for work, didn't that mean I was okay? If I had a cute white girlfriend who took me home to meet her family, didn't that mean I was normal? If I could get hundreds of strangers to sing the songs I wrote, didn't that mean I was a success?

Life at the turn of the twenty-first century accelerated into a breakneck rush of ways to escape. And I filtered it all through my masks: Michael Downing, Mic Dainjah, Molasses. They were spaces where I could hide in plain sight and express the hopes and fears I had tucked away into the furious corners of my soul. It was as if I was running towards something I could never catch.

"So what the fuck is a BlackBerry, anyway?" Chachi blew smoke clouds, slow as the Cheshire cat, and they drifted up over the outdoor patio at Ethel's Lounge and unwound in the lazy Sunday chatter. His baby face was quizzing me.

BlackBerry was just a little pager then, but the company would soon invent the smartphone, that thing we were all destined to become obsessed with. It was also my new corporate employer.

"Yeah, man, either I do cover songs for a living or I get a day job and keep the music sacred. Yano?"

He nodded approvingly. "Cheers, Chavez," he said, saluting and raising his glass. Chach was a Mennonite, a Snyder, direct descendant of the people who'd founded our city. Shrewd with money, Mennos did not believe in credit. Chach had bought each of his cars in cash. So he appreciated my decision to become a corporate flunky: it was a crafty move. And it kicked off the most decadent decade of my life.

Kitchener was known Berlin before the Queen's patriots forced the name to change, so my rap-punk band called our debut album *Berlin Boot Camp*. That entire time felt like a sprint. Like running after something desperate. Like chasing smoke. Like Jumbie coming through the bush.

It started with a job, blazed into a band, survived off a parade of girlfriends, bourbon, and boarding passes, and ended with my writing a book.

In 2003, my life was a bubble building up to burst.

## I I

Asking my parents to do something for me was like getting a tooth pulled: you knew it would be painful, so you did it only when you had to.

"Mom, how yuh going?"

I was calling from my desk at BlackBerry corporate headquarters, leaning back in my fresh-out-the-plastic ergonomic chair, my shirt-sleeves rolled up for the afternoon grind.

"Not good, boy. Trinidad haaard. We ketchin we tail down here."

Gloria was in full self-pity mode. Being back in Trini after running businesses, owning cars, and making good money in the US and Canada was a heavy blow. On the other hand, Michael Downing's future as a corporate sales dude was off to a brilliant beginning, except for one hiccup—I needed a passport to travel.

My solution was to call Gloria to see if she and Al could go to the Red House, the parliament building in Port of Spain, and get me a Trinidadian passport. I'd send extra money for their time; all they had to do was show up. It would be a fast, straightforward, and profitable way for them to do some parenting.

A slam dunk, right?

"Yuh son get a big job," I said cheerfully.

"Yeah? Yuh still with de same company? BlackBerry?" I was happy she sounded so proud of me.

"Yeah, but ah have to travel to de States. Ah need ah Trini passport and ah visa."

"Okay . . . "

"Yuh mind going to get me one? I'm a citizen by descent, and you guys are right there, right?"

"Of course! Yeah, we will handle it for yuh. Ah will get Al and he good-for-nuthin ass down to de Red House tomorrow." This was good news. She was perking up.

"I will send you the money to pay for everything."

"Okay, let me look into it and tell yuh how much money to send."

I hung up the phone full of hope.

Two years later, I was at my Canadian citizenship ceremony, hand on the King James Bible, giving my oath of fealty to the Queen: "I swear that I will be faithful and bear true allegiance to Her Majesty Queen Elizabeth II, Queen of Canada, her heirs and successors, and that I will faithfully observe the laws of Canada and fulfil my duties as a Canadian citizen." Finally, I could get a Canadian passport.

My parents never tried to get me my Trinidadian passport. What they did do was take more than $5,000 from me and send back a lot of tall tales, stringing me along for two years. Two years of stressing daily that I might be fired. Two years before my benevolent corporate bosses found work in Canada for a grateful me. I kept calling my parents, they kept promising and promising, "Doh worry, tomorrow we going down to the Red House to take care of dat for yuh."

Slowly, excruciatingly, it dawned on me that they weren't going to do anything. I kept thinking of my friends' parents—Chachi's parents, Benfoot's parents—and their eagerness to sacrifice to help their kids. I kept dreaming that Al and Gloria would care for me the same way. But they were as broken as I was, and that kind of caring was just not in their nature.

It was a sobering lesson: my parents would never help me; they would only take from me. To them, children were like cash machines: you put in your guilt and pressed the right buttons, and out spilt the money.

My anger froze over. I didn't scream or cry or shout. I simply looked coolly at the facts. I replayed my years of knowing them, from their absence in Trinidad, to my dad's neglect with Hailey, to my mother's greed and lack of interest in who I was or what I needed. I hated them. I loathed their selfishness. And I despised myself for still loving them, still seeking them, still choosing to be their victim.

I stopped calling. I stopped answering when they called. That was 2005, and for the rest of the decade, I didn't speak to either one of them.

### III

My band, Jen Militia, could make me vanish like vapour. It was a tele-portation device, a furious sleight of hand, a potent elixir for what I craved most—to forget.

"Brothers and sisters!" I shouted with my arms spread wide, as if inviting the crowd to hug me. There was a sprinkling of cymbals and the electric guitar singing a high lonely note. "If you came tonight to look cool, you're at the wrong show." The bass and the little drums we called toms joined the bubbling crescendo.

"If you came tonight to be a wallflower, you're at the wrong show!" A few screams came back from the crowd. The intensely white light hid those assembled, and dribbles of it dripped from my eyelashes so that all I could see were the feet of those closest to the stage. They shuffled towards our summons, crowding ever closer now. A few hollered back: "Yeaaaaaaah! Jen mul-lih-shaaaaaaaaa!"

"If you're not here to lose your minds, you're at THE WRONG SHOW." And as the vibrations shook the room awake, faces began filling the front. Suddenly everything seemed to fade into the sting of sweat in my eyes, the shaking and rattling of the kick drum off our bones, chasing down my breath to send another chorus bellowing at the night.

We forgot ourselves, there under the hot lights as the club filled with the sweet stink that only a hundred people approaching insanity can bring. My bandmates leaned, bounced, and gyrated, faces twist-ing in the agony of every note. "Danger knows full well that Caesar is more dangerous than he," Shakespeare wrote in *Julius Caesar*. So I named myself Mic Dainjah (Mike Danger), but I was thinking of little Tony winning the nitroglycerin award in Wabigoon. "You're small, but you're real trouble."

Dressed in an army green surplus jacket, I strutted, collapsed, and postured like a lunatic, like a preacher in his rapture, like my soul depended on it. I goaded, pleaded, and surrendered to the vibrations rolling over us. The decibels split my atoms into a trillion points of light and reassembled me somewhere else. I vanished.

I vanished to a place with no father, no mother, no corporate bosses, no good kids to keep up with—just the certainty of being alive and somewhere I belonged.

## I V

In 2008, at the height of my double life, I was a traveller moving at warp speed, blurring the lights of foreign cities, my sleepy head drooping on the tour van window as the boredom rolled by, drooling on myself at thirty thousand feet, truck stops and boarding passes, propane vans and the rich venison of my corporate VISA.

Mic Dainjah wore an army surplus jacket whose collars slowly accumulated buttons and patches of punk bands, trophies of stupid things done proudly. Michael Downing, sales associate, wore a crisp blue blazer with gold buttons and a fuchsia silk pocket square. Two jackets, two names, two lives colliding into each other with relentless velocity.

For BlackBerry, my territory was the South, all the states that fought to keep slavery. Way under Dixie, the bush was loud and the air was breezy. The night felt familiar. Like Zora Neale Hurston running from hurricanes. Like plantation white. Like the small house behind the big one. Like the rum shop and the fields of cane.

My job was to charm, collude, and imbibe in order to convince our partners to sell more BlackBerry products. I shucked and jived my way through the old Confederacy: Biloxi, Gainesville, Fayetteville, Jackson, Macon, Birmingham. Places where everyone talked slow and thought fast and put nicknames like Bubba, Skee, and Buck on their business cards.

The previous summer I had quit BlackBerry to go on tour with Jen Militia in Western Canada. Our album, *Berlin Boot Camp*, came out in January 2007. It was rock, it was hip-hop. It was Black, it was white. It was neither. It was me. We toured for an insane ten weeks before I ended up back at BlackBerry anyways.

I remember the tour in fits and snatches, night after night after night. In smouldering summer, we whipped across the dark never-ending plains in a twelve-seater propane van, laden down with our bags, our amps, our drums, and our guitars. The fields of wheat dissolved like a golden ocean into the broad, unbounded sky. Then the flatness of the Great Plains gave way to the splendour of the Rocky Mountains. Great blue, jagged behemoths streaked in snowdrifts, rooted in the bones of the world, staring down, icy and impartial, as we climbed and dipped and turned like a tiny caravan of ants snaking through their majesty.

I felt my father's presence out there. I felt the broken 1970s footsteps of Al the player whipping across these lands, chasing his vanity through Winnipeg, Regina, Calgary, Edmonton, Vancouver, and back again. Cajoling his team of whores and snorting his way through the adrenaline of the wild west. "I'll be home soon," he used to call Ami and say. That was a lie.

When we drove through Wabigoon, I had shut my eyes and waited for it to pass.

## V

That same year, my brothers Junior, Nigel, Adrian, and I had one of our rare get-togethers. We met for dinner at a Kitchener steak house and sat grinning and jovial in the dim table light. Junior was in his storytelling mood, screwing up his face, gesturing at the air in front of him, and of course, offering the classic Junior stchuups, an epic teeth-sucking sound that could mean exclamation, satisfaction, or just punctuation. *Sssscccccchttttttups.*

"This guy, man," he said pointing at me. "We used to call him Tony back then. This guy was hot like a pepper." Adrian, Nigel, and I were already cracking up. "He used to fight big man in de road, and when they cuss him, he would bawl out, 'Stay right dey! Ah going for mih cutlass to chop yuh!'"

We were all losing it, shaking with belly laughs.

These meetings were rare. Whatever struggles Junior had survived—whether hustling on the streets or in the prison cell blocks—they showed in the creases at the corners of his eyes. Yet we were all light as air and happy to be there that night.

"That sounds just like him playing basketball for Glenview," Nige added, his deep voice rumbling into a chest-shaking laugh. Nige had quit Waterloo and was working at the Keg restaurant full time. He'd gone from kitchen staff to kitchen manager to serving to server manager.

"So when am I gonna see this girlfriend, Nigel? Yuh getting married soon?" Junior asked.

Nigel was engaged, but he ducked the question. Adge visibly winced. He did not get along with the bride-to-be.

Adrian had just moved back from Calgary, chasing his childhood ghosts. Serving salads to prairie people had left him skittish, a bit flighty, yet he was still wide-eyed and charming. He had just made a mad dash across the country in a blizzard. When I asked him why he had to leave Calgary in such a hurry, he looked down, touched his nose unconsciously, and said, "Oh, you know, it was nothing." I let him have his secret files.

"Man, I was bad as a kid, but our grandfather Horbutt used to call himself the God of Negro," I declared.

Nige shook his head, Junior repeated the phrase to himself, and we all guffawed, floored by the audacity.

"Man, Horbutt was the *nigrium nigrius nigro*."

"The WHAT?!" everyone yelled at me simultaneously.

"The black that is blacker than black. It's Latin."

"Is that a real ting?" Junior asked doubtfully.

Nigel was nodding; he knew what it meant. "In alchemy, it's the point when the metal loses its structural integrity and falls apart into a boiling soup, like birth fluid."

"The *nigrium nigrius nigro*," Junior repeated to himself. He was impressed. We now had our own expression for Black excellence.

"We should do this more often," Adge said. "We should do this regularly."

We all agreed, wistfully remembering that this was what we always said.

Junior, at his magnanimous best, paid for dinner from a thick wad of cash.

## VI

A year later, in 2010, 305 BlackBerry salespeople were offered a choice between a new position and quitting. 304 of them accepted the lateral move. I did not.

The mad dash had ended. The sprint towards something I could never catch had ceased. It reminded me of an incident from Trinidad.

I'm a boy again, pedalling a bike I'd borrowed but couldn't ride, pelting down the main road, wind roaring in my ears, hurtling me towards some uncertain fate. I hit a pothole and jam on the brakes and go flying over the handlebars, chipping my front teeth. Suddenly, just like that day, I was pitched over my corporate handlebars. The bike kept going, but I would have to find my own way. As always, for me, this meant turning to art.

I decided to write.

My novel, *Molasses*, was scribbled down on the back deck of my Kitchener home with the summer wind riffling through the trees. I wrote in black, blue, and red pen in an unlined notebook. I sat in a sketchy lawn chair that kept collapsing under me, and the words bled out of me as if I had opened some secret artery.

I conjured a malevolent all-seeing God, the wildness of the southern night, zombies and voodoo burials, pistols and absinthe, preachers bringing brimstone, the bliss of a lover's warm skin, heartbreak with no closure. The Abandonment. The terror of feeling alone.

Soon I was performing as a smooth soul character named "Molasses," crooning a seductive kind of pain. Strong as Death, Sweet as Love. I learned to wear this skin by watching Al Green perform for his congregation one Sunday morning in Memphis. He shouted some verses for a few minutes then sang for three hours, wailing and warbling his falsetto into every corner of my existence. The shambles he left my soul in became Molasses.

Suddenly, I was on stage as a southern preacher. It felt as if this Blacker, bluesier version of myself offered me the grand tapestry I needed to stitch my stories together. As the book expanded into my imagination, so too did my soul-singing Molasses mask, tumbling me down, back into myself. I sang the words I wrote for my grandfather: "Grandad in '73, his ghost is haunting me, faded picture, eyes afire, is this what I'm meant to be?"

Inevitably, reflections like this sent me back to my childhood, back to Monkeytown.

Back to the family I had tried to forget.

As Molasses unlocked hidden pockets of feeling within me, I started to call my siblings more often. Eventually, I went to visit Shanice in New York City. One night she suddenly asked me, "Brother, why don't you call Mom? She want to talk to you."

"Who me? Never. Not after what they did to me. They always take, take, take and never give, Shanice."

"But what if Mom were to die tomorrow? Wouldn't you feel guilty that you'd left things on bad terms?"

I stopped and took a breath. Shanice's children were sleeping in the other room. We were sitting at the kitchen table as the city hummed outside with a million petty dramas, a million wayward dads, a million bitter mothers, a million resentful sons.

"I have never had a mother. She doesn't even know me. She has never seen me sing, never seen me play basketball. She wasn't there in Trinidad. She isn't here now. How can I miss something I never had?"

The question hung between us for what seemed like a lifetime.

Of course, all these family roads eventually led back to Joan Cynthia Guevara.

"When are you getting married?" my aunt asked in her gossipy voice. This was one of her favourite themes, along with dating advice: "Boy, you need to stop dating those white girls. Those Staceys and Amandas." Dietary advice: "Michael, you need a Crock-Pot. Slow-cook some legumes and lentils." And enticements to go back to church: "Why don't you go to Seventh-days and find a nice Caribbean girl?"

"Child, we should go to Trinidad together," she said, happy that I was calling more regularly these days. She was by this time an ordained minister and the chaplain at two large New York City hospitals. Her job was to counsel the dying and the bereaved.

"Young, young people, I see dem dying every day," she told me. "No man knoweth the time nor the hour. Just last Tuesday, a girl, twenty-two years old—pretty pretty pretty, if yuh see pretty. DEAD. Brain an-huu-rizm. DEAD. Lord have mercy. Dead. Dead. Dead. If yuh see how she father bawl. Rich man, a banking man, drive to the hospital in Rolls-Royce, and he say to me: 'Pastor Joan, why couldn't God take me instead?'"

My auntie Joan and I agreed to go to Trinidad together. Maybe it was all the deaths she talked about, but I felt as though time was running out. Sooner or later, I had to do it. I had to go back to Trinidad for the first time in twenty-four years.

The ghosts shuffling in my head were about to be resurrected.

## Chapter Twenty

# SWEET BY AND BY

I

Home? Home. What did this word mean to me? I had been away from Trinidad for so long. By the summer of 2010, I had lived in Canada for twice as long as I'd lived there. What was I? Trinidadian? That seemed like a faded photograph, a distant lover calling. Canadian? That seemed like the thing I was always trying to be but never could. I was both. I was neither.

I'd always assumed that the longer I stayed away, the less Trini I would feel. Yet as I stepped off the airplane at Piarco Airport that July and smelled the bush on the air and felt its heat on my cheeks, I was at ease.

My soul would always live on that island.

"De crab runnin' tonight," said an old Indian man leaning on a stick by the southern sea. That night, we drove around the coast to bright Point Fortin, the oil refinery glowing like an alien spaceship. Across the water, I could see Venezuela hovering. Close enough to swim to? Close enough to row to? Close enough to dream of.

I ate the Indian man's blue crab stewed in curry and dumplings. A thunderstorm rolled through at three in the morning and transported me back decades to watching the storms of my childhood white-out the world. It drummed on the galvanized roof; it washed down the drain in an unstoppable flood. It filled the world with the fierce, all-powerful hand of God. The power and the glory.

After twenty-four years I was back "home."

The summer of writing had been electrifying, but just reaching for metaphors about my inner life wasn't enough. I needed to taste it in the food, hear the music in its voices, look it in the eye and call it by its name.

Auntie Joan and I had made a plan to meet in Trinidad. For her, the trip was normal—she went back often and always stayed connected to home. But for me, that place was a faraway shore, full of shadows and light.

Trinidad was not how I had idealized it in my child-mind. I leaned in front of my deceased uncle Boysie's shop at the junction in Fyzabad and watched life move by. Jammets, rumbos, and saga boys galore. Everything was strange. Everything was familiar.

"Yuh don't know how to palance?!" my cousin Candace said.

"What is palance?"

Her twin five-year-old daughters started laughing at me and put on the video, and we all hopped to the left four times and back four times, screaming: "Palaaaaaaaance! Palaaaaaaance!" Clearly, I had been missing out.

Joan and I sat on Candace's front porch and smiled until our faces hurt. She had her head wrapped in an African print cloth; her cheekbones were high and magnificent.

"Boy, yuh happy to be home with yuh auntie?"

"Yes, Auntie Joan." I rode the children's tricycle at least twice a day. My heart felt full of joy and life.

In San Fernando, we caught a maxi taxi in New Grant's direction. "Two for Prince's Tong," the driver called out. Taxis didn't leave until every seat was taken. I saw the emblem of Presentation College high on the hill, and a wave of recognition flooded over me.

Once under way, we cut through the Tasker Road, through sugarcane fields as far as I could see, and I was plunged back into the smells and sounds of the night I had run away and faced the void. That moment had never left me: the blackness, the boundless buzzing of insects, the certainty of my aloneness. All these years later, I would often wake up in the night and the darkness would take me back there. Now, here at last, my body was in the field.

Monkeytown burst into my senses like a movie I adored and had somehow wandered into. I was filled with the smell of the bush, the kobo on the tall trees, the cemetery overgrown with grass. It was mango season, and there was a sense of ripeness everywhere. Pools of rainwater evaporated in the sun as I passed the place where Olsten had caught me and my brother. I heard my grandmother calling, "JuniorandTony, come here!"

Miss Excelly's house was now Steve's Bar, a long dark tavern filled with liquor bottles of every colour. My cousin Steve had followed Boysie into shopkeeping, except that his main item was rum. The veranda where I'd learned to read was gone. The garage where the rumbos drank at wakes was now part of the building, yet it was still set up for drinking and All Fours.

Everything had changed. Nothing had changed. I walked the length of Monkeytown and could almost hear the turkeys coming for me in the road. I got used to old people staring at my face as if they were seeing a ghost. Al and I had the same face and build.

Inevitably, I ended up at Miss Monica's house. Monica, the woman whose son and brother had raped me, and whose partner was the sadist who beat Junior and me. I had to face them. I had to see what time had done to them and let them see me: strong, hearty, and full of defiance. They needed to see that Tony was still Tony, except now he could defend himself.

I sat in Miss Monica's living room. "White woman?" she was asking. "How can you kiss white woman?"

I was shaking with rage. "How can you birth a rapist?" I heard myself say, and I wasn't sure if I'd said it out loud. I hadn't. She birthed a rapist and lived with a sadist, and I didn't want any of it to matter anymore.

"Dextah, look! Tony come back from Canada," she called to her son.

Dexter looked like a possum caught in a headlight. He was frail and panicked. He froze. Looked at the ground, then at her. Looked at the ground, then at me, then scurried away. Had I come to expose him? I'd wanted to beat his head with a calabash stick, but when I was finally face to face with him, I realized that there was no justice to be had here. He was a limp, disgusting thing. He, too, had probably been molested by his uncle Larry. All of us had been plucked at our most vulnerable. There was no justice anywhere for Black boys in the Commonwealth. Where was Miss Monica's brother? I wondered.

Olsten Hodge, the man who beat us, was nowhere to be seen.

These people were pathetic. They preyed on the weak and scurried like cockroaches from the strong. I could feel the hold that those awful days had on me slip just a bit. I could feel the child running out of the bushes towards somewhere safe as the wind shook in the tall grass.

"Child, what is wrong with you?" Auntie Joan asked, and I told her. I had never told anyone about it, or so I thought, but Joan knew better.

"Mama told me," she said, sad and serious, slicing a green pomcetay, the juice spraying the air with that freshly cut smell.

"She told you? How could she know?" I was dumbfounded. I had convinced myself that nobody knew.

"When I came once when you were a little boy, she said, 'The little one tell me dat Dexter touch him in his bottom.'"

Miss Excelly knew? Auntie Joan knew? Still no one did anything.

"Child, we can't dwell on these things." My aunt could see the dark clouds brewing in me. "I'm sorry that your poor grandmother couldn't help you."

I was baffled and stunned. Not that no one did anything, but that I had convinced myself so well to forget that I'd told.

"She did her best," was the only consolation Joan offered, and I took it and tried to forget all over again.

Boboy still had a house full of birds in cages. Teardrop white stones were clipped to the wires so the birds could sharpen their beaks. His face was rough and black and his smile suggested wickedness, but he was happy to see me.

Between him and Hodge, he was the male role model I preferred.

The distance from the house to the junction, which had taken my little legs so long to run, now seemed like ten steps. The schoolyard of New Grant Anglican School I crossed in what felt like a single step. I had to beg the guard to let me in. It was like walking in a memory: the creamy banana-coloured paint, the rows of water taps at the back, the field beside the shop where I would get poulourie. These were all like doorways into some lost part of my head. Every site unlocked a rush of knowing. How had I arrived back at this mystical place?

Inside the school, I heard, "So you muss be Al son?" The woman with the broom was cleaning, getting things ready for September.

"Yeah, I is Tony—"

"Miss Excelly grand-chile," she interrupted. "You is de oldah one or de youngah one?"

"Youngah."

"I am an Ayres. We is familee. All a we connected, yuh know? The Ayres, Downings, Richardsons. We in dis land ah long time."

She seemed to know the whole history of the families of Monkey-town, the descendants of those hardy West African, American, Canadian slaves who chose to fight for the Queen and for their freedom.

"Yeah, I went New Yawk, but I didn't like it. I come back home. Alladat runnin' around, stressin' out, killin' yuhself—for what? I live wit my two daughters and my son in one house. We eh rich, but we happee."

It felt as though she had somehow passed something to me. Something so old, so delicate, and so intangible that if I breathed, it might slip away.

At the sickbed of Miss Stella, Auntie Joan and Stella's daughter, Joyce, laid hands on me and prayed for my deliverance. I don't know if it was the moment, the place, or the storm that pelted the galvanized roof with God's wrath, but I was thankful and accepted this ritual of Christendom.

"Praise the Lord," Miss Excelly would have said.

I listened as car by car, taxi by taxi, the news of the suicide of a twelve-year-old girl who had failed her Common Entrance exam travelled all the way to Chaguanas. This was how news spread. This was Third World CNN. Chaguanas was a few maxi taxi rides away from New Grant, passing through San Fernando into central Trinidad, where my brothers Kurt, Cardo, and Ronald, lived.

In Chaguanas, I surprised Gloria by showing up unannounced. She cuffed me in shock. "Yuh see you! YOU SEE YOU!"

It had been almost a decade since we'd been together.

"Oh, Lawd! Yuh kno how much ah pray to see dis boy? Let mih look at yuh. Yuh put on weight? Yut muss be eatin good!"

She was merry and happy to see me, and I stayed with her a few days.

Al had gotten his Canadian passport back from her, she had snatched it out of fear that he would do exactly what he did when he got it back: abandon her. Gloria took Al's passport just like she had done to Junior and me at the airport in 1986. Al, not to be outdone in the repeating of family cycles, promised her, just like he did in 1975, that he would get set up in Canada and "send for her." Yet, just as he did in 1975, he landed at Pearson Airport in Toronto and promptly forgot all about her. Hearing her talk about it that week in Chaguanas, it was hard not to feel sad for her and somewhat ashamed of them.

Whenever he was the topic, in that dark living room, her face became clenched and stormy. "Yuh faddah and he good-for-nuthin ass gone an left me here, not a red cent, not a postcard, not a 'hello, how are you?' Then she asked, watching me sideways, "Yuh know which part he is?" I wouldn't say even if I did know where he was. Between Al and Gloria was not somewhere anybody with sense wanted to be.

Ronald, Cardo, Kurt, and I hung out, and I was touched by how much they looked up to me. Kurt, as always, was boisterous. He told me about being in the army and being in shoot outs. Ronald wanted to be a minister. From rapper to gangster to pastor, he was always looking for something to believe in. He said to calm the sense of loss I had from being so far from them. It felt strange that we had spent so much time apart yet I could feel their admiration, the same admiration Nigel and Adge had offered me so freely, I felt like I didn't deserve it.

Cardo was calm and quiet as usual. "Even if we don't talk so much, we always breddahs right?" And he was right, I thought, as we picked through the noisy market in Chaguanas eating fresh oysters in pepper sauce. Fate had separated us physically but as the sun fell spraying across the galvanized rooftops, I felt no space between us. Always brothers.

Several times Gloria and I sat and talked like co-conspirators. We were both beaming. When the topic was not Al, she was actually bright and cheerful, genuinely happy to see me and this made my heart glad. I was still wary of all the disappointment that came with loving her, but it made me feel light and warm to see her smile.

"Boy, I ketching mih tail!" She was complaining, but she was grinning. Nothing seemed to stop her. Dressed in her white nurse's uniform, she left early and came home late. We sat by the kitchen table, laughing and drinking rum.

"Ah happy to see yuh, Mom." All the years had swallowed my anger and dissolved my wrath. Just hearing her laugh was worth it. I was bathing in the feeling of being a Trinidadian again. Of having a mother again. For however long it would last.

"Boy, ah is yuh muddah—"

"I can't forget, Mom. You tell me every time ah see yuh."

The visit was too brief, but it left me feeling buoyant as air. My heart was full, as if nothing could ever take this feeling of being home away from me.

Just as I had in 1986, when we were leaving for Canada, I stayed at Vio and Steve's house in Trincity before my flight home. The next day, Vio drove me to the airport. She was a practical, professional, capable woman who seemed to think her way through the Third World chaos. The more I talked to her, the more I realized that maybe not all Monkeytown people were destined to be damaged. It was reassuring.

"Some dramatic scene last time you were here, boy," she said.

A tidal wave of memories crashed into me: the tension of the airline people, wanting to send us to our "better life" but running out of time; the defiance on Gloria's face; and the feeling of helplessness in me.

"I was there that day," Vio reminded me. "If Gloria hadn't agreed, what would have become of yuh, boy?"

"I did it for spite," Gloria would tell me years later. "Joan always tryin' to act all high and mightee. I wanted she to know who was boss."

The last thing I did before I left was put a hibiscus flower on Miss Excelly's grave. Fifth Company cemetery was empty, and the light was falling into grey. Night was coming. The air was singing with the hissing of insects. Fireflies hovered over the tombstones like bright lights suspended in time. The grass was silent and high.

"If God don't come, he does send a man," I could hear her say, and it made me smile. Wherever she was, that was my home. It felt as if I had come to seek her blessing. Maybe some part of me knew that calamity usually followed meeting my parents. A great storm was gathering on my horizon. If I was going to survive, I would need all her lessons.

Before I knew it, I was singing one of her hymns: "In the sweet by and by, we shall meet on that beautiful shore. In the sweet by and by, we shall meet on that beautiful shore."

And I felt as if somewhere she, too, was singing and smiling as if she knew everything I did not.

## Chapter Twenty-One

# BRUZEN VI GADA

I

I punched my girlfriend.

It was a left hook, and it was in front of all her college friends one chilly Friday night in January 2011. I really wish that my first thought had been: "Are you okay?" But as the son of a felon, I thought: "Dude, you just committed a crime in front of twelve witnesses. Run!"

And that's what I did.

I fled the scene. Head still drunk and spinning, I launched myself into the frostiness of January. My whole left side was throbbing from rib cage to shoulder to temples, as if my arteries wanted to leap out of me. The horror. What had I done?

Why did I hit her? I checked my swing. Why does she always get in my face like that? They all wanted to fight me. I checked my swing, though. Was she hurt? Fuck, they called the cops. Fuuccccccck! What have you done? What is wrong with you?

I boarded a train back to Kitchener and breathed a sigh of relief when I saw that the cops weren't waiting for me at the station. Nothing good ever happened in London, Ontario.

Kayleen and I had met two winters before, while I was on tour with Jen Militia. We met at a bar in northern Alberta, four provinces and thousands of kilometres away from home. The place was filled with pool tables, a scattering of slot machines, and a slew of pickup-driving, shit-kicking toughs from the Alberta oil patch.

She did not seem to belong there.

She was nineteen, in a sharp, fire-engine-red cocktail dress. I was thirty-four and the lead singer of a rap-punk band. "Hi, Mic Dain. Jah," she teased, her mouth twisted into a secret joke. But there was a fierce, vulnerable tension in her tiny eyes. Those eyes and her perfectly lined bangs made her face feel like a mask. "You always say exactly what you feel, don't you?" she wrote to me in the note she slipped me later. "Who DOES that?" I read it, picturing her twisted mouth teasing. I didn't think it was true, but the way she said it made me swoon.

Two years later, we were involved in a desperate, compulsive melodrama. Two weeks before I punched her, we had spent New Year's Eve yelling, raging at each other for hours, sleepless, frustrated, bawling. It was one of those fights over something so silly that you never remember it after. But there were always deeper reasons. Her wrath. My wrath. Taking our absent fathers and mothers out on each other. Brokenness had brought us together, but like every good drug, it lost its potency over time. Each time we fought and made up, we got a little less high.

On that crisp mid-January night, the stars were icy white. Our New Year's Eve fight was still hanging over us. A few hours into the party we'd gone to, I was alone in a corner of the basement, getting

more and more agitated. "Why the fuck am I even here?" I hadn't seen
Kayleen for a while, and I couldn't quite figure out how long. "Man,
I got friends with kids older than these people." A sure sign I was at
the wrong party. The loudmouth kids were playing beer pong, toss-
ing ping-pong balls into red plastic cups of beer. Loser drinks, winner
drinks, everyone drinks. I stood off to the side, guzzling long throat-
fuls of the Famous Grouse Scotch whisky and boiling over like a pot
on a stove.

Kayleen reappeared suddenly. By her lisp and her lurching steps, I
could tell she was wasted.

"What the fuck are you doing?" she asked, and pushed me.

"I'm sitting here waiting for you! What the fuck are you doing?" I
replied, my spleen up.

She stuck out her jaw and pushed me again, saying, "Shut the fuck
up!"

I felt the room turn into an audience, an auditorium, gathering
round and moving in. She moved to push me again, and I punched her.

For a moment, the whole place was paralyzed. Time seemed to
break hard and slow down to a crawl, leaving a vacuum in which no
one—not her, not me, not the room full of post-teen partiers—knew
what to do. Her face winced, then grimaced.

"Why did you push me?" I justified.

"Fuck. YOU!" she yelled back, still stunned.

The basement closed in on me. These fuckers wanna fight me, I
thought.

Some kid behind me said, "You better get outta here, man, before
we call the cops."

I huffed and held my arms low and open, as if to say "But she
attacked me," or "But I didn't mean to," or "But she isn't hurt." But
nothing. Only huffs of hot blended-whisky breath came out of me.
And then I ran.

My train to Kitchener couldn't move fast enough. I sat with my forehead to the window, collapsing into a pit of panic. What have you done? How could you have done that to her? Why were you even there?

My shame and guilt hovered over me like the angry clouds rolling over the farmers' fields outside. I had become what I swore I'd never be: a violent loser on the wrong side of the law.

I had become my dad.


## I I


The afternoon after I punched Kayleen, I woke up in Kitchener to the sound of police in my kitchen, asking my roommates where I was. They arrested me immediately and slapped me in handcuffs before I could get my shoes on.

We drove half a block to the station, and they led me through one set of massive doors and then another massive door, which opened to an inner room, which looked like a loading dock. When this second door closed behind me, I felt as if I had passed through the gates of hell.

My encounters with the police were never good. This lifelong revulsion was about to get a major dose of reinforcement. I remembered sitting at the back of the cruiser when I was busted for shoplifting, or getting stopped and searched on my way home from school in Scarborough. That's when I learned to call them "The Beast"—and I could never forget them beating down Al when he came to pick me up at the station, or choking Junior in his basement apartment. There were no members of society I avoided more. Which might have been the biggest reason I had no adult police record. This was about to change.

My temples were still thick with tension from the whisky. My stomach roiled. When I sat, my left leg refused to stop shaking. I asked for a pen and paper so I could write to calm down, but the guard chuckled and said, "I don't think so," with no explanation.

In my long history of deplorable behaviour, punching my girlfriend was the lowest point.

My cell had nothing but a small, uncomfortable wooden bench. I was in a cage, and except for the video cameras, I felt forgotten. The walls started feeling too close. Every direction I turned, I breathed in sharply. Every breath I took made me turn in another direction. Claustrophobia and self-pity made me feel nauseous.

After passing out for a time, I was awoken and placed, handcuffed, in the back of a cruiser, and soon we were cutting through snowdrifts on our way back to London. The plexiglas barrier pressed me into the back seat until there was no room to move. The officers treated me with blithe disregard. They were young and obviously did not want to drive to London during a snowstorm.

In London more double doors, but the atmosphere was decidedly worse. Cops stood around everywhere, barely looking at me. Their complete lack of acknowledgment of my humanity scared me the most. "Turn left. Turn right," the voice behind me seemed distant and emotionless. There was a sanitized, fluorescent glow to everything, bright enough to light up the shady corners of my soul. I was presented at a desk where a tall constable, whose neck seemed to reach up to infinity, said to me in that same flat tone: "I am about to read you your rights. I am arresting you for one charge of Domestic Assault. You have the right to retain and instruct counsel without delay . . . Do you wish to call a lawyer?"

My heart was in my mouth. My spirit descended into utter distress with his every sullen syllable.

Below the desk was the list of names of lawyers and their phone numbers. One had my last name. I took that as a good omen. He explained that I was going to spend the night there, and that in the morning, the judge would see me. He said I should not tell the police anything at all.

It was seven o'clock by the time I found myself in another cell. This one was made up of a huge chunk of dirty concrete and a reeking toilet. The claustrophobia returned. My mind caved in. My breathing turned to panting like a trapped animal. The inescapability of my cell closed in around me like fate itself.

It occurred to me that I needed to calm down or I wouldn't survive. Al and Junior, I knew, would have been laughing at me. This wasn't even prison. My dad and brother had both spent years on the inside. All these dramatics over one night in a holding cell? That thought strangely comforted me.

Sitting in the lotus position, I tried to meditate. Sucking air and heat into my diaphragm, I tried to breathe deeply. Barely three seconds would pass before some horrible sound or thought entered my head. Then six. Then eight. Then ten. Breathe in. Breathe out. I opened my eyes and stared about. Calm at last.

There was nothing much to see, but I could hear the sound of cells opening and closing, yelling and crying, drunken Saturday night prisoners screaming in rage, and tired Saturday night cops barking in anger. It was the whole horror show of the London downtrodden venting their futility at the night. The sounds echoed off the concrete and in and out of my sleep. I had reached the inner circles of Dante's hell. Nothing good ever happened in London, Ontario.


III


"Who don't hear does feel," I could hear an old Trini lady say.

Three days after that fateful punch, I woke up in Kitchener, determined to get fit and focused after the mess I had made of my life. I had been given a trial date six months hence, and in the meantime, I was required to complete a court-approved anger awareness program. I was determined to make amends. As part of the court-mandated rules I was not allowed to have any contact with Kayleen. In truth, I didn't want to. I wondered how she was doing, but the work I really needed to do was on myself. I needed to prove that I was not my father, that I could be better, that an old Trini lady hadn't given her last strength to raise another jailbird.

As was my ritual, I pulled on my sweats and spent the next hour running steadily towards Waterloo and back. I returned in a flush of endorphins.

My street, Ahrens, was one of the oldest in town. Tall broad trees fanned out on each side like sentinels. My roommate and I shared a kitchen between our bedrooms. The house had been in his family since the 1800s. When I had called to inquire about the room, I slipped and mentioned that I was a musician. Bad move. But he seized on this. "Perfect," he said. "Then you won't mind if my band jams at the house?" We were both relieved.

After my run, I met Barry and Elaine Lillie for a late breakfast. When they asked what I'd been up to, I said, slyly, "Oh, I was hanging out in London this weekend, with friends." I was hoping for the moment to pass. By this point, Coach was in his sixties, and teaching and coaching were fading into the rear-view mirror of his life. As the vacuum of Al had gaped wider over the years, I began to see Coach as my unofficially adopted father. Elaine was enjoying her third career as a teacher at the university's school of pharmacology. What I saw was classic Elaine, a well-read lady with brown-and-whitening hair, large-framed glasses, and a razor-sharp tongue. Perfect.

Even after fifteen years, it was still disorienting to be loved by them.

Typically I would have celebrated Christmas with them, but I had missed it that year, so they gave me presents at breakfast: Cineplex movie passes and a book, *The Measure of a Man,* Sidney Poitier's auto-biography. Elaine and I laughed about how she always used to get me *Madame Bovary* and *Dubliners,* forgetting that she had already given me those books a half dozen times before.

We clicked in a way that perhaps she didn't with Barry's three children. I was the closest thing she had to a son, and being with them always made me feel loved in a way I felt I didn't deserve. They would sometimes say to me, teary-eyed, "You were the first real decision we made together."

We had come a long way since 5:00 a.m. Greyhound buses and Eggo waffles in the freezer.

When the wheels came off my life, music was the refuge I ran to. It was—like basketball had been so many years before—my escape, my church, my confessor, the only place I could go to feel worthy again. In the early months of 2011, my life needed a makeover. And the woman who would wield the mascara brush was named Gada.

Gada Jane and I collided with all the force of fate. There is a photo of our first meeting. She is talking with her hands, her blue eyes alive with intelligence, her head tilted, absorbing my reactions. I look completely fascinated, my eyes bulging, listening, confounded. She seemed to me, in that moment, like a fierce, doll-faced fairy. Not the gentle Disney kind but the mischievous Shakespearean ones, the impish, omniscient tricksters. Little did we know that this encounter was about to rearrange our lives.

That January, Gada asked me to join her art collective, which was called Predella, a term for the platform on which an altar is placed. Predella consisted of four white women and two brown men going artsy to the maximum. Gada was the driving force behind everything we did. Our meetings started with a ritual, during which we ceremonially burned little slips of paper describing the things we wished to let go. We would end by each chanting: "Struggle is not an option—it's a necessity."

"What does the name of your company mean?" I asked Gada about Bruzen vi Gada, her fledgling film production company.

"It means 'bruised by a mace,'" she said, her pretty cheeks flushing at the mention of violence. She adored Quentin Tarantino levels of gore, and would often explore how bruises look under lights and the different techniques for making fake blood. (She preferred corn syrup and Jell-O.)

"I love how things that are ugly can be beautiful."

She and I declared ourselves siblings and began to transform the ugliness of my life into something beautiful. Looking back, it is easy to see why I wanted to become someone else. But that day, joining Predella, I had no idea what was to come.

This was the group from which John Orpheus would be born.


IV


At the John Howard Society, the circle of plywood chairs was like another circle of Dante's hell.

"She was drunk, and her friends attacked me," I confessed defensively.

"Try again, Antonio Michael. Use her name so that she is fully a person."

"Kayleen was drunk, and so was I."

"It is natural to want to minimize the action. Deflect from it. Justify it. But you can't allow this. You must face what you did without hiding. Don't run, Antonio Michael."

"I punched my girlfriend, Kayleen, in front of all her friends."

"Well done. You see, everyone? There is no reconciliation without truth."

I had started my court-ordered anger awareness program in February 2011. It was life-altering. At first, as I looked around at the hapless deflated figures seated near me, I thought, Is this really where I belong? Mikey, a plumber, was sure his girlfriend was cheating on him. Stan was a middle-aged unemployed guy with multiple domestics against his long-time partner, who also had multiple domestics against him. "Sometimes it's just a matter of who calls the cops first," he told me on a smoke break. Johnny was twenty-one and wore a red ball cap backwards over his shifty grey eyes. "I just pushed her once," he said defensively. "Now I can't go home. I can't call. I need my tools to work." Ahmed was a quiet Iraqi immigrant with a trimmed moustache who seemed as if he had stumbled into the wrong play. What little he said expressed bewilderment.

The facilitator was a neat fortyish woman with an impossibly tender voice and bags under her eyes that makeup didn't fully cover. "First, we have to learn that our bad actions are just that—things we did," she explained. "They do not define us."

I looked around the circle, clear-eyed and grim. The men were all slumped with shame, and ridges of worry creased their faces.

"If we can understand our actions in this way, we can learn from them and leave the feelings of guilt and shame behind us. We can grow."

The words seemed like the solution to some inscrutable puzzle, like the unlocking of some forbidden door; it was as if I had been struggling to play a game and had only just learned the rules. No one had ever spoken to me like this. It was as if she had turned a light on and suddenly Guilt and Shame, which had been pulling my strings from the shadows, were now clearly and irrevocably exposed.

I wanted to despise these men, to feel that I was better than them.

These tough, haunted men, facing the chasm of their awfulness, mostly for the first time. Instead, I found something in them to admire. I couldn't help seeing the genuine remorse and confusion. Perhaps I was exactly where I belonged.

I thought about Chachi, who had picked me up from the London jail that day. When the glare of Sunday freedom hit my eyes, the paralyzing self-loathing began. We drove east through the back roads and fields, as we had done so many times before. But something had gone terribly wrong. He was the owner of a thriving business and several properties and had a happy marriage to a wonderful woman. I was a criminal—and worse than that, a guy who had hit his girlfriend. Yet I suppose we were both following in our fathers' footsteps.

"So even if I punch a hole in the wall, it's abuse?" Mikey was asking.

"Can anyone help him? Antonio Michael?" Our moderator nodded approval at my eager-beaverness. I had become the guy who translated the psychobabble into dude-speak. The male voice they could believe.

"Yeah, man, it is. It's a threat. It's like you're saying: 'This is what I'll do to your face.'"

I noticed the men's hands. They were hard, sinewy, stained hands—working men's hands. Did white-collar guys like my BlackBerry bosses never hit their spouses? Or were their properties so large that no one could hear them do it? I became determined not only to learn and internalize everything myself, but to help every last one of these men learn too.

"When people say, 'I exploded,' that's not how it happens," the facilitator explained. "There are always triggers and signs along the way. We just have to know how to recognize them and de-escalate."

We were learning how to manage our emotions, to acknowledge and communicate them constructively. We were learning how to separate the person from the act: not "you're an asshole," but "when you yell at me, it makes me feel hurt and betrayed." It was like watching fully grown men learn to walk. Like babies, we just didn't know how. It wasn't a class I had ever been offered. How could I know something no one had bothered to teach me?

Day after day, the men fell apart and reassembled themselves. They could use their partners' names now. State unswervingly what they did. Name their triggers and coping strategies. "Everybody should be taking this course," said Stan, and we all agreed.

I felt like some hidden sun had peeked over my horizon. We had been given more than a court-appointed penance, or even skills for life—we had been given permission to feel. I took to it with all my schoolboy zeal. Some part of me unclenched in those classes. I left lighter and unburdened, as if a great mystery was starting to unravel. My very long path to healing had begun.

"You should really consider doing this as a career. You're a natural!" our facilitator said to me.

"Thank you," I replied, staring at the dark shade of tiredness below her eyes. In my head I thanked Auntie Joan for her therapy books. As a first-time offender, I'd only had to complete the program and a short period of probation in exchange for a suspended sentence. Jail was never gonna see me again. Walking home after that good news of successfully completing the program, I felt like the black cloud that had been following me had moved on just a little bit and perhaps life could be clearer skies from then on.

If only things were ever that simple.

V

The last time I saw Miss Excelly was in a dream that week. I know some will say that doesn't count, but it was so gripping and real that I woke up rattled to my core.

In the dream, I was crossing Monkeytown, coming up the hill from Boboy's towards our house, where Mama's wake was happening.

"She left you everything!" a woman yelled. She pointed at me, accusing. She was some family member, a woman with a baby in her arms, a child holding her hand, and another trailing behind her. "She left you everything," she spat at me in disgust. I knew that by "everything" she meant Mama's silver and gold bracelets in the heavy box at the bottom of the wardrobe, but the dream whispered what treasure Mama had really left me: her resilience, her songs, her wisdom, her unquenchable spirit.

As I left the woman behind and crossed the road, I looked towards the cemetery, and there was my grandmother, risen like the Nazarene himself, striding calmly towards the house in all her glory. O death, where is thy sting? O grave, where is thy victory?

She wore a serene look and the spotless white toga of a campaigning Roman senator. On her head, made of sticks and leaves, sat the grass crown, the symbol of a conquering general returning in triumph. I rushed to her and buried my face in a hug, and all creation disappeared.

"What are you doing here?" I asked and started to weep.

In the real world, my body had not hugged her for decades. That hug was the home I had been missing.

"What are you doing here? You can't come to your own wake!" I said, as if bad manners were the problem and not the fact that she was undead.

She remained silent.

"Oh." It dawned on me. "You're not staying, are you?"

Her eyes watched me lovingly and she said, "I am always with you, especially when you can't see me."

When I woke up, I was still weeping.

# VI

"Get it over with and fuck already!" some guy yelled out of the pile of bodies in the living room. Eryn and I had been talking for hours; the whole house was full of her friends crashed out on couches. Outside, a blizzard had buried the world in snow.

She was showing me her high school dance videos, the pageants and the costumes, the dad dances and her moves. Like many dancers, she was clumsy when not dancing, but her clothes were tucked and proper. Everything in its right place. There was a sensitivity under the neatness, some quiet vulnerability reaching out to me.

In hindsight, I realize I was exactly the kind of person twenty-five-year-old women from good families should avoid: a thirty-six-year-old unemployed musician with a drinking problem and a domestic violence charge.

We took it slow. I felt dangerous, and I wanted to run away even from myself. With the John Howard Society lessons rattling around my brain, I was direct and honest with Eryn about my past. That didn't faze her. For the first time in my adult life, I was resisting the temptation to fall into a relationship to get over another relationship.

Eryn lived in a massive old house backing onto Victoria Park in downtown Kitchener. If she and I left our homes at the same time, walking, we'd meet roughly in the middle of the park, by the bridge where the man-made lake froze and the lights glowed yellow. Her presence felt like a soothing potion for the turmoil I was going through. We kissed in her parents' driveway one night in early March, when the snow caught the light and threw it everywhere until the lake, the houses, the sky, even the air seemed to glow. I sailed back home, exhilarated, unable to feel the frost or the wind or hear the snow crunching under my feet.

"Don't mess this up," I warned myself.

## Chapter Twenty-Two

# WHITE LADY, BLACK ORPHEUS

I

Cocaine, the "white lady," ran through the veins of my family like a lover that would not leave. She brought shame, she brought comess, but mostly she brought the false promise of escape. Something we were all seeking.

"I'm going to work at a new restaurant," Adrian said.

We were cutting across Highway 401 towards London at breakneck speed.

"How come? You just started four months ago."

My brother loved to drive, the faster the better. He weaved in and out of traffic, shifting the gears and touching his nose compulsively.

"Well, there was an incident with some drugs. They think I have a problem."

My eyebrows lifted. "Do you have a problem?"

He didn't answer. He just sniffed at the air, pointed the car towards the horizon, and shifted into high gear.

Adge, the boy who'd turned his life into a piece of performance art when he saw the movie *Scarface*, was now truly coked up, without the Cuban accent. By 2009, the parody had become the reality.

He'd fled to Calgary, to the streets where Al and Ami had met; some pungent nostalgia pulled him there while his burnt bridges pushed him out of Ontario. "Alberta is just better," he would say, longing for a new start. Except that being coked out in a Calgary oil boom was not paving his own way; it was following in his father's footsteps. When he came back later that year, he was a mess.

He told me what his days were like in Cambridge in that year when he had briefly returned from his western exile: "I used to be in my room, sweating, wide awake, can't sleep, just snorting a little bit more, a key here, a bump there, another line here, until the sun came up. Then I'd drive around the corner and watch Mom leave for work, then go back home and snort all day."

I had never seen Adge so unenthusiastic about life. A light had gone out in his eyes. But that didn't stop him from heading back to Calgary that spring.

"Cocaine is a helluva drug," declared Dave Chappelle's Rick James. Rick James was one of our favourite singers from the tapes we used to listen to in Al and Ami's basement—the place where Nigel, Adrian, and I had first bonded over our father's tastes.

Al's tapes. Al's tastes. Al's life.

For two decades, since he'd left me outside Junior's apartment and driven off with Hailey, Al's most consistent relationship had been with the white powder.

The worst he got was shortly before the family was deported to Trinidad. Gloria told me: "My-kaal, if yuh see yuh faada. If yuh see de sad state yuh faada reach. He livin' in a crack house, with all dem haunted peepul. For days in de darkness like some vampire. If yuh see yuh faada, yuh would weep till yuh eyeball drop out."

That same year, Junior was in the back seat of a car crossing Jane and Finch when he yelled out: "Stop, stop! Lemme out for a second." The shaggy homeless man he had seen was Al. He couldn't believe it. "He looked right through me like I wasn't there."

That year, Junior would see Al, dirty and desperate, many times, but he would never stop again. He just pretended not to notice and shut his eyes, waiting for our father to pass by.

A few years later, Junior became strung out on the same drug. I didn't know what was happening until he called from Vancouver, where he'd fled to escape his habits.

"You fight with it at first," he began slowly, and I felt as if I could see the lines of his brow rumple. "You don't want to accept that it's happening to you."

He paused and sucked in air deeply.

"The first week I started using, when I came down, I used to cry. 'What the hell? Is this what it's gonna be like now?' Then I set up another dose and said to myself, 'You shouldn't be doing this.'"

I could hear him pause again, remembering. He had since found Jesus, the other family obsession, and had got clean. His voice was serene.

"Then I thought: 'No one gives a shit anyway,' and I swallowed the smoke."

When we were kids I thought we were so different, but talking to him that day, I felt like I was talking to myself. Except that I had made different choices.

"What was it like?" I asked him. "Did it make you feel better?"

"At first it was peaceful, but then the peace would fly away faster and faster, until there wasn't no peace, just doing it to do it."

When I heard that Al had given him the drugs, my heart swelled with spite. Like a Caribbean storm, the white lady ran through my family and left only shambles.

## I I

Auntie Joan continued to live in New York City in the years after our trip to Trinidad. I had not seen her since, but it was nice to get her phone calls every month or so.

"Child, your aunt is getting old." It had been two decades since she put me on that train from Grand Central Station to Cambridge, but I could never see her as old. She existed in my mind as a monument, an indestructible thing that would stand and keep its shape no matter what.

"Yuh grandmuddah would sing, 'For the Father waits over the way. To prepare us a dwelling place there.' You know that one?"

I sang the refrain: "In the sweet by and by, we shall meet on that beautiful shore."

She was still working at two large hospitals in NYC. She flourished as a chaplain—the person the house of medicine called when medicine could not save you. She had two types of clients: those about to be deceased, and the loved ones of the recently deceased.

"What do people say when they are dying, Auntie Joan?"

"What do they say? Child, I will tell you what they don't say: They don't wish for more money. They don't wish they'd worked more. All they want is time. More time."

She was always preaching. The stories, sayings, and Bible verses tumbled out of her in sighs and warnings and exaltations. Not in a condescending way but the way of someone who had seen the naked face of death and had to speak some sense to it. All those dying eyes, all that wailing and shouting and gnashing of teeth. She was out there on the mountain, under the fierce gaze of the Almighty, and her prayers shook the heavens.

"Father, Gaaawd, we come before you to ask your mercy. For you say in your Word: 'They that wait upon the Lord shall renew their strength.' Yes, Lord. 'They shall mount up with wings as eagles; they shall run, and not be weary.' I bring this child, Michael, before you. You know his heart. You know the prayers of his grandmother and the trials and tribulations she went through to raise him up. Be with him, Lord. Ring your angels around him, Lord. Show him the path of righteousness so that his feet may never stray. Amen."

"Amen."

## III

Gada and I would talk with all the fury of exploding stars, night after night, day after day, for months on end. Her hands would dance through an explanation, her shockingly blonde hair tied back, eyes crackling with life, animated with the force of her surging synapses.

Before long, we decided that we had to change the world.

One night after a Predella meeting, which was when many of our marathon exchanges occurred, she stood in the kitchen as I plopped down my tired bones.

"This chair! A proper Roman *lectus*," I declared, reclining like Caesar.

Her eyes lit up. "I'm always having identity crises just like you. You know, for five years I thought I was Bill Clinton," she said without any irony.

"Really? Bill? Not Hillary?"

"Isn't it fun becoming someone else? I've never had a time when I wasn't trying to become someone else."

Gada lived in a parallel universe where all my weirdnesses became normal.

"Oh, I have some thoughts about you," she continued, watching me closely. "You keep telling me these stories of your life: about your grandmother, killing your brother's fish, the bush, the entrance test thing. They seem so important, as if you're trying to figure yourself out."

She was right. My conversations never strayed far from Trinidad. I was fixated on the sunken memories of my past. As if they could explain why I'd punched my girlfriend, and why I wanted to be anyone but me. Those stories would become my greatest attempt at not being myself. His name would be John.

"Maybe we need to make you a new identity?"

When I wasn't with Gada, Eryn and I were inseparable. We rarely slept apart. Her friends became my friends. Her parents made sure that I was always invited for dinner and family get-togethers.

Eryn loved to dance. Her anxiety seemed to fall away like a caterpillar's cocoon, and her confidence butterflied into bloom. These were my favourite moments, watching her bounce and twirl, effortless and free. In the caress of an endless summer, our bodies discovered each other. We followed each other's skin like a treasure map. And as our hearts unravelled, our craving evaporated the space between us.

Except when it came to all things Gada. Gada was just a friend, not competition for Eryn, but it was a friendship that consumed us both. A mutual admiration society. Who wouldn't have been jealous?

I was once again setting up Al's pattern—two women at war for my soul.

The night John Orpheus was born, Eryn sat quietly in the corner while Gada and I gushed about the movie *Orfeu Negro* (*Black Orpheus*). It was the myth of Orpheus set against the Brazilian Carnival in Rio de Janeiro. In hindsight, there is no real mystery as to why the movie fascinated me. Rio's Carnival was just like Trinidad's: it was a slave's triumphant holiday, with music, bands in the street, wild abandon, a pageant of masquerades rolling through the hills, strange characters, costumes as elaborate and lush as the jungle itself. Brazilians loved to "play mas," as the Trinis would say.

Black Orpheus was the bandleader, strumming his raucous and then delicate songs while Death chased his lover through the streets. He was everything I worshipped: guitars, orphans, tragedy, and Black people dancing in the tropical streets.

"'This is perfect," Gada proclaimed.

I agreed. It was as if we had found a window into the enigma we had both been trying to solve.

Orpheus was the *nigrium nigrius nigro*.

## IV

Weddings always made me feel inadequate. Uncomfortable, like when someone is crying in front of you but you don't feel sad. Weddings made me feel certain that deep down inside, some part of me wasn't quite human.

One day, sometime in the 1990s, my friends from university just moved on with their lives. While I was still burning scrambled eggs and sharing houses with undergrads and trying to keep my guitar player from drinking bourbon before the photo shoot, they got married to long-term girlfriends and were soon on to their second mortgages, complete with salt-and-pepper goatees and snotty kids calling me "Uncle."

In my mind I was still a kid, still figuring it out. I had no love handles, mutual funds, or middle-aged pot belly. But my friends were just one screaming toddler tantrum from getting old. I told myself that I would never want their lives. But secretly, I was filled with envy. They had the things I thought I could never have: family, consistency, a place to belong. I felt the same sense of inadequacy and experienced the same sense of longing as when Aunt Joan had left me with that Christian family. Their stability reminded me of everything I lacked. Like the fact that I had no relatives cheering in the stands at my basketball games, or that when my girlfriend's mother insisted I stop staying over, I passed out on Chachi's parents' couch, and his mom, seeing me curled up and shivering, placed a blanket over my shoulders. "I never thought of him as having parents," she would say much later.

All those things were confirmation that something was wrong with me. And at weddings, all those things bubbled up and became a raging torrent of self-loathing. Except for two weddings in 2011: my brother Adrian's in Mexico, and Coach's daughter's in her Kitchener backyard.

Ally was a slight prairie girl who stared at Adrian as if he were the source of life itself. She had no qualms about the mad pace he wanted their relationship to move at—in fact, she preferred it. Adrian had met his match.

Adge got married to Ally in Playa del Carmen, Mexico, the week after Eryn and I started dating. The night before the wedding, I stole him away for a drink at the cabana. We inhaled the salty Gulf of Mexico like sailors who had survived some dreadful voyage.

"What was the worst you ever got with coke?" I asked. I often had the perverse need to get "deep" at awkward times.

He looked over playfully. "Why? You thinking of starting up?" And we both chuckled. Ally was pregnant and she and Adrian had just found out they would be having two girls. "You gonna come back and see us again when the twins are born?"

"Maybe I'd like to go to-booze-ning down the hills again!"

The year before, all of us had gone out tobogganing in Calgary in the biting wind, freezing our fingertips on a steep, iced-over hillside. Warm Scotch whisky spread out like wings inside me, and we barrelled down the hill on a piece of red plastic and laughed and laughed. It reminded me of that day in Sioux Lookout, when I had first met the cute little boy with the chipmunk cheeks who apparently looked like Herbert. Now a grown man, he'd squeezed me hard when we hugged and said, "Ally and I would really like you to be part of our family, Uncle Mike."

The next day, the wind almost lifted the wedding and blew it straight across the gulf to Cuba. It was pitching and heaving and threatening to storm all day. The men in the wedding party wore soft purple dress shirts and worried frowns. At thirty-six, I was the only single man there. It was as if adulthood had skipped me completely.

Finally, in a sliver of sunlight, Ally and Adge were married. My delightful, lost, romantic little brother had found the holy grail of family.

That summer, Coach's youngest daughter, Kim, got married in her backyard. She was the Lillie child I was closest to. When Jen Militia broke up in 2009, Kim and I grew closer, mostly because we had the same approach to surviving breakups: large bottles of red wine.

Kim had Coach's sense of duty to the ones she loved. They were always the two quickest to cry at the slightest sentimental moment. Coach would cry at Tim Hortons commercials and she was her father's daughter, so perhaps it was inevitable that we would get along.

In the tent behind Kim and her soon-to-be spouse's house, the whole Lillie clan gathered, crisp in their wedding gear. Coach arrived already weepy, with Elaine and her widest smile supporting him. Kim's brother and sister and their families were there, as well as her uncles, aunts, and cousins. This was the very definition of family: you show up. When important things happen, you are there. My heart could feel this, but my brain fumbled to grasp it.

I sang and played two songs on acoustic guitar as the couple walked up the aisle, and another as they signed the wedding certificate.

That night, Eryn and I lay cuddling, listening to the sounds of the rain outside and musicians plucking their joyful songs nearby. My mind was buzzing from the day's events. My body felt like it was floating, seeing them all together and happy. Could I have a wedding like this one day? Why was it so hard for me to picture myself happy? To allow myself to deserve happiness?

I was so busy mourning the family I'd lost that I was blind to the one that had found me.

Act Four

# JOHN

## Chapter Twenty-Three

# THE QUEEN AND LIAM GALLAGHER

I

Becoming someone else was my drug of choice.

My personas were the cure for my self-loathing. It was no coincidence that as I abandoned all hope in my mother and father, I threw myself into my aliases one after the other: Tony, Mic Dainjah, corporate warrior Michael Downing, soul preacher Molasses, and finally John Orpheus. Even as the hope of love and stability was offered, I escaped instead to the all-consuming spaces I had created. I wanted to be devoured. I wanted to be reborn. I wanted those disguises to digest the frightened immigrant boy and spit out someone worthy.

We named him John, after John the Baptist and the Gospel of John ("And the Word was with God, and the Word was God") and the preacher Johnny Richardson, my great-grandfather, who was the pastor at Fifth Company Baptist Church and preached fire and brimstone, power and glory, while the congregation ketch powah and the teeming bush sang on like a tropical jungle choir.

And the deeper I went into John, the harder it became to be Tony.

## I I

The Hippy Mafia was the finishing school for John Orpheus. Before I could fully become J.O., I needed to experience a sliver of what I was chasing. I needed to see the dream made flesh. To this end, Mic Dainjah went on tour as the lead singer of the British band the Hippy Mafia. We toured with rock stars, ketching powah and getting a raw dose of the Queen's England, which had stalked my imagination since I was a schoolboy in the backwoods of the empire.

The best part about being in a Manchester rock 'n' soul band was the accents. Everything was a sing-song, with rhythms and melodies that turned regular words into gibberish. "Fookin 'ell, mate," "raaa-ight," "naice one, mate," "sort yuh knacker out," "dem jeans are the propah darrks," "got to polish de suedes, mate," "you aaight?," "I could murdah a curry," "not fookin avindat," "top geezah, dat one," "fucken muppets." It wasn't the Queen's English that I'd been taught. It was northern slanguage greased up with Irish and pronounced deep in the gullet. I spent a year trying to decipher what my bandmates were saying.

Gaz, our drummer, was the undisputed leader of our band. He was a joker at heart, a nervy, Irish-descended Mancunian with a Beatles haircut. "So how come you're a vegetarian?" I asked him once. He deadpanned from behind his shaded glasses: "You like to kill things, mate?" Gaz was a proper UK son of the stage. Since he was seventeen, his only job had been playing drums in a rock 'n' roll band. He'd lived the life I'd always craved but had never seen.

I had become his new band's singer over eleven tall cans of Guinness—"the black blood," as he called it. It was a rock and roll job interview. Both of us were plastered by the fourth round, but we kept going so as not to look like lightweights. Except that we were both lightweights. Gaz reported back to the rest of the band in England, "Well, hiz tunes are shite, but ee drinks like a fish." Which apparently meant that I was hired.

I was still in Kitchener and living off my BlackBerry severance. Touring with rock stars seemed like a great way to pass the time. I signed up right away.

"Right, then, we need a bass playah," Gaz declared. This was his way of asking me if I knew anyone cool enough to join our band. "No fookin white guys. We need a propah dreadlocked bass player, a Rasta." That's racist, I thought, but as it happened, I knew the perfect man for this job.

I introduced him to Fitz Dvyne. Fitz was a tall, dreadlocked Bajan, a fellow "West Can-Indian." He wasn't "long" as they say in the Caribbean to mean "slim and lanky," or "diesel" as hiphop heads say, meaning muscle-mag built, but something in between. His voice was deep and slow, his eyes wise and watching. "Yow, Dainjah, 'preciate the call to play in this band. Good looking out," and he gave me dap, a hand slap with a shoulder hug, and I felt like I had never left Scarborough. To me he was an impressive dude, he painted chiaroscuro blues singers and Black history heroes, his fabrics, his colours, his kicks were always flawlessly on point. And the biggest connection: he was a Caribbean kid who played in punk bands. So we got along.

It was a different feeling receiving respect and acceptance from a dope Black artist like Fitz. There was an understanding. Like seeing someone Black in a very white area, there's always a head nod, an encouraging grunt, a shared experience. For me he personified that feeling. "Run de Guinness," he answered in his smooth, low voice when Gaz asked if he'd "fancy a pint?" Gaz was thrilled. He'd grown up idolizing poetic, roots men, Caribbean dudes in England. Fitz was in and the band was getting Blacker. Perfect.

Gaz's connections landed us a gig opening for Beady Eye, which was the famous Brit pop band Oasis minus Noel Gallagher. I was flabbergasted. What?! We were going to open for Liam Gallagher? Oasis was one of the foundations of my rock 'n' roll dream in the 1990s. And brothers Noel and Liam had become legends: seventy-five million albums sold, massive acclaim, immense wealth, and earth-shattering star power.

But first we had to prove ourselves by opening the night at the Toronto stop of Beady Eye's North American tour. The show happened that summer at Sound Academy, a large club on the Toronto waterfront. We were enigmatic: black-shaded, dark-jeaned, suede shoes brushed and clean. We were Black. We were white. We were equal parts Manchester, Toronto, and the Caribbean. After the show, we hung out with Liam and the band. He was dressed in a leather jacket, his strong jaw framed on either side by tufts of hair like coutured horns. His eyes were clear and steady and light blue as lightning. A Titan made flesh. He said he had loved what we did. "We gotta get you lot over on tour in England in November." Yessir, Mr. Gallagher!

I was about to be tour-mates with one of my rock 'n' roll heroes.


III


I got a phone call from Al that fall.

"Hey, Michael, it's yuh father . . . Michael? . . . Boy, you there?" My breath stuck in my lungs. I was struck dumb. We hadn't spoken in more than six years. Ever since I had done the hard math and realized that no matter where I was, he would bring me down lower. "You there, boy?"

*Click.* I hung up.

My heart had no room. My life had no space for Al and the inevitable calamity that followed him. He'd left Gloria in Trinidad with the same promise he had given her almost thirty years before: "Once I get set up, I will send for yuh." Just like those early years, when my mother slept on a park bench with me in her arms, he forgot about her as soon as the plane took off. It was a full circle, complete in its callousness.

My parents had separated again. But being in touch with them was hard. It was easier to pretend they didn't exist. I'd had a lot of practice doing that, but being close to them and watching them fall apart were not things I knew how to do.

After our reunion in Trinidad, Gloria and I talked on the phone regularly. She was always having some problem that required me to send money. Just thinking about her made me weary. She didn't care about what I was doing, and I never sent her money again. Over time, the phone calls came less frequently but I still called her occasionally. Although I would never admit it, I still nurtured a dream that included her in my life, until one day, on one such a call I said:

"Hello, Miss Gloria."

"Miss Gloria? Who yuh callin' Miss Gloria? You need to show some respect. I am yuh muddah."

"Okay, sorry, Mom. How yuh going?"

"Things hawd. Things very, very bad for me. Yuh could stay Canada and hear I dead."

"Yuh see dem boy? Ronald, Cardo, and Kurt?"

"Yeah, dey good. Everybody good. Yuh could send a flat-screen for mih? Buy a flat-screen TV and send it for mih, nah?"

I chuckled before I even realized what I was doing.

"Yuh laughing? Why yuh laughing? Yuh see you, you nevah do nuthin for me. All these years. Yuh nevah do a damn thing for me. I don't have time to talk to you."

*Click.* She hung up.

## IV

England, the great Queen Motherland, changed me.

It felt like a return to places I had never been, a memory of things I had never known. It was all brand new, second-hand. But I had always known this land, hadn't I? The white cliffs of Dover, Buckingham Palace, Sandringham. Its pomp was my circumstance, its language the very blood and sinews of my mind, the tendons of my ambitions, the sauce that marinated my first thoughts.

From the back of a rental van, listening to dirty jokes and dub reggae and speeding past fields and neighbourhoods of ancient mouldy bricks, I saw this familiar country for the first time.

Is this the same place that Churchill said would never surrender? Are these the fields of Lancasters and Yorks? Of medieval carnage soaking the ground in pulpy, bloody death? Is this the England of Chaucer, Dickens, Wolsey, the Spice Girls, *Coronation Street*, and Ali G? This blessed plot, this earth, this realm, this England?

We were based in Manchester, where we rehearsed.

Fitz and his cousin Slay laughed their heads off. They woke up bussing jokes in English accents and went to bed cracking up about the day's events, which were somehow always hilarious. Mostly I stayed quiet and went for runs along laneways of mossy brick. The feeling of familiarity was surreal.

The tour loomed like a great crossroads in my life. Either all the daydreaming had been a waste of time or I was born to be on stage. I would either rise to the occasion or collapse. Ever since a fake Alice Cooper plucked me from the crowd as a mouthy little twelve-year-old, I had believed in the power of the stage to transform me. To sanctify all the awful away. To redeem my life into something worthy. I wanted to win. That defiant heart of mine wanted to return triumphant, like the conquering Roman general. Like Caesar, I wanted to win the grass crown.

The Beady Eye band was Liam's move to step away from his older brother's legacy. The rabid Oasis fans wanted to know whether Liam could do it on his own. For that reason, the tour meant a lot to both our bands. The security guards were the only other Black folks at almost all the shows. They would give me, Fitz, and Slay a nod of surprise, like "I see you, brother."

Eryn met me in Manchester and travelled in the van with us. She had been touring Europe on a trip she'd booked before we met. She was quiet and sweet as always, but it was weird to be reunited so far from home. We stayed at a hostel, laughed and fought and fucked and ate English breakfast with baked beans and delicious coffee. I inhaled her kisses deeply and ran my fingers through her hair, which was curly and yellow from the European sun.

Party-wise, the tour was a snooze. Liam disappeared immediately after each show and never drank or smoked. The boys would pull on strong joints of marijuana, sip short drinks, and chat in low voices while break-beat mixes played in the background. It was middle-aged-rock-star shit. And why not? They all had children and wives and were over forty. It wasn't the heady Oasis days of getting kicked off airplanes for demanding scones, crashing the Brit Awards wasted, snorting and cavorting and taking on the world one screaming stadium at a time.

"It's like I'm me dad," Liam said. "Drop the kids off. Peck the missus on the cheek. Off to the pub. It's like I'm me dad."

The final show was at Brixton Academy in South London. It was an old theatre with a sloping floor and windows high up so Juliet could look down on her Romeo. The walk to backstage was intimidating. Along the walls were pictures of artists on the very stage we would be gracing: Lauryn Hill, Dave Grohl, Smashing Pumpkins, and on and on. The photos were a reminder that this stage was hallowed and blessed.

After the show, Liam was actually partying for the first time, so there was a carnival atmosphere. There was one room for him and another filled with "the wives." The wives' room was packed with women, many of whom seemed vaguely famous. My mind was ablaze with booze and adrenaline, and I drifted naturally to the couch at the back. Liam's wife gushed: "You know, you were fabulous. So different!" She leaned in close enough to whisper and touched my wrist in a way that disarmed me. It was as if I had been blessed by royalty.

In the so-called men's room, there was Guinness and gallivanting galore. The intense pace of the tour detonated into a circus of fun. Music blasted from the outer room, and when I penetrated the chaos, I found Gaz and Liam holding court, banging on about how Coldplay was "utter shite."

"This is either the biggest thing I will ever do or the new normal," I said to myself with a headshake. England had been a waking dream.

Liam watched almost every set of ours from side-stage. "You're a fookin top front man, mate," he said to me. "Youse are special, and it's not just dat white-boy noise, right?"

Whatever you say, Mr. Gallagher. I had been too stunned to speak to him the whole tour.

Eryn didn't enjoy the final night. It was full of drugs and alcohol and celebrities, and I had all the access I wanted. Perhaps that was what frightened her. She seemed clingy and quiet, and she wanted to leave when the party had barely begun. A friend from Waterloo who was doing a PhD in neuroscience at Oxford offered us MDMA.

"I understand you don't do drugs," I said to her, "but this is good clean stuff. I tested it myself. If not tonight, then when?"

So I did it. I popped the molly and starting sweating.

Eryn was hurt and pissed off. My high and her anger crashed up against me all at once. She wanted to leave; I wanted to stay and soak it in. It was the biggest night of my life. My eyeballs were tingling, and the noise of the party buzzed like a hive in my temples. I realized that I had to choose: my girl or the stage. Of course there was no real choice. I stayed.

I put Eryn in a taxi to my friend's place, where we were sleeping, and stayed to bask in the champagne glow.

When I climbed out of Brixton Academy and into the back alley to wait for my cab, the party was long done. Wasn't Bowie born in Brixton? As I got lost in this thought, a lone fox trotted out of the fog, sniffed at me, unimpressed, then jogged off into the London night.

## Chapter Twenty-Four

# THE BALLAD OF
# JOHN AND YURI

I

I came back from England wanting to do one thing: get out of Kitchener. In the spring of 2012, Eryn and I both moved to downtown Toronto. She moved in with two of her best friends, and I moved in with Kwame on the word of Fitz: "Yow, Mic Deez, if I was gonna move in with anybody, it would be Kwame." Which was all the convincing I needed.

Kwame was a thick Black man in his forties, always hip to new music, always with a twinkle behind his thick black-framed glasses. He called other Black men "cat" and women "queens," and he welcomed me with open arms. Kwame loved to throw parties. He was a scientist in the art of bringing people together. His parties were loud, bouncing affairs and he met folks at the door. "Mah brutha, mah sister, the dance floor is cooking," he'd say, aglow with gregariousness. "No stiffs, no squares, no wallflowers."

Kwame was a Black Scotian—which is what we called Black Nova Scotians—and he was always introducing me to cool Black people. "Mic Dainjah, aka John Orpheus, is a baaaaad man! He plays bass, raps, tours with rock stars, and rumour has it, he will cross you up on a ball court! Beware!"

Drummers, comedians, painters, DJs, lawyers, entrepreneurs, all fly ebony intelligentsia. He was my passport to a constellation of Black stars shining. There was oxtail and plantain from the kitchen, and the music he played was a cauldron of everything ecstatic and Black. There was an old school soul set, a soca set, a dancehall set, a 1990s hip-hop set. Earth, Wind & Fire side by side with Buju Banton, Machel Montano, Biggie Smalls, and Fela Kuti. It was a whole galaxy of Black music cooked up in a stew, a pelau, and if you didn't watch yourself, it would swallow the entire evening in sweat, hoarse throats screaming their joy.

With few exceptions, I had lived my life as a minority ever since I'd left Trinidad. For those few hours of rapture, I could finally be West Indian, Black, and Canadian in one space. And set all them free to rejoice. It was nourishing.

Eryn sat silently by the fire, intimidated at being the only white person at the party. "They don't like me," she said sullenly. "It's weird being in a room of people where I'm a minority."

I couldn't leave the irony alone. "You mean, like how I feel every time we hang out with your friends?"

The question hung tensely in the air between us.


11


"I'm bringing balance to the force," I answered when Nigel asked about my new job in Toronto.

"Huh? Like Star Wars?"

"Exactly."

We were sitting on his living room couch, tucked away in the suburbs of Brampton. Nige was looking round and happy.

"Usually when people meet lawyers, they hand over thousands of dollars. My new job is to get the lawyers to hand *me* thousands of dollars."

Nigel smiled, and his chipmunk-cheek dimples pushed out.

"And they hate it," I concluded with a grin.

My new job was a sixty-hour-per-week grind in the heart of Toronto's financial district. In my dress clothes and blazer, I spent the days calling, emailing, and meeting with barristers and solicitors and selling them technology. Which is a lot like trying to sell vegetables to a kid with a sweet tooth. They needed it, but they had no idea why they should want it. My job was to provide the why.

"So should we call you Antonio or Michael?" my new boss at the Bay Street tech firm asked.

A difficult question at this point. We were sitting in the tiny boardroom, and I was trim and shiny in my new blazer and pants. I didn't mention that I could legitimately be called any of three other names too: Tony, Mic Dainjah, and John Orpheus. But none of these were appropriate for the boardroom.

My new boss had printed off our emails to show me that we'd agreed to meet at 1:00 p.m. and not 1:30. It was important to him. A forty-something, somewhat-white, somewhat-brown man in a suit and glasses, he had the practical air of an IT guy with a lawyer's love of details. He would be tough and candid, and he would hold me accountable. I would always know where I stood. Working in sales felt like performing: another room, another stage, another mask.

Nigel and his new partner, Corrine, lived five minutes from her parents' house and from each of her three siblings. They were tight-knit and loyal to a fault—Nigel's kind of people. Nigel, like his mother, Ami, loved totally and forever.

Well, almost forever. He had married the first woman he ever dated, and now he was living with the second. The strangest conversation we ever had was when he called to inform me that he'd cheated on his first wife and had left her for Corrine. It was the most un-Nigel thing to do. Which is why I didn't question it. He had to have had a good reason, I thought.

This was a pivotal moment in the life of SuperNige. Ami had taught him to love forever, and he followed her example right into a miserable marriage. He could have spent his life there, but when the time came, he took a page out of Al's book and jumped ship for the sake of his own happiness. He broke both their cycles. Nigel was always clever with the heart's arithmetic.

III

Death, Gada and I would say, is the perfect way to start a career in show business. So when we decided to invent John Orpheus, killing him was an obvious first step. Gada emailed: "Can you send me the backstory for J.O.? We need to know who he is."

My response to her was taken from one of my journals, which I still kept as my diaries and workbooks. The John Orpheus description rings loudly with familiar names and places: Trini (my first atrocity, the void, Miss Excelly, airport drama, rumbos and wakes, Larry and Dexter); Wabigoon (the ice, Billy); Sioux Lookout (Adge and Nige, powwow); Thunder Bay (basketball, Mr. Yaciuk); Scarborough

(Al and Hailey); New York (Westbury, Agnes); Cambridge (Benfoot, Coach Wyman, Coach Lillie).

The best lies often begin with truth. So becoming John Orpheus started with becoming Tony all over again. Gada called them my cornerstones: "You have these fragments of stories that are like cornerstones of your life. Your grandma singing, you running away, the bush, you and your brother pretending to be preachers. They're so clear. This is where we have to start."

The movie script she wrote around the character of John Orpheus was a dystopia. In the not-so-distant future, iconic, eccentric pop star John Orpheus and his lover, Yuri Orsi, a wispy savant who never wore pants, chat, confuse, and champagne their way into a violent protest movement. Police then mortally wound J.O., but his adoring fans, rather than helping him, whip out their phones to post pictures on social media.

As Yuri declares, "Everyone interesting is hooked on fantasy."


IV


"Will you stop introducing me as Mike?" I asked, yawning, when I answered the door for Eryn. Her knocking had woken me up again. She worked at an upscale restaurant a block away. It was eleven thirty; she had got away early. "In Toronto, it's John."

"Why can't you just be yourself?" she said, curling up her mouth sourly as she did every time I spoke about the movie we were making. Something about it made her implacably insecure.

"Which self?"

I sighed hard as she concentrated on folding her work apron. Not another fight, she seemed to be saying.

I preached at her: "When you're at work, you dress and talk one way. When you're on the town with the girls, you dress and talk another way. A family gathering? Same thing. A wedding? Same thing. Everyone is always changing clothes and becoming new people. I just give mine names."

January had turned her hair less blonde and more straight. I reached for a stray strand and carefully tucked it behind her ear. For a moment, her stony blue eyes softened.

"I have to do this. Can't you just trust me?"

Her eyes hardened and narrowed again. "No. You don't."

As we curled up in bed, her sleepy voice asked, "When will this movie thing be done?"

"I don't know," I said. Shit, why do I always sound defensive about this? We both sighed and released our bodies' tension into the waiting arms of sleep.


V


Sabotage is sexier than commitment.

On my birthday, June 3, 2013, Eryn walked in on me having sex with another woman. Sofia was a charismatic Spanish singer I knew through mutual friends. We sang at her kitchen table in the east end, and I was captivated by her fiery style. I didn't mention that I had a girlfriend.

On my birthday, with Eryn working a block away, Sofia dropped by to surprise me.

"Do you want to hang out for your birthday?"

"Nah, I'm busy. Maybe another time?"

"But I got you a present."

The present was a bottle of wine, which I felt obliged to drink with her. Then I felt obliged to kiss her. I did this knowing that Eryn would arrive at any moment. It was an act of such brazen stupidity that I have come to believe some part of me wanted to be caught. From my room, the lights muted, the heat of Sofia's nipples against my ribs, the sound of her gasping in my ear, I heard the front door unlock.

The next few minutes were as sordid and predictable as all such breakups go. Eryn determined to see me exposed, me furious to stay hidden. All our lies dissolved. All our illusions melted. The dark of my room versus the light she would let in; the person I wanted to be versus the mess that I was. Then, suddenly, she gave up. Sobbing and despondent, she walked away. Sitting on my bookshelf was the unsigned lease to our new place. It had sat there for weeks. I was scared to sign it. Eryn's mom said after, "I knew he wasn't going to sign it." I was afraid that I didn't know how to be with someone that way. That it would all fall apart. Or more likely, I was afraid that I would have to stop living so selfishly. It was a classic Al move: when the home, the stability I had told myself I wanted for so long was within my grasp, I sabotaged it so I could run away.

It took us almost three months to actually break up. Neither of us wanted to let go but the memories of that night echoed loudly in our heads. When we did break up that September, within a few days, Eryn's dad was diagnosed with late-stage lung cancer. The next time I saw her was at his funeral six weeks later. I walked to the front, hugged her family members one by one, and then took a seat behind them. That's what families do: they show up.

But I was sitting on the outside again, close enough to understand what family did but still infinitely far away.

## Chapter Twenty-Five

# *NIGRUM NIGRIUS NIGRO*

I

"That's your niece," Auntie Joan said when I asked who the young teenage girl was.

"And who is that baby she's holding?" I was hoping to goodness it wasn't hers.

"That's your sister, Eve."

Al, at sixty-three, had made up for alienating all his older children by creating new ones, and the teenager who was holding my new baby sister was apparently Junior's daughter. Junior had never acknowledged her before. This was our first-ever sort-of family reunion.

It was the Christmas before Eryn and I broke up. Auntie Joan, the family matriarch, was moving to Toronto, and we had all assembled to welcome her. Ray, Uncle Boysie's son, was there, grey and beer-bellied, looking like his dad. He still talked slow and in a heavy Trini accent, just as he had when he first landed in Aurora and suffered the wrath of Hailey the Hellcat. He had Boysie's everything.

Auntie Joan seemed to have jogged her way into immortality.

A lifetime of the Adventist way—vegan, no booze, no smoking—had left her a stately, energetic, and clear-headed seventy-year-old.

"Yuh not going to church, boy?"

"No, Auntie Joan."

"Yuh get too big for church? Remember they that wait upon the Lord shall—"

"Run and not be weary. Yes, Auntie Joan."

"Your grandmother's prayers are still watching over you."

"Yes, Auntie Joan."

Then in came Al, dreadlocked, belly round from beer, and smiling his schoolboy-prankster smile, but with a few missing teeth.

"Heya, kid," he said sheepishly.

"Al, how yuh going?" I said, then retreated to the living room before he could answer. I kept my distance.

What had become of the trim, clean-shaven, Jheri-curled super-man I had known? Al looked round, fattened like a calf, his beard grey and unruly, his head full of dreads, clean but tangled. He also looked unburdened, almost peaceful.

Aunt Joan and Eryn met—my two worlds collapsing into one.

"I'm so scared to meet her," Eryn had said beforehand. "You make her sound so scary."

"Do I? Don't worry, she talks like a schoolmaster but she's harmless."

They met and my aunt watched her with a cool eye, her face giving away nothing. "A very special girl," she told me after. She had given up advising me to find a good Adventist girl or a nice church girl or a pretty Black girl. At this point, she was just happy to see me stable. A small victory for stubborn Tony.

Al cradled baby Eve with adoration. His daughter was around the same age as Adrian's twins, Al's grandchildren. He held her in the crook of his arm, her soft neck turning, her chubby little fingers stretching up to brush our father's face.

Watching how attentive and doting he was with Eve, I wondered if he was trying to make up for all the nurturing he had failed to give us. Jealousy rippled through me. Where was this for me? Where was this for Nigel? Where was this for any of us? And yet, I understood it. After a life of abandoning his kids, Al had a blank slate with Eve, a chance for redemption. I watched how carefully he laid her down on the bed to change her. Those clever hands gently tucking her in for a nap. I resented it, but I understood it. I, too, longed for redemption.

That image of him felt like a premonition of future me. I asked myself, Is this where I'm gonna end up? A sixty-three-year-old with a toddler? The thought made me shudder.

Junior never acknowledged that the young girl was his daughter, never named her mother. Gloria said he was ashamed because her mother was a white girl and a notorious big-mouth, but who knew? When I asked him about it, he got angry and I let it be.

This was my family. This was the patchwork of broken things that had spawned me. No matter how much I ran, how much I pretended, who I toured with, how many songs I sang, or how many fans admired me, I could never escape this: the absent fathers, the children scattered. The bush. The brimstone and the King James Bible.

Eryn and I instinctively found each other. We clasped hands. She was nervous. I was overwhelmed. At least we had each other. But this, too, was not to last.

## 11

Life returned to normal, but nothing was the same.

In the months after Eryn and I split, in the winter of 2013, I was still working at my corporate sales job, talking lawyers out of their money, and still living with Kwame in Toronto's Entertainment District.

Hippy Mafia had fallen apart over money, but I was busy working with Gada on the album and movie we would call *John Orpheus Is Dead.*

Despite all the activity, I felt hollow, pitted. It was the feeling of living with what I'd done. I was as empty as the oil drum after I'd killed my brother's fish. "What is wrong with you, child?" I heard my grandmother asking across the empty alley off Queen Street West. As I reached the top of my staircase, I thought of Eryn that night, her mouth twisted, her face boiling with anguish and tears. What is wrong with you, child? I muttered to myself again.

Eryn was more than a girlfriend. She was my last chance to feel fully human.


My room is a wizard's lair. Three guitars hang from a stand like conjurers' staffs. I have only one small shelf so I stack my books on the floor, chapters on top of chapters, like condos made of pages, like spellbooks promising wisdom. By the windowsill, hard black journals, Bic pens, and headphones. My walls are pasted with posters and pictures of bands and tours, and above the bed, enshrined and elevated, are the faces of my family.

In one picture, taken in 2008 at his wedding, Nigel is buried under a hug from me and Adrian. Our arms enfold each other like overlapping roots of a giant tree, our faces are joy unleashed. In another, taken in 1992, Ami, Nigel, Adrian, and I stare out of a posed studio portrait, our various heights arranged into a perfect family diamond, mother and her baby-faced teen boys. In 1989, Al is crouching among all of us, swagger and smiles. Teenage Junior is also there. Al's eyes, as always, are filled with chaos.

I fall asleep to fierce dreams. Running, always running. Savage things calling me, hunting me down. Wings that won't fly. Guns that won't shoot. Legs turning slowly into heavy planks that anchor me to a land of nightmares. A raft, a river that trickles and then widens to a flow, hungry creatures submerged in the water. Soon they will tip me over and there will be no way out.

When I wake up, the city is full of terror. Even the traffic lights go dim. The family faces on the wall become phantoms leering at me. My chest is kicking stallions at my ribs; the whole night is hissing, a dull, sizzling ring. I'm breathing shallow and fast, brisk and sudden. Panic seizes me stiff. I am certain of my complete aloneness.

When I fall asleep again, the river has spilled me into the sea. The night roars with thunder. Far from land, the bottomless merlot-coloured sea, pitching and heaving, endless and indifferent. The waves rise up towering and crash down with omnipotence, smashing my existence into bits.

Awake again. The clock says 6:22.

I force myself to go for a run. January whips me like a dominatrix. It is raining, a heavy, sleety kind of rain, the dangerous kind that freezes suddenly and ices the world. My head is swimming in a soup of dark thoughts, my guts scrambled with creamy rose tequila, IPA beer, and blue vodka cocktails. I pump my arms, lift my knees, and run as if I can chase down hope.

Down John Street, over the Union Station tracks, around SkyDome, onto Queen's Quay, and east towards Cherry Beach along the grey, mushy shoreline to land at the bridge that lifts to let ships through. There, wet and soaked through to the bone, I yell King Lear at the storm: "Blow, winds, and crack your cheeks! Rage! Blow!" I scream until my throat shreds.

There is nothing left of me, just the raw, unpasteurized spite I have for the universe.

And yet I turn around, check the time, and point my knees towards home. If I run hard enough, I might just catch up to the person I hope to be.

I have to admit that I have lost all control of my life.

## III

Junior called me, sounding buoyant and full of jokes. "We should plan on going back to Trinidad, man. We have to reconnect with we roots." This is what he always says when he is happy.

That Christmas, 2015, I flew to Vancouver to see him. He had married a Hispanic woman, and they lived together in a small, neat apartment while the sky over the Rockies and the Pacific frowned down on them and soaked the streets with never-ending rain.

"Papi," which is what she called him, "are we gonna go to church tonight?" They attended a non-denominational church three times a week. Junior worked construction. He helped build condominiums. His hands were steady and strong, and he looked jailhouse fit.

I couldn't stop smiling. So many years had separated us. Being close to him, I felt like I had plugged into another lung and was able to fully breathe again.

There was no alcohol in the house. Substances were a no-no. Junior still attended his weekly Narcotics Anonymous meetings for recovering addicts and had a circle of support buddies.

"We just hold each other accountable, yuh know?" His mouth twisted and his brow knotted. "We get together outside the meeting sometimes and just talk and keep each other up." It reminded me of the John Howard Society. All those rough men learning how face themselves. Junior sounded like he could lead the class. "It's not the substance that hooks you, it's the emotions," he explained. "There is a crack somewhere in our spirits, and we have to heal that before anything."

Not long after that, he had a relapse.

He called me, insisting he needed me to send him money right away. His wife called me separately: "Don't send your brother any money." Aunt Joan called soon after: "Don't send him any money." Then the calls stopped. I felt terrible for him. I tried to picture him lost in some hellish place, some dungeon, some hole he couldn't get out of. A horror show on repeat. It broke my heart. I couldn't fathom that tough spirit being broken. But I knew how good we all were at pretending. I knew there was nothing anyone could do for Junior until he was ready to do something for himself.

When he eventually got back on his feet, Auntie Joan paid for him to go to a therapist for the first time in his life. She said it helped him tremendously. "That boy said, 'Auntie Joan, you saved my life.'"

Yet he didn't call me for a while. He felt ashamed. When he did call, I was relieved to have him back, to hear that warm certainty in his voice, and to know which number to reach him at.

"I'm sorry, you know, for that little bad time I had." He was struggling with his shame.

"Nothing to apologize for," I said. "I'm just happy you're all right now, you know?" I could feel him relax on the other side of the phone.

"The psychologist was the best thing that ever happened to me. Just to talk about everything: the family, Al, Gloria. Everything." He sounded hopeful.

"Yeah, I been a few times. It's helpful."

"Did you know dem boys had molested me?"

"Who?" I was stunned, breathless.

"Some big boys from down the hill."

"Not Dexter and Larry? Did you tell Mama?"

"No, only Auntie Joan knew. I didn't tell anyone. Just she."

My brain was flipped upside down. There was no direction up. I was surprised but not surprised. Was this what was eating at Junior all this time? His darkness had a source too: this bottomless evil covering both our lives. Where was Al? Where was Gloria? What did they have to do that was so important they weren't there to protect us? Aunt Joan knew?

I inventoried my head and found a frightening cloud stretching back to the tall grass and the wind. How much wasted life had my brother spent fighting these demons? How much had all of us paid?

The wide expanse of hurt opened up before me and seemed to stretch back forever. So many bodies, so much flesh. So many scars that cannot be seen. I wept silently.

"You're a lion," I finally said. "You're the strongest person I've ever known."


IV


At first, my therapist told me nothing.

His voice was a steady call that lulled me into spilling the beans. We met in a small, dim room just off busy Bloor Street and Avenue Road. I'd hustle to get there on my lunch break, a light glaze of sweat soaking my shirt from dashing up the subway stairs three at a time.

It was our regular time, one hour every week that I spent pouring out the entire sordid tale of my being. Massive monsoons of stories. I told my life frantically, eyes fixed on nothing, reeling off towns and family names and tragedies as if hypnotized.

It took three weeks, but finally, during the fourth session, he stared at me and said: "You should be proud of yourself."

"Huh?" That was not what I was expecting.

"By the stats on people who survive things like this, you should not be doing nearly as well as you are."

I was immediately skeptical. This is what he's paid to say, right?

I was apparently a poster child for what happens to adults after childhood trauma: poor impulse control, difficulty controlling emotions, shame and guilt, feelings of hopelessness, sleep disorders, depression, sexual compulsiveness. The list was much longer, but those were my particular poisons.

"I would say that your grandmother and your art are what saved you," the therapist continued at the next session. "Art is sometimes the most effective therapy. All this music and writing you've been doing was not discretionary. You needed to do it. You needed it to survive."

Art was my cure? I did it to hide, to belong, to let out the fury inside, to be the *nigrium nigrius nigro*. But as I dashed to catch the subway, the thought rang through me like a giant bell tolling: while I was busy hiding from myself, words and music had saved me.

I was still living off an old lady's prayers.


V


I lived in Toronto's Entertainment District, the rowdiest part of town, but when I rose every morning to run before work, it was usually silent and empty except for a nasty cutting wind and the early garbage trucks on Wednesdays.

Over and over I ran in the cold before dawn.

I ran hard, but I never seemed to catch the thing I was chasing. Frozen air stabbing at my lungs, wind biting at my cheeks, body screaming at the morning, mind turning over and over in every direction—this was my penance. This was the price my body had to pay for redemption.

Gradually, things got better. In the grey gloom of the evening, when I awoke in complete panic, I would smile. This panicking time would happen every night, but now instead of fearing it, I embraced it. "Welcome," I would say. "There you are, buddy. So glad you could make it." And I felt like I could hear the colossal symphony of the darkened canefield. The gloom, the weight, the emptiness, the sheer terror of being completely alone. It felt familiar, like the spots on a lover's skin. I started to become detached and still.

Is this why Miss Excelly rose up so early to pray? Was she too fighting hordes of devils she could not see?

"Miss Excelly . . . " The thought of her cooled my skin, and goose bumps swelled up across my naked shoulder. "Well, girl, ah don't know if you can hear me, but ah know what yuh would say: 'De race is not for de swift nor de battle for de strong, but he who persevere shall see de victory.'" I had never spoken to her like this before. But it made sense.

Maybe I was just Al with no jail cell. Maybe I was just Gloria throwing another selfish tantrum. Maybe I would never be anything more than the scraps they had left for me. Or maybe none of this mattered. I would wake up tomorrow and still be alive, and just like my grandmother, I would have to get myself up and crack on.

My chest filled with breath. Inhale. Count to twenty. Exhale. Count to twenty. Then twenty-five. Then thirty. Then I let go. I let go of myself. I let go of my cravings. I let go of my shame. I let go of everything, and yet somehow I felt connected to everything: to the city humming quietly outside, to the faces of bands and brothers staring at me from my walls, to the night and the solitude and the great reeking mess we all must endure.

The void seemed a little less lonely then.

VI

My new therapist saw only men.

"You're addicted to sex," he declared firmly. He specialized in helping men who had suffered sexual trauma as young boys. "That's my opinion from everything you have told me. How many women are you sleeping with? What do you think this means?"

His uptown office looked south towards the Toronto skyline. We hovered in a noisy corner with jackhammers whining beneath us. Yet being twenty-seven floors up felt peaceful. The view offered a panorama of the city; from the forest of skyscrapers to the condos of nouveau riche Mississauga, the city spread out before us.

"It sounds like you blame yourself for what happened. But look at this."

With a black Sharpie, he drew a pyramid and labelled them from the foundation to the pinnacle: "Rape –> Powerlessness –> Insecure masculinity –> Sexual orientation confusion –> Isolation, a struggle to trust in relationships –> Sexual compulsivity, addiction." His pyramid exposed my compulsions. He had drawn a straight line from my shame to my trauma.

"Is any of this resonating with you?"

"A lot of it."

I felt as though he had exposed the monster lurking at my core. He had explained my relationships with women and with music. Like my brothers and my father, I was always trying to be good enough. Yet whenever I was given the choice between family and more attention, meaningless sex always won.

My dad and brother snorted and smoked the white lady; I dated her. And it had all begun that day in Monkeytown, over a bag of peanuts.

I'd spent my life pretending that I'd never been raped. Yet such facts do not disappear because we ignore them. They feed and grow fat on our avoidance. A part of me was still stuck in that Trini bush, listening to the tall grass, floating above the smell of the broken stalks. There was a part of me that had never left that grass.

That night I did something I rarely did: I read through my old journals. I had kept them since 1989, twenty-four hardcover books marked up in pen and pencil and marker like arcane spellbooks. They were the Bible of me. And the Word was God. They were filled with my thoughts, feelings, ideas, poems, sketches, storyboards, fantasies, dreams, memories—the full inventory of my presence on this planet. I had never looked back like this.

There were frightening poems about being chased by creatures in the grass. Savage, murky things that took many shapes and filled me with terror. Haiku obsessions. Anne Frank diary drama. Prayers to Caesar. Pep talks. Dark things lurking between great splotches of ink. My journals were a mirror, a window. Together they formed a portrait of my struggle to articulate myself into something coherent. And it was equal parts Miss Excelly—songs, psalms, and prayers—and the Queen—sonnets, plays, and soliloquys.

It made me weep. It made me hold my head and bawl for the confused child I had been. I wanted to reach out and hold him in my arms. I wanted to tell him that he would be okay, to stay calm, to pay attention and show up. I wanted to love him the way he had always hoped someone would love him.

I fell asleep amid those pages, but my last thoughts were clear: Something had to change. Everything had to change.

Somewhere deep in my belly, a little hardened boy started to believe.

## Chapter Twenty-Six

# PLAYING MAS

I

I had a diagnosis, but what was the cure? Overwhelmed by this question, I started speeding up into manic mode again. I stayed up, hiding from sleep, bathing in gin cocktails, singing in four bands, having vacuous sex, sex that hollowed me out, sex that left my skin crawling. Then I'd change into suit pants and blazer and smile my way through the boardrooms of the Financial District. I felt shattered, like splinters of myself, like a mouthful of dust.

How do you reframe an entire life spent cornered by something as horrible as rape? Under the influence of something so toxic and malign? The answer, like all good endings, was to go back to the beginning. To remember who I was before I'd caught the rapists' eyes. To recall the thing they could not crush. The answer was to become Tony again. And the idea originated from the most unlikely of sources.

———

Howard was a short, middle-aged Jewish man with a wispy Afro and a grin like a co-conspirator. He came up to me after a Jen Militia show in 2008, when Mic Dainjah was a hot mess of sweat and breathlessness. "Wow. Just amazing," he said in his sweet nasal voice. "So many things come to mind: Public Enemy, Red Hot Chili Peppers. Just wow!" He wore a patterned red-and-white shirt and hundred-watt white jeans and sneakers. He looked like he was on his way to a Caribbean fete.

"So you're from Trinidad, eh?"

"Yeah, New Grant. Down south," I answered, wondering if he had any clue where that was.

"I only got as far as Princes Town, but I love soca. I go to Trinidad all the time for Carnival. You must really love this year's soca songs!"

This was embarrassing. This eccentric Torontonian knew more about what was happening in Trini culture than I did. So I went for my go-to move.

"You know, I went to school with Machel Montano." By this point, Machel, the little kid I had spent a few months with in Trinidad, had become the greatest soca singer of all time. His first name was all you needed to identify him. Howard was impressed.

"You went to school with Machel?! Incredible! Tell me more . . . "

I had no idea that this conversation was the beginning of my becoming a Caribbean man again. After that night, Harold took me to soca shows with names like "Soca or Die 7." I was ashamed to admit it, but my own culture was so unfamiliar to me that being surrounded by it made me nervous. Years later, though, after my catastrophic breakup with Eryn and in the middle of my midlife meltdown, Howard and I found ourselves in Barbados. And this activated something in me.

The party was Crop Over, the Bajan version of Trinidad's Carnival. Soca music was booming in all directions, while sweat, mud, paint, and rum fuelled the tens of thousands of people partying in the streets. From the time we landed, I became fully Trini again. My mind was set ablaze: "You mean I can just talk like a Trini?" It was on. It brought me back to my beginnings. It brought me back to life.

The maddest portion of Crop Over was an all-night street party called Foreday Morning. Howard and I met around ten o'clock and jumped into the crowd of people fete-ing behind the truck with our colours: a bright yellow bag, T-shirt, and drinking mug emblazoned with a blue Roman eagle and the words "Caesar's Army." Which, of course, made me feel like I was in the right place. Behind the truck, people were dousing themselves in mud and paint, and the sound system was already blaring that year's soca hits. Then the insanity began. We rolled through the streets of Bridgetown, thousands strong. Girls in skimpy bathing suits, asses out, dancing and enticing; men shirtless and flexing. Our heads were on fire with the sizzling energy of the night and the hot breeze blowing in off the Caribbean Sea.

Abandon. Liberation. Bacchanal.

When the party goes from incredible to insanity, we bawl out "Bacchanal!" for Bacchus, the Roman god of wine and song. European myths and dark-skinned bodies—what could be more Caribbean than that?

The real playing mas happened the following Monday. As in Trinidad, it was a pageant held under blistering sun, music pounding in the road and people in costumes, colourful and elaborate, marching through the streets in broad daylight. It was a rushing river of bodies and colours: peacock-bright feathers and the full palate of the flora and fauna of the bush, but also the devil's horns, the goat's hooves, the bloody red body paint. A Bacchic, primordial, reckless kind of ecstasy dissolved Black and brown and white and made Africa and India and Europe the same place. God lived in heaven, but the Devil lived everywhere else.

"Yuh fraid de devil? Jab Jab! Yuh fraid him bad? Jab Jab! Well, look de devil—Jab Jab!—right in yuh yard." And he could drink rum, gyrate half naked, scream and carry on, dress up and misbehave. The devil was all the fun things.

I learned that there were similar carnivals in Grenada, Cuba, Guadeloupe, Miami, New York, Berlin, and London, as well as, of course, our Toronto Caribana festival. Everywhere there was a Black diaspora, there was a carnival thriving. It made me feel like I was swimming in that river and that it had no bounds, that it reached back into the smudgy depths of time and across the broad landscapes of space.

Playing mas made me think that this is what it felt like for a slave to be free, to hold nothing back, to lose himself in an electrical storm of firing synapses. This is what it felt like to forget the master's rules, the insecurity, the struggle to fit in, the ghosts calling from the cemetery, the preacher in my head wailing. Playing Mas allowed me to become myself. To bypass my trauma and to reconnect with the lost ancestry coded into my hardy hips, my plum smooth skin, the thickness in my ass and lips, my voice, my blood. It allowed me to be free.

This was Mic Dainjah's madness, Molasses's raging poetry made flesh. John Orpheus, the prodigal son, returned and redeemed. For the first time in my adult life, I felt complete.

The Soca Monarch finals that year shocked me. This was a massive concert watched by thousands and broadcast live on radio and TV. The singer Red Plastic Bag, who had already taken the crown more than any other act, was favoured to win. For Bag's second song, "Royal Visit," he brought out the Queen herself. Decked out in white dress, handbag, and tiara, she trotted about and waved at the crowd maternally. I was stunned. If this had been Port of Spain or Kingston, half the audience would boo and hiss, but the Bajans went wild. They loved it. Bag won another crown that year.

That night, as we careened down a country road on our way to yet another fete, I put down the van window and stuck my head out into the darkness. It was a Caribbean bush, which meant it was alive with the symphony of critters and smelled fresh and endless.

We went to Crop Over every year until Howard passed away in 2015. Each time we flew home, I returned a little more whole, a little more rooted, a little more comfortable in my skin. A little boy inside me was grinning himself silly.

## Chapter Twenty-Seven

# JOHN ORPHEUS
# IS DEAD

I

John Orpheus died on Devil's Night 2014, the night before Halloween.

It was not his first death, nor would it be his last. He died as only a performer would: under hot lights and ovations, covered in sequins and sweat. He died for the only reason a performer should: to feel alive.

In a stairwell topped by a door leading to the stage, Gada fussed over my eyeliner with one hand as firm as a claw and the other as delicate as an artist's brush. Her electric-blue eyes were dancing. She wore leather pants, and her bare cleavage was lined with gold spikes. Her round face was painted with glitter and framed with blonde. This was Gada Jane: my Dr. Frankenstein. She had built me from the ground up. She wrote the script, shot the film, designed the clothes, and was about to dance backup in the show. But first, she needed to make sure my makeup was on point. This Queen designed my face.

The character of John Orpheus had completely taken over my life. Most of my friends had no idea my birth name was not John. J.O. was a contradiction, a hyper-masculine man who wore lady's sunglasses and bracelets. A grimy punk rapper who preferred sequins and glitter. The movie and the music bled into each other. Actresses danced and sang at Orpheus concerts; John O's video shoots played out as scenes in the movie. It had taken us nearly five years to birth this charming abomination. Gada blew on the embers of my own messy story, and we cobbled together a character, a fever dream, a champion of both our imaginations. And on this night, as we were releasing his album, he was finally ready for his close-up.

Being a shady bitch, I was fussing right back at Gada. The show was late, the soundcheck too short, the band a hot mess. Would enough people show up that I could pay the musicians? In my mind, this was all somehow Gada's fault. I needed someone to blame for all of it, and she was the one who'd chosen to be there. I sulked as she focused. This was what I did at every show—I channelled my stress into a snippy, petty place while the tension of what was to come hatched in my belly.

It began as a funeral procession. In a blood-red cloak that dragged ominously, flanked by furies wearing gold spiked bras and followed by the solemn band, I entered. We walked at a wedding-march pace, as if we were on the way to marry the devil. Emilee, a svelte, alluring young woman, walked in front, carrying my totem: a motorcycle helmet bedazzled with gemstones.

Picture Lady Gaga as a Black Baptist preacher and there you have it. The music was a cauldron of energy and pop. The lyrics brimmed with sex and death. The show careened out of control, somewhere between Johnny Rotten and John the Baptist. The spectacle ended suddenly when I collapsed backwards into the waiting arms of my pallbearers. They covered me in the cloak and carried my corpse out on their shoulders.

It was messy, but it was a good death.

"Give him a mask, and he will tell you the truth," said Oscar Wilde, another clever boy from an island colonized by the Crown. Playing mas had been scorched into my consciousness as a child. The mask was the slave's freedom. Whether in Rio, Barbados, or Port of Spain, the act of becoming was an act of revelation. I had put on a costume so I could show the world who I really was.

Before the show, Gada slipped me a handwritten letter, which I unsealed later that night:

> Dear John, my brother and my friend,
> I wanted to write to congratulate you on how far
> we have come and wish you the best for tonight.
> The Christening. The Baptism. The Beginning . . .
> I remember the child who was running away
> through the bush in the dark, the man who told
> me in the kitchen about his dreams of Caesar and
> his grandmother. Let that person always be the
> centre, and remember that though J.O. is a gift, you
> are enough on your own. Always remember that
> J.O. was meant to serve the person, Mic Dainjah,
> Antonio Michael Downing, Tony.

## I I

There was not much traction for the *John Orpheus Is Dead* album.

The Devil's Night show was supposed to celebrate its launch. We supported it with a press campaign and a college radio campaign, and I sent a Grim Reaper in my blood-red cloak to deliver hand-signed invitations to a music industry rep who chuckled but didn't show up. It was supposed to be a coming-out, but it felt more like a falling-down.

Rock stations said, "Too urban for our audience," while hip-hop blogs countered, "This isn't rap enough for us." Once again, I was simultaneously too Black and not Black enough.

My grand ambitions as a musician had failed. Jen Militia, Hippy Mafia, and this first attempt at John Orpheus had all broken down. There would be more successful incarnations of J.O. later, but in the months following, it was hard not to feel deflated. Like basketball, music was more than just a job or a creative outlet for me—it was redemption. It was the dream that was born in Sioux Lookout with the fake Alice Cooper and his boa constrictor. If I could just be successful, wouldn't everyone forgive me? Wouldn't I finally feel good enough? Wouldn't I finally feel at home?

In two short weeks, I had spent my entire life savings to launch the album, only to watch it crash and burn. I was thirty-nine years old. The music business was a demanding, fickle mistress. Junior's words about doing crack came ringing back to me: "At first it was peaceful, but then the peace would fly away faster and faster, until there wasn't no peace, just doing it to do it."

How long could I keep doing this?

Six months later, when we launched the *John Orpheus Is Dead* movie, it was Gada's turn to show and tell. Four years in the making, *JOIsD*, as we called it, had consumed our time. It was all we had ever done together. We had no idea how to hang out, have fun, or talk about something trivial. We were always planning a show, a movie shoot, a recording session. We started as pretend siblings, but by the end of it, the sweat and struggle had bonded us forever.

I hid outside as the movie had its first and only public viewing in Canada, at a theatre in downtown Kitchener. Gada couldn't stop smiling after. And I couldn't have been happier for her. How stunning she was, clad head to toe in black leather, gaudy gold chains dangling. I felt like we had swum an ocean and had by some miracle survived to see the other shore. We had made it.

The after-party was at my old place in downtown Kitchener. In between cocktails and congratulations, I smoked a blunt with my young Eritrean homie, then slipped out the back door to the deck. I sat down in the same shaky lawn chair where I'd written *Molasses*.

"That is high-low hang jack game to goooooo!" I cackled at the moon, remembering the old All Fours saying. Then I slammed some imaginary cards down as hard as I could.

The trees whipped and roared in the wind, and my smile floated up into the darkened sky.

III

In winter 2015, we were sitting in Junior's van in Vancouver as raindrops pounded the metal roof. We were under a big leafy tree facing Trout Lake as it quivered under the onslaught of the storm. I was watching how the lines on his face trailed down his cheeks when he talked, how he twisted his mouth sideways to hold in a laugh. Droplets of water raced down the windshield as lightning blasted us with white light.

His eyes were so much like mine.

"You remember when we used ta make fun of preachers?" I asked him.

"Yea, man! Ooooh, death, where is thy sting?" he said, putting on his shaky preacher voice. "Ohhhh, graaave, where is thy victory?"

We keeled sideways, laughing. The deluge seemed like it would never end.

Junior was single again. Work, church, and Narcotics Anonymous meetings were all he did. The discipline suited him. His eyes were clear.

He looked fit and focused. He was explaining to me why the bottom floors of condos are always built bigger.

I told him that I had been travelling to Brampton to play with my niece McKenzie, Nigel and Corrine's daughter. She had Nigel's cheeks and a massive curly Afro like he had as a baby. Nige, ever the most stable of my brothers, was thriving as a dad.

"Nigel's good, you know," I was telling him. "He still doesn't say much, but I can tell that he's happy. He daddies like how he does everything: total commitment."

When Junior took me to the airport, we talked about land in Monkeytown that we should've inherited, and about Al and Joan.

"They been corn and husk since they were kids," Junior said. And we laughed and laughed.

Somehow it was hard picturing little Al and Joan. To me, they had never been kids.

In early spring, Adrian saw our father for the first time in fifteen years. It happened because I, after wrestling with it for a day or two, offered to arrange a meeting. Knowing the damage Al could cause, I didn't want to be the one who initiated such a meeting. But Adrian hadn't been to Ontario for almost a decade and Al, now in his mid-late sixties, was starting to show the signs of five decades of hard living. "Last week, your Fah-Ther went to the Doc-Tor," Aunt Joan had said the month before. She weighed down the statement and the pause that followed with great pathos, inviting me to comment. When I refused to take the bait, she asked, "Did he tell you anything? That boy is so secretive." Even in her seventies, she couldn't help feeling anxious about Al. Perhaps I was a bit too. I didn't want to deprive Adge of his last chance to see his father. For that reason I decided to broker their reunion.

We met at Auntie Joan's apartment in Toronto. Al had a head full of silver-grey dreadlocks and a prominent paunch. He was missing several of his teeth, but that didn't stop him from flashing his best smile. Adge melted. He had always missed Al the most because he had known him the least.

Auntie Joan fussed and made way too much healthy Trini food. Bake, a salted fish dish called bulgoi, zaboca, brown rice, ackee, sweetbread, and mauby to drink. I sucked the salted cod and olive oil off one long bone. It reminded me of the meals she made back in Sioux Lookout.

"So these are my little girls." Adge was showing pictures of his twins; they were the same age as Al's daughter, Eve, the little sister I had never spoken to.

Al said, "Oh, so these are the girls." His voice was full of guile. There was more to this story. "Someone used to call me and just leave the phone on so I could hear two little girls in the back. I think it was Ami."

"You think?" I said. Obviously you know, I thought.

"She did what?" Adge couldn't believe it. Neither could I. Ami did not know how to not help Al.

There was no drinking allowed in the Reverend Auntie Joan's house. When she left for her "retired" counselling business, where she worked thirty hours a week, Al, like a circus performer, produced eight beers out of thin air.

We sat with our chairs pointed at the afternoon sun, which was falling over the greenest stretch of the wooded West Don Valley. It streamed in and bathed our faces. We basked in this unusual occasion: the three of us, the ease, the feeling of being connected. It felt deceptively normal: father and sons gulping beers and having a laugh in the fading light.

# IV

The only time Aunt Joan and I ever fought was terrible and rattled me in a way I would never forget. It was after Adrian's visit, and perhaps seeing Al had triggered me. There was so much we, the children, didn't know. Aunt Joan would say it was for our own good. Al would just wink and raise his eyebrows slyly. It was hard to shake the feeling that they wanted to keep their secrets to protect themselves, not us.

On the phone, she said, "So I hear you tell Adrian not to give his father his phone number?"

"That's not what I said at all," I replied. "I said he should wait twenty-four hours, and if he still wanted to, I would provide it."

"Adrian has a right to decide for himself. You can't speak for him. Al is his father."

The question at the tip of my tongue spilled out: "Auntie Joan, if you always take Al's side, at what point does that make you his accomplice?"

"His accomplice? Me?" I could hear her spine straighten with indignation. "He is my brutha. My bru-tha. I am supposed to be on his side."

Maybe my recent reconnection to the Caribbean was bringing back little Tony, but I was not in the mood to let it drop. I was feeling hardened and own-way.

"Who sticks up for the people he hurts?"

There was silence.

"Adrian is *my* brother," I carried on. "You never lived with him like I did. You have no idea what he's been through."

I could hear her huffing and puffing on the other end of the phone. Then her voice got cool as a breeze and she went all clinical-therapy condescension on me: "Well, I am happy you have found these projective narratives to help you heal."

I wasn't going to be belittled. "Auntie Joan, who knows better the dangers of toxic fathers? Who? How can you sit there and say that Al is the one who should be protected? Is that your professional opinion?"

"Boy, why are you so angry?" Now she was angry too.

"You know." And I paused before asking another question that was eating at my head. "Why did you never send Junior and me to therapy?"

The quiet on the other end ate a hole into our souls, but I wouldn't stop. I was sick of it. Sick of the hurt, sick of the excuses. Sick of the folly of people who were supposed to protect us but instead left us to the wolves.

"Our grandmother was dead, you knew I had been molested, we were in a whole new country, and we were showing all the signs of trauma. You knew all of this and did nothing."

"Boy, how long have you been saving up this poison for me? How long? I did my BEST. Maybe it wasn't good enough for YOU. But I did my BEST." Then Auntie Joan went to her ultimate weapon: she called on the Lord. "Well, I guess, you have your opinion," she preached. "And I have my opinion. But there is a third opinion—GAAAWD's opinion. HE sees my heart, and HE knows I did my BEST!"

*Click.* She hung up. The sermon had ended.


We never argued. I respected her too much. She was Auntie Joan, the family matriarch, our guardian angel. Yet how could a woman with so much education and experience in trauma not see the obvious?

The answer was pride. Her colleagues would know her business. She would have to face the awful devils lurking in her own past. She would have to face her own abandonment by "Horbutt," her wandering father.

I felt a swell of protectiveness for my brothers. They hadn't asked to be born into this. None of us had. My heart was kicking like engine pistons. My eyes stung; they grew hot and misty.

She, too, was damaged. My auntie Joan—this remarkable woman who had spent her whole life trying to save her troubled little brother and his broken kids—she, too, needed saving.

Joan might as well have been Miss Excelly, my grandmother, who was deserted at thirteen years old and then turned to care for six younger siblings. Or Gloria, my mother, abandoned by her parents to fend for herself before she was even a teenager. Or Wilton's mother, killed in the road while rushing about, trying to take care of five children alone.

They were Caribbean women, mules of the empire, forced to carry the burden of the Crown's dreadful legacy, of Black bodies chained to the spines of ships, of broken families, of men disempowered, stripped of their status in the home, sent to roam the earth with only their sex to prove their manhood, slaves by blood and by circumstance, saga boys.

She had done her best for the children of the Queen's Black soldiers, abandoned to the predations of hurricanes and man-eating snakes; in the deepest, darkest jungle, she had done her best.

She had done her best.

Chapter Twenty-Eight

# FIRE AND BRIMSTONE

I

The corpse of John Orpheus was resuscitated by a lightning bolt of miraculous news in the spring of 2016. A year after we'd finished the movie, it was accepted into the Nice International Film Festival. No one had expected this, and while the festival was not nearly as prestigious as Cannes, who cared? We were flying to France, to the glittering Côte d'Azur, to host the second screening ever of our movie.

I had packed all of J.O.'s regalia: a bright chalk-blue blazer, two pairs of tight leather pants, two shiny, long-sleeved black shirts, a pair of gold-laced Michael Kors sneakers, two shimmering silver shirts, four pairs of sunglasses with lines of pearls across the lenses, and at least fifteen gold chains.

On our third morning in Nice, at 5:00 a.m. Toronto time, I got the phone call from my roommate, Kwame. He'd been trying to reach me for two hours.

"Are you sitting down?" he asked, his voice tense.

"Sure?"

"My brother, there's been a fire. It started in your room, and all your stuff is destroyed."

I inhaled. "A fire? How did it start?" I thought: Is he angry with me? Is this my fault?

"We don't know all the details yet. Are you hearing me? No one was hurt, but all your stuff is gone, brother."

I smiled for some reason. He wasn't mad. He was worried about me.

"You mean to tell me that all my worldly possessions are gone?"

"Yeah, man."

And I felt so light that I began to laugh out loud.

My body weighed nothing, it seemed. I could've floated away on a soft Mediterranean breeze just then.

Gone? Gone! GONE. All of it. All that remained was the contents of the two bags I had brought with me to France: my old black travel case and a carry-on loaded with John Orpheus's shiny things. Gold chains were now 50 percent of my net worth. I couldn't help but feel liberated. Did I even need to go back?

In Trinidadian folklore, a Soucouyant leaves her skin and flies about the night as a ball of fire. But she needs her skin to return to, and without it, she will die. My skin had burned—now what?

Fire cleanses, fire purifies, fire burns and destroys, fire warms and provides. Fire is the giver and taker of life. Fire is the active agent that in alchemy boils everything down to its essence: the *nigrum nigrius nigro*. The black that is blacker than black.


That morning in Nice, France, I accepted the truth, but my body had not itemized the staggering cost:

I lost the letter Ami had written to me when I was a boy in Trinidad. I lost the Bible and hymnal that Auntie Joan and Auntie Agnes had given me at my baptism. I lost the only copy I had left of *Children on*

*Cato's Mountain*. I lost my closet full of jackets I had donned like super-hero cloaks—Mic Dainjah's army surplus jacket, Michael Downing's navy blazer, the suede jacket taken from Junior's stolen stash in that basement apartment. I lost the ratty, faded leather basketball that Benfoot and I had dribbled through Cambridge all summer. I lost the handwritten manuscript of *Molasses*. I lost seventeen of the twenty-four journals I had kept since I was twelve.

Everything I owned was sent hurtling into the underworld of ash and nothingness, leaving me weightless and soaring and free.

John Orpheus was dead, but he was now all I had left.

# EPILOGUE

## Her Majesty's Gifts

You can only become the person you always were.

The thing I most regretted losing in the fire was my Venezuelan birth certificate. It was the first place anyone had written my original name: Antonio Michael Downing. Tony, that boy who was sweet, smart, and a little bit crazy—he was where I belonged. And he had been with me this whole time.

I never needed to become John Orpheus. I needed to become myself.

I can see now that John was my conduit, my way of throwing off the whips and chains of my trauma. I understood the communities of slaves and their descendants who embraced Carnival, the ones who needed to play mas to become their other, freer selves. John Orpheus was my mask, my window into myself. But Carnival always ends. The rum and bacchanal turn into hangovers. The memories fade. The slaves return to the fields, a little more able, a little more themselves.

I rediscovered Tony when my drummer recommended an alternative healing community called Alternity. They did things like crystal workshops, reiki master training, past life regressions—healing colonialist karma—and the class I went to: shadow work. The idea was to do a guided meditation into your darkest past.

"So you're John Orpheus," came the greeting when I arrived out of the drifting snow. I was expected. White ushers in flowing Hindu robes with bright smiling faces led me to a meditation cushion in a room full of spiritual "seekers."

"Now try to reach back into your childhood."

The room had gone silent and was slowly filling with sighs.

"Try to go towards the shadow you can't see. Breathe in. Breathe out. Breathe in. Breathe out."

Just like my 4:00 a.m. nights, staring at the void, I thought.

I had been doing this for twenty minutes, waiting for terrible things to arrive, when four-year-old Tony popped into my head. He was grinning in his khaki shorts, with eager eyes. I shooed away the mental image. I was trying to take the shadow work seriously.

The room was echoing with sporadic weeping.

"Now as you breathe in, can you feel where in your body the trauma is?"

Tony kept coming back. Finally I realized that perhaps his shiny forehead was the reason I was there.

"Tony, wey goin' on, boy?" I said to my younger self, in my head.

His face lit up. All cheeks and teeth. He beamed a smile of pure joy. "Yuh know we can let all of dis stuff go, right?"

"Yeah, I know that." And I sat in the room with his face in my mind. We were like two kids who already knew the teacher's lesson.

"I've missed you so much," little me said, and he hugged me so completely that the entire room vanished.

Now I, too, felt like sobbing.


"We'd love to have you there," Coach said, inviting me to his and Elaine's twenty-fifth wedding anniversary. The celebration was a classic Lillie family brunch. Coach met me at the condo door. He was dressed in a sweater so well styled I knew it had to be chosen by Elaine. "Michael, you came early for sausages, I see," he wink, winked, nod, nodded me.

Elaine was beaming behind her large frames, tiny and delicate, yet full of sharp jibes. Karen was late. Ken drove from Stratford. Elaine nibbled a salad while we feasted on cheesy, egg-scrambled goodness. Kim got weepy even before her dad did.

"We're just so thankful for our crazy unorthodox family. You've each made our lives very special," he choked out as little rivers of tears dribbled onto his ketchup-free sweater.

After Coach's kids and their kids left, he and Elaine and I sat chatting in their living room. Twenty-five years had passed since the era of chicken fingers and Eggo waffles in the freezer.

"You were our first big decision together," Elaine said, as she often did.

How startled and happy this made me every time I heard it. Their love for me had become intertwined with their love for each other. I left, as always, floating on a cloud of disbelief. This is what family did: they showed up.

Family.

What did the word even mean anymore? The ones that had me did not want me, and the ones that wanted me, I could not accept.

Eryn and I, our romance long over, became friends.

She had forgiven me, but more importantly, she had forgiven herself for loving me. And I, too, was ready to forgive. Gloria, Joan, Al, Ami, Agnes, Miss Excelly—they all had done their best. We couldn't change what was written, but we could still make the story mean something.

The rain doused downtown Toronto that day. The bleak clouds bubbled over and cracked into a storm surge that flooded the subways and drowned the skyline in smudgy grey. Watching the lightning split open the sky, I wept. The faces of my family floated up before me, and I knew that I couldn't continue anymore. I needed to forgive them all. I needed to forgive myself.

"Praise the Lord," I heard Miss Excelly say.

And I felt like I finally understood her God. God was not a hiding place. God was not a thing in churches or books or pews. God was the darkness that shook the cane. The noise roaring over the tall grass. The mighty Rocky Mountains staring down. The wolves with their haunted eyes in the Wabigoon trees. God was the song I was always trying to sing, the word I needed to write, the prayer Mama summoned into the pitch-black stillness of the morning.

I had just sat down to Christmas Eve dinner with Auntie Joan when Al pulled up. He wasn't driving, though—his chauffeur was a twenty-three-year-old white girl. Classic.

"But where you find dis gurl, Al?" Auntie Joan big-sistered him. "Lord have mercy, wat trouble is dis?"

We left her there muttering a prayer, doing what she had done since he was born: worrying about Al. We dropped the white girl off at her parents' house by Lake Simcoe, then we drove together for days on end. We spent Christmas touring the scrappy homies he hustled with and called his friends. They were beautiful and broken, just like we were. I could tell how much they idolized him by how hard they worked to impress me.

"How's it going?" my friends kept texting to ask me.

"Well, he's the most charming, most mysterious, and cleverest man I've ever met."

"Oh, so he's your dad." The unanimous response.

"I have something for you," he said slyly, and he gave me a large mouldy book.

A rush of sensations flooded my brain. It was Miss Excelly's Bible, the one I had learned to read from. "How did you get this?"

He was grinning with satisfaction, like a cat in cream. "Hailey kept it. I was driving by her aunt's house one day and decided to drop in. Her uncle gave it to me."

It was a miracle.

I dragged my fingers over the cover, feeling every groove, remembering all the times I had done the same thing as a child. I flipped to the pictures, stopping at the one called "The Prodigal Son." The son had his hands clasped in prayer, penitent, as his father put his arms around him. This was after the son "took his journey into a far country, and there wasted his substance with riotous living."

In the front of the Bible, the inscription read "From: Mama, To: Tony."

We drove on in silence.

The snow covered the trees and the farms like a soft blanket as we rushed by. Al's strong hands lay gently on the wheel. Those same hands had picked poor people's pockets at Carnival, rebuilt engines from scratch, and stabbed a woman on the Prairies.

When I looked over, he was smiling the same mischievous, boyish smile he often did. It was just like mine. It occurred to me that we were alike in so many ways, but his choices were not mine. I was not him.

All of my playing mas, all of my wearing masks, all of my becoming had finally allowed me to become myself.

I eased the seat back as he smashed down on the gas and we shot towards the horizon, two Trinis, two West Indians, two Canadian men blazing through the Commonwealth.

Miss Excelly came to me then, smiling like there was a joke we hadn't got yet. Miss Excelly in Caesar's toga. The vision made Tony chuckle. What a bizarre image: the woman who'd loved me most, dressed in a conqueror's costume.

But then again, the Queen designed my brain.

# AUTHOR'S NOTE

*Saga Boy* features many of my family and friends. I am grateful for their cooperation and for the aid of numerous people who helped tremendously but have not been named. To wrap my head around the task of writing this memoir, I engaged in over 250 hours of interviews with people; often sad, often hilarious, always indispensable. Yet, in some cases, due to matters unrelated to this story, I have not used everyone's real name or have changed certain biographical details out of respect for their privacy.

# ACKNOWLEDGMENTS

*Tell it plainly, let the sweet be sweet, let the sour be sour, let the Truth ring its own bell.* This is what I wrote in the cover of the plain blue notebook Coach and Elaine had given me to hand draft this manuscript. *Saga Boy* began, as most of my projects, as an attempt to understand myself. To reclaim my history. It has been my immense privilege to have the time and emotional resources to grapple with the history of myself and my people in this way and there are many to thank for it being in your hands today.

Firstly, I'd like to thank my family and closest friends. Auntie Joan, who never stopped praying for me. Al, who in this process became a friend and a father. Gloria, whose side of the story this process made me truly appreciate. Ami, for your sacrifice. Coach and Elaine, the most decent and loving people I have ever known. My brothers in Canada: Junior, a lion of a man who taught me to never fear the darkness; Nigel, a true Jedi who taught me that silence often speaks best; Adge, who taught me how to love strong and never regret it. My Trini siblings, Shanice, Ronald, Cardo, and Kurt, you are always close even when you're far. Wilton Gillard, who spared no effort in helping me piece together the stories from before I was alive. Gada, for teaching me that when I'm uncomfortable, I'm probably growing. Chachi, somewhere in my head we are still rolling through the existentialist night. Dion Fitzgerald, my brother in Blackness and art, we still in a band, mate. Benfoot, all summer, all summer. Howard Hacker, who believed in the Trini in me before I believed in it myself. G. Brong, Karen Daniels, and Natalie Ricard, 344 forever. Eryn Handley, who was generous enough to teach me forgiveness. And my bestie, Eva Schubert, for always being my co-poet, companion, drill sergeant, and never letting me stop climbing the mountain. Zahra Mohamed, my love, for always feeding my face and my soul. You have all been my heroes.

Secondly, I'd like to thank my marvelous team of book people who have made this happen. Ida Hallidri, who was careful to blow on the embers of this idea when it was only a fragile flame. Becky Blake, without whose vision and recommendation of me as an Emerging Author at the wonderful and sadly defunct Taylor Prize, this would not have happened. My mentor, historian, and great Canadian thinker Max Wallace, whose appetite for a good yarn and a good roti sustained me. Diane Turbide, Publishing Director at Penguin Canada, whose calm wisdom and guiding hand took this from a few scratches on a page to what you see here. The exceptional folks at Penguin Random House Canada and extended team: Helen Smith, Janice Weaver, David Ross, and designer Emma Dolan. My agents at Westwood Creative Artists, John Pearce and Chris Casuccio, whose careful attention, pep talks, and gentle scoldings saved this book more than a few times. And Wendy Morley, whose passion, capacity to hear me talk things through, and careful editing was instrumental. Your faith has been a humbling lesson.

Thirdly, I'd like to thank my John Orpheus music team who have been patient with my self-imposed literary isolations: Chaenel Matise, Sarah Jane Riegler, Mike Schlosser, Adrienne Elkerton, Patrick Hodgson, Ola Mazzuca, Dynesti Williams, and Bryant Didier. To Seth Bernard and Jordan Hamilton, for being great musicians but great men first. Last Poets, Amber Hassan and Heavy Color. To the Haus Orpheus, Speak Ya Truth and AfroHaus crew. SO WE DO IT.

ANTONIO MICHAEL DOWNING grew up in southern Trinidad, northern Ontario, Brooklyn, and Kitchener. He is a musician, writer, and activist based in Toronto. His debut novel, *Molasses*, was published to critical acclaim. In 2017, he was named by the RBC Taylor Prize as one of Canada's top emerging authors for nonfiction. He performs and composes music as John Orpheus.

milkweed
editions

Founded as a nonprofit organization in 1980,
Milkweed Editions is an independent publisher. Our mission
is to identify, nurture and publish transformative literature,
and build an engaged community around it.

Milkweed Editions is based in Bdé Óta Othúŋwe (Minneapolis) within
Mní Sota Makhóčhe, the traditional homeland of the Dakhóta people.
Residing here since time immemorial, Dakhóta people still call Mní
Sota Makhóčhe home, with four federally recognized Dakhóta nations
and many more Dakhóta people residing in what is now the state of
Minnesota. Due to continued legacies of colonization, genocide, and
forced removal, generations of Dakhóta people remain disenfranchised
from their traditional homeland. Presently, Mní Sota Makhóčhe has
become a refuge and home for many Indigenous nations and peoples,
including seven federally recognized Ojibwe nations. We humbly
encourage our readers to reflect upon the historical legacies held in
the lands they occupy.

milkweed.org

Typeset in Arno

Arno was designed by Robert Slimbach. Slimbach named this typeface after the river that runs through Florence, Italy. Arno draws inspiration from a variety of typefaces created during the Italian Renaissance; its italics were inspired by the calligraphy and printing of Ludovico degli Arrighi.